not so big remodeling

not so big remodeling

tailoring your home for the way you really live

sarah susanka *and* marc vassallo

The Taunton Press

The Taunton Press, Inc.
63 South Main Street, PO Box 5506
Newtown, CT 06470-5506
e-mail: tp@taunton.com

Editor: Peter Chapman
Copy Editor: Diane Sinitsky
Indexer: Jay Kreider
Jacket/Cover design: Jean-Marc Troadec, Design & Typography
Interior design: Chika Azuma
Layout: Chika Azuma
Illustrator: Martha Garstang Hill, except as noted on p. 327

Library of Congress Cataloging-in-Publication Data

Susanka, Sarah.
  Not so big remodeling : tailoring your home for the way you really live / Sarah
Susanka and Marc Vassallo.
      p. cm.
  ISBN 978-1-56158-827-5 hardcover
  ISBN 978-1-60085-824-6 paperback (with flaps)
  1. Dwellings--Remodeling. 2. Small houses. I. Vassallo, Marc. II. Title.
  TH4816.S98 2009
  643'.7--dc22
                              2008046632

Printed in the United States of America
10 9 8 7 6 5 4 3 2 1

for Linda and Nick
and for Margaret and Brian

acknowledgments

We would like to thank the hundreds of architects, designers, builders, and homeowners who honored us by sending in their remodeling projects for our consideration. We received far more book-worthy Not So Big remodels than could possibly fit even in these many pages.

This book was a long time coming, but better to make it good than quick. It's a point that can be applied profitably to remodeling as well. We'd especially like to thank everyone whose work or home appears here, for your willingness to share, your enthusiasm for our collective endeavor, and your patience. It's through the examples set by your design work, construction projects, and homes that all of us have the opportunity to explore and learn about Not So Big remodeling.

As always, we owe a debt of gratitude to everyone at The Taunton Press who worked on this book, in particular art director Alison Wilkes and our good shepherd, editor Peter Chapman, who guided this book home over hill and dale. This is Peter's sixth collaboration on the Not So Big series, and a lot of the credit for each book's readability and user-friendliness goes to his careful attention to detail. Thanks also to the many photographers, illustrators, and graphic designers who contributed their efforts.

Marc would like to thank his agent, Phyllis Wender, for her unwavering support.

Sarah would also like to thank her agent, Gail Ross, as well as her assistant, Marie St. Hilaire, who adeptly orchestrated the process of finding suitable projects for inclusion in this book, and who helped Marc and Sarah coordinate their efforts as they assembled this jigsaw puzzle of over 100 remodeling projects.

From Marc, a special thanks to Linda and Nick, for whom he dedicates this book.

And from Sarah, a continuing appreciation for the support of her husband as she lives her not so big and not so private life.

contents

introduction

When I wrote the first edition of this book, the economy was booming, and many homeowners were using the increasing value of their biggest asset to secure lines of credit that allowed them to make substantial improvements, add extravagant luxuries, and buy pretty much whatever they wanted. There was also a lot of house flipping going on as entrepreneurial individuals made a business of buying, improving, and reselling houses that were growing in value, even without any remodeling. There was nothing to lose—or so it seemed at the time.

I felt like a voice in the wilderness, trying to bring some sanity to the legions of eager remodelers. I watched in horror as houses in neighborhoods I knew and loved were added onto in monstrously unappealing ways, with additions that dwarfed the homes they were attached to.

"Why do people do this?" I wondered. "What's the appeal of BIG when that bigness is so graceless?" It was clearly time to introduce the concept of a "Not So Big Remodeling"—a remodeling that fits both the residents' needs AND the scale and character of the existing home; that begins with the repurposing of existing space, rather than with a giant addition that leaves you wondering what to do with the old part of the house. I wanted to get this book into the hands of those who were trying to capitalize on this most certain of investments—their home—so that the money they invested was a benefit not only for them today, but for all the residents of future decades as well.

But then of course the universe changed. The hardcover version of *Not So Big Remodeling* came out in early 2009, just a few months after the subprime mortgage crisis began, and pretty soon all of us were holding on to our wallets, uncertain about what the future would hold. Though the book sold surprisingly well given the state of the economy, I had no way of knowing when I wrote it that its real value would be for this post-recession era.

Like the people of the era following the Great Depression, the post-recession consumer is more cautious, and more sensible about expenditures. People want quality, but they're not as convinced as they once were that quantity is so important. Which is fortunate for me, because that's what all my books are about. Build better, not bigger. Focus on quality, not quantity. Design for the way you really live, not for some imagined formality of a bygone era. Make your home your own, designed to inspire you daily. And make it fit you to a tee—not too big, and not too small, with every space in use every day. That's what Not So Big is all about, and it's the perfect message for today.

What you'll discover as you work your way through this book is that, with a little creativity, you'll be able to change your ho-hum residence into a place that is a delight to dwell in. In fact, you may discover that the house of your dreams is actually hiding right where you live today. No matter how plain Jane your abode, there IS hope, and there really is a way to transform her into a real beauty.

Sarah Susanka
Raleigh, North Carolina

1. my not so big remodeling

When my husband and I first laid eyes on the house we now live in, we both knew it was the one for us. As we drove around a neighborhood of Raleigh, North Carolina, looking for potential candidates, suddenly there it was—a lovely cape with a big front porch and three perfectly proportioned dormers. The house stood on a piece of property that looked like country, even though it was in fact quite close to all the amenities we needed: only 15 minutes from the airport, a half mile from a good grocery store, and a few blocks from a beautiful lake with ample walking paths. What more could we ask?

Although the interior of the house left a lot to be desired in terms of décor, it had good bones, with a sense of flow from room to room, and I could instantly envision the simple changes I'd implement to make it more livable and appropriate for my and my husband's needs. Since both of us work from home, we needed enough space that we could each stake out an area to call "my office," each with some separation from the rest of the house. Bringing to bear the attitudes and sensibilities of the Not So Big House, we decided to make the home's original living room and dining room into my husband's office quarters, while I would occupy two of the four bedrooms on the upper level. With this decision made, we were ready to begin redesigning the parts of the house that needed some remodeling to meet our needs.

keep it simple

I've worked with thousands of individuals, couples, and families over the past two decades, so I knew exactly what was needed to keep costs down and livability up on my own house. Although a remodeled house is rarely as personal, architecturally speaking, as a house you design from scratch, there are lots of small things you can do that will make it much more closely aligned with your visions for a dream home than you've probably ever thought possible.

My goal with this book is to show you how to make a little remodeling go a long way. In fact, the informing attitude is one of "Keep it simple."

Instead of showing only high-end architectural solutions, I will be revealing good ideas that can make average houses a lot better.

My own remodeled home isn't a "great" house in architectural terms, yet for the time being, while my life is as busy as it is, it serves me very well. Although I may someday build a new one that is of more architectural significance, for now I'm living in a house that, although by no means stellar, is really personal and comfortable.

If I were not the owner (and the author), the house I live in now would probably never make it into a magazine or book, yet compared with the way it was when I bought it—the way most average houses are—it is vastly superior. It is comfortable like a well-worn shoe or a favorite

The house we chose to call home had good bones: a classic Cape form, an ample front porch, and three perfectly proportioned dormers.

not so big remodeling

There are three options for remodeling your home in a Not So Big way.

OPTION 1 WORK WITHIN THE EXISTING FOOTPRINT

When people think about remodeling, they often begin in the wrong place. They immediately assume that they have to add on and end up doing nothing because they also assume it will cost more than they can afford. But there are literally thousands of small alterations you can make to your house or apartment as it is right now, without having to change the original footprint at all. Removing or opening up a wall, adding some storage, or rearranging the way you move through a room can solve all sorts of spatial problems without resorting to added square footage.

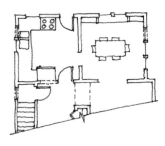

within the footprint

OPTION 2 BUMP OUT

It's only after you've considered every possible change that can be made within the existing footprint that it's time to consider a bump-out or two. Any time you cut through the exterior envelope of the house, you're likely to be looking at a bigger investment of remodeling dollars. This is because the exterior surface is the weather barrier—the home's raincoat if you will—and it consists of an intricate combination of components that usually make it significantly more challenging to remodel than interior space. But the extension of a space by just a couple of feet can make a big difference to the utility and aesthetics of the room in question, so it is important to understand where a minimal modification to the existing footprint is worthwhile.

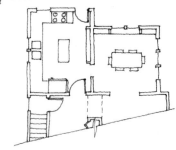

bump out

OPTION 3 ADD ON JUST A LITTLE

This is the last step in a Not So Big remodeling, and yet it, too, is often overlooked as an option by people who are planning to modify their house to fit them better. The usual approach is to start with a big addition. In Not So Big remodeling, adding on just a little is the step of last resort. It is a solution that inevitably costs more money because it involves more square footage. But when it is accomplished in a Not So Big way, even a small addition can be a cost-effective strategy when compared with the alternatives—a substantial renovation, moving, or building new.

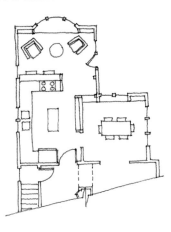

add on a little

The primary purpose of adding a front door with glass was to bring light to the dark entry foyer, but the new door also improves the welcoming quality of the porch.

cardigan, neither of which you'd ever likely see walking down the runway at a fashion show but which is in fact a lot more practical and satisfying than any article of runway clothing will ever be.

getting started

The remodeling moves I've made to this house can be broken into three categories:

- What needed to be changed right away to make the house more livable.

- What we decided to do to improve the character of what was already here.

- What we changed a couple of years later because of some new developments in our lives.

And then there's a fourth category:

- What would be nice to do someday but which we haven't done yet either to avoid life disruption or because it seems to cost too much for the added benefit.

I'm going to take you through each of these categories in turn so you can see the thought processes involved. In this chapter, I'll describe my approach to the first two categories, and at the end of the book, after you've learned a lot of innovative remodeling techniques, I'll describe my approaches to categories three and four. I've divided them up like this because if I were to describe all of them here at the beginning, they would in all likelihood blend together, when I want you to appreciate the substantial differences between the first two categories and the second two. By making this distinction, you'll avoid a lot of unnecessary adding

on, and you'll learn to identify the most cost-effective, functional, and aesthetic improvement strategies right off the bat. That's what the first two categories introduce.

what needed to be changed right away

Before we had decided to buy it, we loved the outside of the house and the lush surrounding garden, but when we first set foot in the house, the first impression was *not* a good one. We stepped into a dark entry foyer that was too small to feel comfortable in. The stairway to the right of the

The saving grace of the original entryway, and the reason for my continued interest in the house, was the view to the backyard through a set of double doors that opened into a hallway leading to the informal eating area. This view had the potential at least to be charming, although the wallpaper, the furniture, the strategically located trash can, and the excessively shiny white linoleum floor all had to be ignored to recognize this (see the photo on p. 10). As we continued to move through the house, although there were plenty of eyesores like the ones cited above, it was easy to see that most of what was seriously wrong was only skin deep—nothing that a little remodeling couldn't fix.

Rethinking the Kitchen Layout

As in so many homes, the room that required the most work was the kitchen. Its layout made it an extremely inconvenient work space. The work surface was set up in a U, with a peninsula separating the kitchen work space from the eating area. This arrangement tends to make an already small space seem significantly more confining. Open the dishwasher here, for example, and you would have nowhere to stand while you put away the dishes (see the before photo on p. 11).

The cabinets themselves were not pretty either, and the soffits— those dropped ceiling pieces above the upper cabinets—stopped and started in odd places, probably indicating there had at one time been some additional upper cabinetry that had been removed. And the overall composition of the room lacked a *point of focus*. For a primary living space, the room was drab and dull.

With the peninsula removed, the room was just wide enough to allow the addition of a kitchen island—a far better solution for a room of this size, improving the flow between kitchen and eating area and making the whole room seem larger as a result (see the after photo on p. 11).

door was in deep shadow, and the hall closet was easily the room's most prominent feature, intruding into the space and making it difficult to maneuver.

By replacing the front door with a new one that included some glass, adding a window at the base of the stairway, and removing the closet, I was able to improve both the room's size and character, transforming it from a squished and dingy awkwardness into a gracious place of welcome (see the photos on the facing page).

If I hadn't been able to find an easy fix for this problem, we wouldn't have bought the house. First impressions during *the process of entering* a house are extremely important, not only for guests but for the homeowners as well. If you don't feel well received by your house each time you return, it is almost impossible to make it feel like home. (Note that phrases in italics are the names of Not So Big concepts you'll be learning more about as you read through the book.)

FIRST FLOOR PLAN

before

Dining room

Kitchen

Eating area

Family room

Living room

Entry

after

Garden room

Office (room 2)

Kitchen

Dining

Family room

Garage

Office (room 1)

Entry

Dashed lines show location of dropped ceilings.

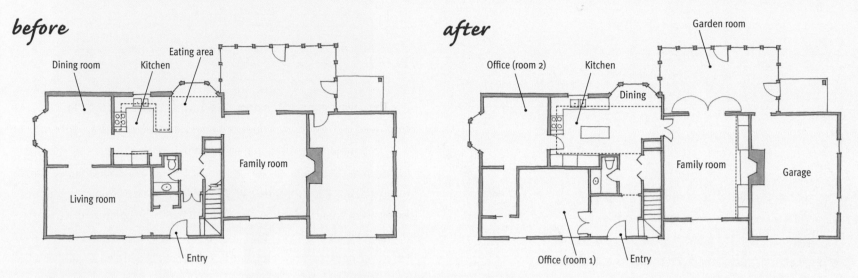

My husband's office, converted from the original living room, sits just to the left of the main entrance. We carved 6 ft. out of the back of the room to create a mailing room and added a lighted painting at the far end to draw people into the room.

shoji screens to nowhere

Shoji screens are typically used as sliding doors or partitions to separate room from room. But they can also be used to give the illusion of more space beyond, where none actually exists. In my husband's office, we took two sets of inexpensive tri-folding shoji screen room dividers, removed the hinges, and reattached each segment of screen to a 2x4 laid flat against the wall. We finished the design with a horizontal cherry trim band above and painted the wall above that.
It appears to be covering a room behind, but of course in reality there's nothing there. It is simply a unique wall covering that imparts a distinctly Asian flavor to the room.

The long view from the front entry foyer to the backyard was enhanced with fresh paint and a darker floor tile to give some visual weight. Lowering the hall ceiling to 7 ft. created a transition area between the foyer and kitchen.

In fact, we decided to replace all the cabinets (with elegant and inexpensive IKEA® cabinets), but to keep remodeling costs down we left the cooktop, oven, and sink in their original locations.

For the new countertops, I turned to another money-saving trick that I've used in many remodelings. Instead of using one type of material throughout, I used a solid-surface material—a quartz composite product called Zodiaq®—just on the island, where it becomes a focal point for the room but requires no special cutouts for appliances (which keeps costs down). For the rest of the countertops, I used a patterned laminate that costs considerably less than the Zodiaq, adding a wood cap atop the contrasting laminate backsplash that's aligned with the existing windowsill to tie the room together and to add a little extra character.

Because the walls between the upper and lower cabinets were already littered with outlets and switches, I decided to avoid the alignment problems that would arise if I added tile throughout this area. Instead, I used a single favorite tile above the cooktop where its placement creates a *point of focus* for the whole room. By surrounding this tile with a design of contrasting standard tiles that match the colors of the island and the laminate, the composition inexpensively adds personality to the whole room (see the photos on pp. 12–13).

But the most important change in the room's design happens at the ceiling plane. The jumble of soffits was in serious need of an *organizing strategy*. I extended the missing soffit across the door to the old dining room, removed the soffit over the old peninsula, and added a few inches

Removing the peninsula and adding a center island instead improves the entire orientation and flow of the kitchen. In addition, extending the soffit above the table to align with the one above the cabinets gives the entire room a more streamlined and coordinated appearance.

A single favorite tile surrounded by contrasting standard tiles creates a focal point and costs much less than a full tile backsplash.

(facing page) IKEA cabinets and new Formica tile flooring (darker and easy to clean) added personality to the kitchen without undue expense.

onto the width of the soffit above the eating area so that it aligned with the one above the kitchen cabinets. I also added a small shelf above the cabinets, refrigerator, and pantry on the other side of the room to disguise the miscellaneous indentations in the wall and to widen the area beneath it to the standard 24 in. in depth.

I made one other ceiling height change that flows naturally from this small shelf decision. Lowering the ceiling height of the hallway linking the front entry and the kitchen creates a transitional area between rooms. Although the ceiling heights throughout the house are only 8 ft., dropping this hallway ceiling to 7 ft. makes the ceiling heights to either side—the kitchen and the entryway—seem taller. This one apparently insignificant change of adding *ceiling height variety* makes a huge difference to the sense of welcome you experience as you step into the kitchen (see the photo on p. 14).

Fixing an Awkward Powder Room Layout

The original powder room felt considerably smaller than necessary because of the placement of the sink and cabinetry directly across from the toilet. As with most powder rooms, the full 8-ft. height of the ceiling also emphasized the smallness, and the dark wallpaper only added to this feeling.

By moving the sink to the wall across from the door and replacing the cabinetry and countertop, the length of floor space in front of the toilet seems greater, which makes the room feel bigger. When a room's largest dimension is its height, it's always worth looking for ways to drop the ceiling a bit in order to accentuate one of the horizontal dimensions instead. So in this room, I lowered the ceiling to the height of the new hallway ceiling and then ran a narrow trim headband of cherry trim around the entire room. Because of the new up-lighting to either side of the new mirror, this creates the illusion of no ceiling at all—only brightness off this broad *reflecting surface* (see the photos on p. 15).

Lowering the ceiling height of the hallway linking the front entry and the kitchen creates a transitional area between rooms. A continuous band of trim ties all the soffits together, while bold colors below the original chair rail and between the original crown molding and the new trim band introduce some visual weight.

what we did to improve the character

We *could* have lived with everything else, but if we'd made no other changes the house would still have seemed pretty impersonal. These next changes are ones that have made the house our own by bringing it into balance visually, so that no matter where we are, there's something inspiring and expressive to enjoy.

Brightening Up a Frumpy Family Room

We liked the size of the family room as well as the shape of the fireplace, but the finishes—grass-cloth wallpaper, fake beams, and dark paneling—made the room seem very gloomy.

In this room, a lot of the remodeling strategies were simply removals. The first things that had to go were the fake beams and spray-textured ceiling, which looked instantly inauthentic. Next was the grass-cloth wallpaper, which was absorbing a lot of the potential reflected daylight from the big square window that looked out onto the front yard. And the last item for removal, at least for this first phase of the remodeling, was the dark paneling surrounding the fireplace brick.

In its place I designed a three-dimensional assemblage of cabinets—also from IKEA, to match the new kitchen décor—with shelves for artwork between (see the bottom photo on p. 17). This composition gives the room more dimensionality, relieving its boxiness and at the same time adding some much needed storage and display space. I still didn't much like the mantel arrangement, which was placed too high on the wall for the room's height, but I decided I could live with it for now. (In this room's final form, only recently completed, the old mantel was removed, a new colored wall panel added, and a simple solid cherry mantel installed; see the photo on p. 322.)

I also ran a second trim line around the room at countertop height, as a *differentiation of parts* of the room, adding some color to the wall surface below this line for *visual weight*—a favorite technique to make less look like more. Two additional vertical trim pieces provide a frame for the mirror. This is a really easy but elegant way to give any small bathroom added character. (One change I wish I could have made was to put in a pocket door, which would have improved the ease of circulation, but the cost of removing the wall and replacing the out-swinging door didn't seem worth the benefit at the time.)

Far from making the remodeled powder room feel smaller, the lowered ceiling does just the opposite, making the room feel significantly larger than it really is.

These were the changes we made to the main level. The one room we barely changed at all, and that played a big part in our buying the house in the first place, was the garden room, a space surrounded by windows and accessed from the family room through a set of wide French doors. This room is a wonderful spot to sit each morning as the sun rises, flooding the room with golden light and shadow patterns (see the top photo on p. 17). The one addition we did make to it was a coat rack to replace the closet I'd removed from the front entry. This is where we take off coats and hats, so it is really a much better location for it than the front entry.

changes on the upper level

All the changes we made to the upper level fall into the category of character improvement. None of these changes were absolutely mandatory for us to move in, but they all made a huge impact on our feelings about the house and in hindsight were without question money well spent.

Revamping an Ugly Hallway

The upstairs hallway, like so many of its kind, was unrelentingly dull, its insipidness affecting not only how we felt about the hallway but also about all the rooms accessed from it (see the before photo on p. 16). The hallway was poorly lit, and its ceiling was decorated with all the mechanical and electrical necessities of house maintenance—the return-air grille, the attic hatch, the smoke detector, and the requisite center light fixture. Not a particularly inviting welcome to the second floor.

The feature of this hallway that bothered me the most was that the return-air grille was placed off center with the axis of the hallway, giving

Adding a grid of trim pieces and a second color to the ceiling transformed the upstairs hallway at minimal expense.

the whole experience of ascending an off-kilter feeling. As a fix, I decided upon a strategy I call *simple pattern overlay*. I took the relative dimensions and locations of each ceiling feature and drew them accurately on a piece of paper. Then I came up with a design that would weave them all together into a composition that looked as though each placement was intentional.

The addition of a simple pattern of trim pieces, and painting the ceiling sections between to emphasize the new *composition* rather than the ceiling acne, created an entirely new feel for the hallway. Now, as you ascend the stairs there's something to look at that has an order and a character to it. It's no longer a purely utilitarian view. This may seem unimportant, but consider the number of times you go up and down stairs each day, and realize that each time there's the opportunity for some inspiration—something graceful to greet you.

Balancing the Master Bedroom

The first thing we noticed when we stepped into the master bedroom was that the area where the bed would naturally sit had a sloped ceiling on one side but not on the other, making that end of the room seem off balance.

Our initial solution was simply to slope the other side of the room to match the already slanted one in order to balance the *composition,* and to create a sheltered alcove for the bed. Although we could have done just this and nothing more, we decided to make the bed *alcove* the *point of focus* for the room by adding a *framed opening* to emphasize the new form, and by painting the interior of the alcove a deep maroon color (see the photo on p. 18). The effect of this change was remarkable, a perfect example of "a little goes a long way."

The garden room, accessed from the family room, Is one space that was largely unchanged by the remodeling.

Remodeling the family room consisted mostly of removing frumpy old things: fake beams, the spray-textured ceiling, and the grass cloth wallpaper. In place of the dark paneling surrounding the hearth, I designed a three-dimensional assemblage of IKEA cabinets to match those in the kitchen.

SECOND FLOOR PLAN

before

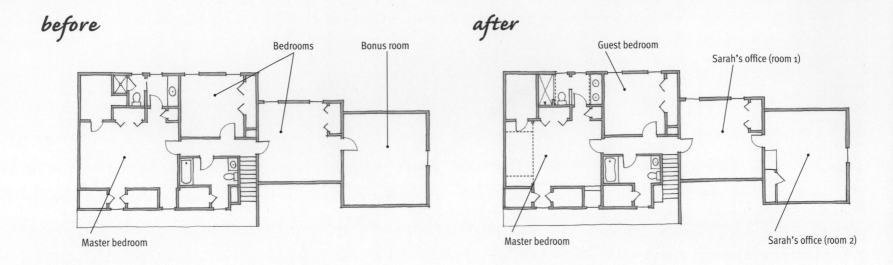

Bedrooms

Bonus room

Master bedroom

after

Guest bedroom

Sarah's office (room 1)

Master bedroom

Sarah's office (room 2)

Angling the ceiling on the right side of the bedroom to match the slope of the left side made a framed alcove to shelter the bed and create a focal point for the room.

Reconfiguring the Master Bathroom

As with so many houses, the master bathroom was very awkwardly laid out, with barely room to turn around. It was separated into two tiny rooms, one containing a long counter with a single sink and the other the toilet and a small shower. The two were divided by a 2-ft.-wide sliding door. Everything about these two spaces felt cramped and inconvenient—hardly the experience we'd want to be greeted by each morning.

Not wanting to incur the costs of a major remodel to this space, I decided to leave the plumbing where it was, but to modify the elements that were making the room feel so cramped. I knew that the dividing wall between the two rooms would need to be changed, but if I removed it entirely I would have to replace the floor tile as well because there would be a space where the wall had been. So instead, I decided to leave intact the bottom half of the wall dividing the toilet from the sink (see the photo at left on p. 20), and then to open up the rest of the wall to form a *framed opening*. The result, of course, was a room that appeared twice the size. (I was also able to make the shower considerably larger by borrowing some poorly used space from the adjacent closet.)

The final shaping of the space took place in the ceiling plane, where I dropped a soffit over the sink area and over the shower to give both a sense of *shelter around activity*. As with the hallway on the main level, although it may seem counterintuitive to make an area shorter to make the space feel larger, it really does work. Keep in mind that it is the *contrast* between the two ceiling heights that helps define one from the other, giving your eye more to look at.

Adding a wall-to-wall mirror above the sink area increased the sense of space in the remodeled master bathroom. Framing the mirror with a 2-in. band of cherry and arranging the tiles on the countertop in an interesting design added some character to a room that had previously been purely utilitarian.

(far left) The original bathroom had a sliding door separating the sink area from the shower and toilet. Rather than remove the wall entirely, which would have forced the replacement of all the floor tile, I converted the sliding door pocket into a half-wall, keeping the remodeling required to a minimum.

(left) Typically we use skylights for light alone, but if they are positioned appropriately they can also let in the view. This skylight is actually two units ganged together and stretches from the ceiling to the new countertop that extends the full length of the office.

Rescuing a Marginal Bonus Room

One of the two bedrooms I planned to use for my own office was a sad affair when we first bought the house, with brown shag carpeting, dark wood paneling, and a single window. Hardly the place to write books about how to make more inspiring places to live. But within this dreary and forgotten room, I could envision the makings of a room I'd love to spend time in.

The carpet was an instant "gotta-go." But then what? This room desperately needed more light, and the dark color of the wood paneling was absorbing what little light there was. Painting it a lighter color would allow the light to bounce around. Although I don't typically recommend painting natural wood, in this case it was a necessity. In addition, I added a skylight for both light and view.

Let There Be Light

As we headed back downstairs at the end of our first visit to the house, I saw another "gotta-do" (which I mentioned earlier when describing the entryway issues). With no daylight to descend toward, the bottom of the staircase was a pool of darkness (see the before photo on the facing page).

The window I added to bring light into the entryway does *double duty* as a source of *light to walk toward* as you move from upper to main levels. By aligning it with the center of the stairway and using a uniquely

A new window at the bottom of the stairs adds light to the entry foyer while providing *light to walk toward*, making descending the stairs a daily pleasure.

shaped window that lends some character to the front of the house as well, this one simple addition dramatically affects the way we experience the house as we move between floors over the course of each day.

remodeling basics

All this work may sound like a lot to accomplish before moving in, but if you look at each of the areas we modified, you'll see that none but the kitchen remodeling required major work. Most of the adjustments were made simply to reveal the full potential of what was already there. And that's what most homes need. Although we assume we'll have to add on or move to find the home of our dreams, we overlook the simple strategies that will bring to the fore the things that could make the house into "home."

Although my husband and I have done a small amount of adding on as well in the intervening years, building above the garden room to expand my office space, I won't describe that addition until the end of the book. That's what most books about remodeling describe—the more dramatic stuff, which is important to consider, but not until after you've implemented the other simpler strategies first.

So get out your notebooks, and prepare to learn the basics of remodeling in a Not So Big way. It's all about looking for the simplest and most elegant ways to pare away what isn't working, retain those things that aren't too objectionable and whose continued presence helps to reduce the amount of remodeling work to be done, and add some small functional, aesthetic, and personal details that help accentuate each space's best features. This is the true art of remodeling, and if you master it, you'll discover that your house, no matter its size, can be transformed into a wonderful place to live without breaking the bank in the process.

PART I

The Look of Your House

2. the exterior

When you decide to remodel a house, it's typically because you believe something needs fixing. When it comes to the exterior of a house, it may not be a crucial functional issue but more of an aesthetic preference, and the remodeling gets put off indefinitely. But if you don't like the look of your house, it can markedly color your life within its walls. So even if you don't really *need* to change the exterior, give yourself permission to consider giving it a prettier face, both from the street and the backyard and even from the sides of the house—the sides your neighbors see. When each face of the house is an integral part of a single house identity, the entire home expresses something more about who you are, both to yourself and to the neighborhood.

Greening up this little house was an occasion to improve its looks as well. What appears to be wood siding is actually 4-ft. by 8-ft. fiber-cement panels with caulked joints concealed by battens made from wood fiber and recycled plastic.

There are several ways to approach a remodeling. One way is to assess what you like and what you don't and to use this as a point of departure for the design changes you want to make. This helps to narrow down the number of aspects of the home's design that need changing. Another equally important approach is to look at the composition as a whole and to evaluate and then propose alterations to its various elements.

what you like, what you don't

To begin the process of remodeling the exterior, first identify the features that you like and then those that you don't like. Even if there aren't many items on the "like" list, they will give you a place to start the design process. Use the following questions to get things started:

• Do you like or dislike the overall shape and character of the house?

• Do you like the arrangement of windows, or is there something about their layout that doesn't look right?

• Are there appendages to the house, such as a porch, stoop, or dormer, that you particularly like or dislike?

• Do you like or dislike the material that the house is sheathed with, such as brick, stone, or clapboard siding?

• Is the front door in a convenient or inconvenient location?

• Is there a welcoming path up to the house from the street or from the place you park your car, or is there a lack of graciousness about the way the house receives you and your visitors?

• Does the house have a pleasing face when seen from the street and from the backyard, or do those faces need some work?

how each chapter is organized

In this and each of the chapters that follow, you'll see a pattern to the design process for remodeling that I'm recommending. First, we'll look for the most frequent causes of problems. Then I'll help you look at the specifics of your particular problem areas, and then we'll review the Not So Big Principles that will most likely provide the solution. Finally, in the case studies that close each chapter, we'll look at how other homeowners, with the help of their architects, have arrived at solutions to some similarly thorny issues to your own.

Although you'll be able to see some solutions to your own design problems instantly, other problems may require professional help. There are many architects and designers who specialize in residential remodeling. Check out the Home Professionals Directory on the www.notsobighouse.com website to find an architect, designer, or remodeler in your area.

As you work through the list, additional questions will inevitably arise that will refine your impressions. Your goal in this phase of the design process is to identify the things that you feel most strongly about—both those you want to keep and those you want to change. For now, you don't need to do anything with your discoveries. Observing them is enough.

With answers in hand, you're ready to consider the best remodeling strategies for the job. I do this by making an evaluation based on a set of design principles that ensures that the whole house is considered at the same time you are working with each separate part. For a home's exterior, these principles fall into three main categories: getting the proportions right, integrating old and new, and connecting to the neighborhood. Let's take a look at each of these categories.

getting the proportions right

One of the most common complaints I hear about house exteriors is that something seems "off," it just doesn't look right. The house seems insubstantial, it looks as though it's squinting, or it's just bland. In almost all these cases, there are simple solutions once you understand the root cause of the problem.

Our eyes are highly attuned to proportion and scale, as well as to alignment and balance, yet we don't have the language to describe these things. So when something is out of alignment or not in proportion, we can't easily put our finger on the problem. By naming the qualities that our senses recognize, we can more easily identify what's not working.

Proportion

When something is well proportioned, it just looks right: well supported, well integrated, with all the elements of the appropriate scale working with everything else. The only time we tend to notice proportioning, in fact, is when a house *doesn't* look right.

In the photos on p. 24, the original house had two elements that seemed out of proportion. The gable end facing the street was too tall for its width, and the roof over the front stoop was so minimally supported that it looked as though it might blow away in a strong wind. In the remodeling, adding a horizontal shadow line to the front elevation of the gable breaks up the vertical face of the house and gives it more pleasing proportions. The addition of thicker columns and a white picket railing make the roof over the stoop appear more substantial. And the construction of another larger gable roof over added space that sits just behind the plane of the original gable makes the proportioning of the whole composition even more pleasing.

Have the courage of your own convictions. If something looks out of proportion or seems precarious, insubstantial, or flimsy, that's where you need to direct your exterior remodeling efforts.

This house was nearly doubled in size, but carefully conceived to remain in proportion to our human scale. The small gabled dormer addition alone tells you that this is still a house whose life upstairs is lived within the gentle slope of its roof.

Human Scale

It is possible to design a house where everything looks in proportion, but when you approach the house on foot you realize that it is out of proportion to our human bodies. It's as though the house has been designed for giants. These days we're all familiar with this type of house.

Several years ago, one of my business partners had a rude awakening when one of his clients discovered that he needed a bit more space than he had originally planned. The client took my partner's plans, enlarged them on a copy machine, and built the beefed-up version. Although he increased each dimension by only 10 percent, the result looked quite ridiculous when surrounded by its standard-sized neighbors. It was out of proportion with our human scale—an expensive lesson for the client.

So in addition to considering the proportions of each element in relation to the other elements of the design, we must also include ourselves in the equation. A house must be in proportion to our human bodies. When adding on, it is very easy to make the addition too big for

In proportion   Out of proportion   In proportion

Beefing up the front porch with a brick base, thick half-columns, paired beams, and deep fascia boards adds character and lends an air of dignity to what is still a small house.

the proportions of the rest of the house. The photos on p. 26 show a house that was doubled in size, but which was carefully conceived to remain in proportion to our human scale.

Solidity and Permanence

Many houses have one or more elements that look tacked on, little more than flimsy afterthoughts. The most common offenders are porches, stoops, and sunrooms. Beefing up the structural elements of these spaces, such as the columns and beams, eradicates the sense of impermanence. In fact, the addition of these heftier forms can help to "root" the whole house, even though only the porch or sunroom has been remodeled.

In the example shown on p. 27, the original front stoop was covered by a minimal lean-to roof, supported by a wrought-iron post that all but disappears when viewed from the street. The architect added a much wider and more substantial front porch whose roof is supported by

Window out of alignment with gable roof above.

Adding a line of glass block or a shutter disguises the nonalignment.

The original house had the basic shape of a Craftsman-style home but lacked its expressive spirit. The remodeled front porch—with its stout, paired columns, rich colors, and vintage details—properly conveys a sense of solidity and structure, hallmarks of the Craftsman style.

oversized columns. The difference in the appearance is notable: This house, it's clear, won't be leaving any time soon.

Alignments

When a gable roof has a window beneath it, we expect the window to be aligned with the roof's ridge in some way. And when there's a series of windows on a main level and a similar series of windows on the second level, we expect the two sets also to be aligned with each other. When they're not, the whole house looks out of whack. For many people the most objectionable problem on a home's exterior is one where an alignment has been missed. Even *almost* right can look awkward, as in the drawing on the facing page. To cure such a problem, you can either move the offending element to its proper place, or, if this is not possible, introduce another intermediate element to disguise the nonalignment.

In the example shown in the photos on the facing page, the original house had a front door and walkway that were not in alignment with a centered lean-to dormer on the second level. By moving the front door and the steps and path to the street, the house now looks properly aligned, both with itself and with the street. Yet on the house we saw on p. 26 where the front door is not centered below the three windows on the second floor, this off-centeredness has been disguised with the long roof of the porch, which balances the composition.

integrating old and new

Our attitudes about the way materials are applied to the surface of a house are very different than they were a few decades ago. If you look at most new houses today, you'll notice that one material is applied uniformly all over the surface, much as a young child with a box of colored crayons might apply color. There's no differentiation between elements, so the siding, for example, is applied everywhere, except where there's a window or door.

Your eye tends to read the trim band capping the brick as the top of the first story, so the house, overall, appears shorter, as though it might be a story-and-a-half, closer in scale to the original single-story house.

DIFFERENTIATION OF PARTS

Uniform siding and trim

lipstick

When you don't have a lot of money to spend but you want to give the existing parts of your house some differentiation from one another, one of the least expensive but most effective approaches is to paint the window sashes (or the storm windows if you have them) a strong color, as was done here. I call this the "lipstick" approach because it has the same effect as makeup on a face: It draws attention to one small element and makes the whole look more appealing as a result.

Differentiation of surface materials

In the past, there was much more differentiation of each surface, and not only on the side that faces the street but all around the building. Older homes might have a base of brick or stone, for example, all around the house. Look at a new house, and there's usually no such distinction between the base of the house and the upper part. An older home will typically have wide trim boards surrounding each window and door, while a newer house usually has none.

This differentiation of parts is largely what makes an older home so much more appealing. One of the keys to a successful remodeling of the exterior of an older home is to duplicate the original differentiations across all the newly remodeled surfaces. If the original house had few differentiations, it will be a significant improvement to introduce some. The following principles explain how the parts of a house can be distinguished from one another to make a more expressive and personal composition.

Visual Weight

In the example I described above of a house with a continuous brick base, the material is used in part to give the house a sense of "visual weight." Because the brick is darker than the siding above it, our eyes actually interpret the density of color as weight. We see the house as heavier on the bottom than the top, and this emphasizes the impression of permanence.

Another example of the same principle is the house shown on p. 29, which was originally sheathed primarily in brick. The architect who designed the new second story for the house used the natural visual weight of the brick to differentiate the lower part of the house from the upper part, extending the brick above its original dimension to the sill of the second-floor windows.

Beltlines

Not only does the brick in this example root the house, but it also creates a beltline—a continuous line that divides top from bottom, much as the belt holding up your pants divides torso from legs. Imagine for a moment if this house had been made all of brick. It might have looked very heavy and significantly bigger. On a street of smaller houses like the original version of this house, the bigness would have looked seriously out of place. Using a beltline reduces the massiveness and adds some differentiation to each surface, making it both more approachable and more personal.

A beltline was also added to distinguish the original main level from the new second floor in the beautiful addition shown below. Here, both upper and lower sections are painted the same color, while the beltline is a strongly contrasting color—in this case, white. It is also possible to paint upper and lower sections a different color from one another (see the photo on p. 26), but it is still important to make the beltline contrast strongly with these in order for the principle to work.

The addition of a beltline below the second-story addition makes the new house look more classically proportioned than the rather plain original house.

Theme and Variations

When the original house already has some charm to it, you can copy details in the remodeled parts of the house, and in so doing weave an addition into the fabric of what already exists so that it appears seamless. The charming little bungalow shown on the facing page was almost doubled in size, which could have ruined its beauty and character if done insensitively. But by replicating the details of the old house, and by getting the proportions of the second floor right, the house looks like it was designed this way from scratch.

By using details from the original house in this way, you are working with a theme and developing some variations, just as composers do when they create a piece of music.

connecting to the neighborhood

You can design a beautiful remodel that is very pleasing to the homeowners, but if the neighbors find it an affront to the character of the neighborhood, then it isn't a good design and doesn't represent a truly Not So Big sensibility. A Not So Big remodel is by its very nature a good neighbor because it is designed as much for the community as for the homeowners themselves.

Being a Good Neighbor

To be a good neighbor, your house should be in proportion with the other structures in the neighborhood and fit without making a big statement. This means that you have to take note of the things that give the neighborhood its character. So, for example, if all the houses on a particular street are story-and-a-half bungalows, converting one of them into a three-story starter castle is not a gesture that is typically received kindly by the neighbors. It looks completely out of place and is seen by most

If a remodeled house is made more appealing from the street, surrounding property values are likely to rise and the entire neighborhood benefits.

Human-scaled details that can be appreciated from the street, day or night, express the personality of the homeowners, welcome visitors, and delight passersby.

as an eyesore that dramatically reduces the charm of the street (and instantly lowers the property value).

Connecting to the Street

Many older homes have little or no connection to the street other than a plain concrete pathway. Even the steps up to the front door look tacked on and unwelcoming. From the street this tends to color one's impression of the entire neighborhood, saying, "You're not really welcome here."

It is a different story when an effort has been made through the remodeling process to make a connection with the street. This is one of the reasons that open front porches are so universally loved. They greet the street, providing an intermediate space that isn't yet inside but is not quite outside; not quite house and not quite street. The house above (and also on p. 28) has made such an effort, turning a rather average and uninviting front porch into a real welcome gesture. It gives

the clear impression that, to the inhabitants of this house, the street is a part of what makes this place home.

The weaving together of all these considerations is what makes a remodeling Not So Big. There are no hard and fast rules about how this is accomplished, and there's no one style that is required—far from it in fact. Houses of all styles can be made Not So Big through the implementation of these principles. The point is to use them to increase the overall beauty, balance, and integrity of the house you are remodeling as you go about making it better fit your visions of home. In the case studies that follow you'll find a variety of successful Not So Big exterior remodelings that will help you learn to think like an architect and see the potential for transformation that lies within every house.

Because the second-story addition hunkers within the original roof, this house retains its much-beloved bungalow qualities: a dominant, sheltering roof, builderly details, and the modest character of a single-story house.

a front porch opens up to the street

Our houses—especially those located close to the street—have an opportunity and even an obligation to be neighborly, to contribute to the streetscape and encourage social interaction.

When Christina and Wayne bought their 1912 bungalow in Minneapolis, it had a three-season front porch encased in cheap storm windows to go with its workmanlike overall appearance. The exterior lacked the details and features that give a housefront personality and visual interest; it lacked color and charm. Worse still, the enclosed porch robbed the living spaces inside of light and a connection to the street.

Christina and Wayne could have winterized the front porch when they remodeled the interior, expanding the living room into it. Instead, the couple and their architect, Eric Odor, opened the porch and made it a kind of outdoor parlor. At the same time, they amped up the house's "bungalow-ness" with stone kneewalls; sturdy, tapered columns; and a sweeping, arched beam.

Christina and Wayne gave up the opportunity to add square footage in favor of connecting their house—and themselves—to the neighborhood. They don't miss the extra space; in fact, they like the idea that their home expands in the summer and contracts in the winter. For private dining and lounging, they improved the back deck, adding a trellis and a more elegant railing, but for mingling with the neighbors, nothing beats their generous front porch.

style and substance

The original housefront—dominated by thin-framed aluminum storm windows—lacked depth, detail, and visual weight. The house's new face has real bungalow character. And it has presence, thanks to the heavy stone kneewall and sturdy columns.

before

after

"The house was transformed from recluse to social butterfly."
—Eric Odor, architect

Christina and Wayne gave up an enclosed, three-season porch but gained a sheltered outdoor area for hanging out in warm weather and a closer connection to the neighborhood all year long.

a welcoming home

The former walkway went straight at the flimsy door to the enclosed porch. You were out and then you were in. Now a curved pathway leads through a gardened front yard and up wide steps to the center of the open porch. A pleasant walk across the porch takes you to the door.

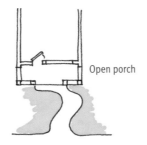

Enclosed porch

Open porch

❶ The complement to the more public front porch is an extended back deck with a trellis overhead.

❷ ❸ ❹ Details such as the brackets on the sides of the house, the trim around the windows and doors, and the tapered porch columns have a unifying effect on the exterior.

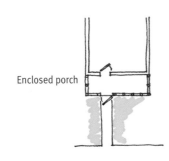

New window and door trim throughout echoes the porch details and adds Bungalow character.

The newly opened porch incorporates the existing beadboard ceiling, refinished with fresh stain.

The arched opening and burnt-orange trim paint add personality in keeping with the original house's Bungalow style.

Thick columns, rustic stonework, and wide trim boards lend the house scale and substance.

At 8 ft., the porch is wide enough for furniture, so it feels like an outdoor sitting parlor.

from suburban blandness to cottage charm

Like so many postwar suburban "Colonials," Gail and David's house in Falls Church, Virginia, felt like a phony. Compared with a well-proportioned, crisply detailed genuine Colonial, their 1940s house looked pretty flimsy. With a growing family, Gail and David's dual challenge became improving the look of the house while adding square footage to it . . . without spoiling its appropriately domestic scale. Their architect, Charles Moore, chose the Not So Big route, converting the garage to a mudroom, adding part of the master suite above it, and tucking the rest of the added space behind the house. He revamped the roof without changing its pitch and made many small changes that, taken together, give the new housefront much greater integrity than the old one.

breaking up the boxiness

The remodeled housefront has fresh paint colors, larger windows, and a trim band that brings its top and bottom halves together. But the two changes with the most impact are the new front entry porch, which is properly scaled to the house behind it, and the overhanging roof and shed dormers, which break up the boxiness of the original house.

The former garage sat back from the original house and looked like an afterthought.

The roof looked slight and insubstantial. It lacked height and any sense of thickness (which would give it visual weight); it also lacked overhangs and so did not appear sheltering.

The symmetry established by the windows demands a prominent element at the center. Instead, the spindly columns and a shallow, pagoda-like porch roof were at odds with the rest of the house.

The windows to either side of the entry emphasized the vertical (with long shutters and a panel below each window), which only accentuated the thinness and inadequacy of the entry.

The overhanging roof adds depth and a sheltering quality; the roof's wide fascia board adds visual weight. Shed dormers break up the roofline and help tie the addition to the main house; the exposed rafter tails add detail, charm, and scale.

Painted brick and thin clapboards in warm, complementary colors tie the bottom and top of the house together, while two sets of paired double-hung windows add visual weight to the bottom half of the house, where it belongs.

Wide trim band across the center of the house helps the clapboards and brick come together gracefully, gives the house a pleasant horizontality, and helps integrate the stepped back addition (formerly the garage) and the main house volume.

The new front porch has a substantial pediment roof and thick columns, befitting the importance of the main entry and the scale of the house.

adding with integrity

The main volume of the house presented a formal, monolithic front to the street, with a strong symmetry its small features couldn't live up to. Although the new house is larger, it takes advantage of the enclosed garage and added space above it to downplay the symmetry and break up the mass of the house. The resulting exterior is more relaxed, playful, and cottagelike.

"The scale of the house is everything."
—Charles Moore, architect

updating the look, respecting the neighborhood

Tracy and Ken chose to live in the city of Austin, Texas, because they liked its humble 1940s-era houses and walkable neighborhoods. Needing room for their growing family, they hired architect Nick Deaver to help them add space to their 900-sq.-ft. home. It's easy for small houses like this to be overwhelmed by an addition, taking away the very charm that draws people to such neighborhoods in the first place. To avoid this, Nick designed a cottage-scale "companion" structure that extends off the back of Tracy and Ken's house, preserving the integrity of the old house form. By stripping away a false gable end at the front, cheap wrought-iron porch columns, and other "insignificant details," Nick refashioned the house as a purer version of its original self.

"Removing corner boards, minor roof gables, and other insignificant details revealed a generous front porch and a clear, simple form."

—Nick Deaver, architect

What isn't seen from the street is as important as what is. An addition equal to the size of the original house has been placed discreetly behind the old house, preserving the cottage scale of the housefront.

At 4 ft. wide, the front door feels generous and welcoming. It isn't a fancy door, but its solid cherry panels and singular slot of glass signal that this is no run-of-the-mill house. The door was crafted by the homeowner, who is a professional builder, and it speaks to his enthusiasm for natural materials and the arts.

The new cupola is a signature element, something people walking by will notice and remember. But it's not there just for looks; its windows bring light into the center of the house and open up to help ventilate and cool the rooms below.

The galvanized metal standing-seam roof and painted clapboard siding are new, but they have a vintage feel. The clapboards look conventional, but for durability equal to that of the metal roof and to save on wood use, they're made of Hardiplank® cement fiber.

Because the front door has been relocated from the center of the porch to one side, there's now ample room for a sitting area.

Fresh exterior elements—a broad, overhanging roof with a handsome cupola, a generous front door, and crisp concrete stepping stones—give the little house personality and presence it never had.

Square concrete pavers and concrete porch steps fit the crisp look of the remodeled exterior and also relate to the native cut limestone of the low retaining walls, neighboring houses, and the addition hidden at the back.

fitting in

The remodeled house has a cleaner, more contemporary look than the original. Gone are the asphalt roof shingles, wrought-iron porch columns, and double-hung windows, replaced by a crisp, metal roof, spare wood posts, and casement windows undivided by muntins. But the basic house form remains the same, its gray-green clapboards are traditional, and new details, like the exposed rafter tails, fit the cottage scale of the neighborhood.

celebrate the new, respect the old

Architect Warren Lloyd and his wife, Jennie, liked the look of their Tudor Bungalow from the tree-lined street in their Salt Lake City neighborhood. But with a third child on the way, they were growing out of two bedrooms and a bath. They decided to add a family room to the back of the house, with two children's bedrooms over it, and to convert the attic into a master suite with a nursery. Extending the house into the deep backyard would also be an opportunity to create outdoor living space and to bring the outside in. From the front, the house still follows the old rooflines and looks almost the same as it did before the remodeling. Toward the back, the addition, with its jaunty red dormers, reads as something new—perhaps a series of additions, like those added over time to a Vermont farmhouse—yet also feels at home with the original Bungalow. The clapboards carry across from new to old, but what really ties the two together is their complementary scale: Both are Not So Big.

maintaining a sense of balance

The addition at the back of this Bungalow doesn't maintain the look of the original in any strict sense. It introduces new forms, new roof shapes, new colors, even new window types. But it does maintain the human scale of the original. In both the old and new, the bedrooms are within the roof, and you sense this life lived within from the street. And in overall size and massing, old and new are proportionate, which is why they feel balanced even though they're not the same.

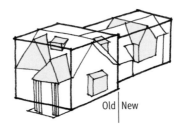 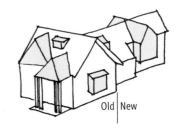

stepping back

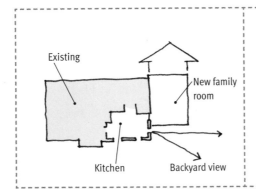

Existing
New family room
Kitchen
Backyard view

Warren could have designed a larger family room, but instead he stepped it back to avoid blocking an existing kitchen window facing the backyard. Stepping back meant a somewhat smaller family room and smaller bedrooms upstairs, but it also meant the kitchen wouldn't be pinned in.

To accent the new dormers and dining room bay, Warren Lloyd consciously picked a rich red color that is dramatic and different yet compatible with the existing brick.

"We wanted our remodel to tell a new story but not detract from the original house as a story of its time."
—Warren Lloyd, architect and owner

The existing house had a fine front porch, but it stepped abruptly down to the grass. The new porch terraces down the front lawn and—in the true spirit of doing double duty— makes use of bricks removed from the back wall of the house.

growing in size without diminishing in character

With enough care and restraint, it's possible to make a small house considerably larger without spoiling the spirit of the original. To make room for his family and their active lifestyle, architect Charles Moore tripled the size of his 1922 cottage home, from 1,100 sq. ft. to 3,300 sq. ft. The house is now noticeably larger, but it still feels like a cottage and it still fits the neighborhood, which is predominated by larger, historic homes. Charles put the question to himself like this: "How do you take a house that you love, that you've already renovated once, change it again, yet end up with a similar kind of house?" The answer lies in embracing the detailing and materials of the old house, in keeping the new look simple and honest, and in breaking down the taller, two-story form of the remodeled house into a pleasing composition of smaller roof sections and dormers.

getting the height right

In a full two-story house, the walls of the second floor are typically 8 ft. tall or taller, just like the walls on the first floor. The rooms inside are like boxes; from within them, you have no sense of the roof. But for the added second floor in this house, architect Charles Moore set the height of the exterior walls at 6 ft., then sloped the ceiling up to 9 ft., where it flattens out. Moore considers 6 ft. a magic number: tall enough that you don't feel cramped, even standing close to the wall, as in a Colonial, but low enough that you feel the sheltering quality of the roof, as in a true Cape. Nine feet is important, too. It gives the upstairs spaces some headroom and it maintains the 9-ft. height of the downstairs rooms, helping to unify the new second floor with the existing first floor.

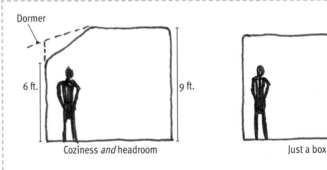

Dormer

6 ft.   9 ft.   8 ft.

Coziness *and* headroom   Just a box

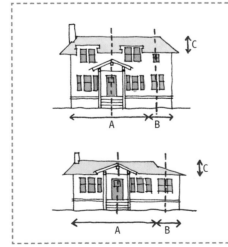

seeing the old in the new

This was already a sweet little cottage home, thanks to a remodeling architect Charles Moore had done previously. So it wasn't a case of saving an ugly house or even of improving on an inferior one; rather, the challenge was to add a second story and expand the size of the house without diminishing the charm and character of the original. Charles succeeded in doing this by maintaining the rhythm and symmetry of the windows, the shallow slope (and thus the low height) of the roof, and the purity of the white-on-white color scheme of the old house.

"The simple, understated approach to massing and detailing doesn't overwhelm the original house."
— Charles Moore, architect and owner

The new roof has a shallow pitch, just like the old one. It sits on second-story walls that are 6 ft. tall, rather than the typical 8 ft., so the whole house is 2 ft. shorter than it might have been and more in keeping with the scale of the original cottage.

The little window plays a big role in the look of the new house, anchoring the area above the pair of sitting room windows without detracting from the symmetry of the larger windows about the centerline of the entry porch and front door.

The shed dormers punch through the overhanging main roof, animating the exterior, breaking the roof into smaller sections, and keeping the house from looking as tall as a full two-story house.

Exposed rafter tails under the broad, overhanging roof add human-scaled detail and cottage character. A wide fascia (the horizontal board that hides the rafters) gives a roof a substantial, sheltering quality that's usually welcome, but here the goal was to lighten the feel of the roof, to downplay the impact of the added second story.

The lower half of the house remains essentially as it was, with the entry porch unchanged. Although the first-floor windows were replaced for better performance and to better match the new ones above, they're identical in looks and set in the very same rough openings as the originals.

3. front entries

The front entry is not usually at the top of a homeowner's list for remodeling, but it is a very important aspect of a home's design. When I use the term *front entry,* I'm referring not only to the doorway itself but also to the process of arrival, the stoop or porch, as well as the place you enter once the door is open—the receiving place.

If the front entry isn't well designed—if it isn't inviting, if it's in an awkward position, or if it looks tacked on like an afterthought—it can make everyone who arrives at the house feel uncomfortable, which is hardly a desirable first impression. By contrast, a welcoming front entry instantly puts visitors at ease. As they step across the threshold, they're already prepared to enjoy the experience of being in the home. So this small and often overlooked improvement can dramatically alter the perceived quality of the house for visitors, for the homeowners, and, when the time comes to put the house on the market, for prospective buyers as well.

The original entry was functional but lacking in character. The new entry features wide trim that echoes the new window trim, a gently pitched roof with personality, and a signature door.

common front entry problems

In my experience, the most common problems related to front entries are as follows:

• The front entry is in the wrong location, so no one ever uses it.

• The front entry consists of a path, a set of concrete steps, and a door, but little else. There's no place to stand at the top of the steps, no shelter over the door, and no separate place to enter once you step inside.

• The front door delivers you into the middle of the main living space, with no receiving place inside. This divides the living space in two, making it almost impossible to furnish, and makes entering a very awkward experience.

• The receiving place, although well located, is dark and unwelcoming.

• There are no connecting views from the receiving place to other rooms and spaces, so the first impression of the house is boxy and confining.

not so big principles

The Process of Entering

When you are remodeling a front entry, the first thing to consider is whether the entire process of arrival is sending the right signals to guests and visitors to make them feel welcome. And if this is also your own everyday entry, the arrival process must also accommodate your needs, such as where to set down your stuff, where to hang the keys, and where to put the mail.

DIVIDED LIVING ROOM

The path from the front entry divides the living room in two.

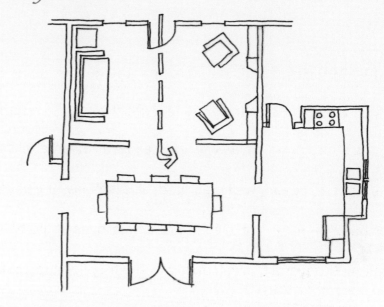

If the path to the front entry requires a long or circuitous journey from parking area to door (as shown in the drawing on p. 49), it's likely the entry point is poorly located. The house is in effect turning its back on would-be visitors. No amount of visual improvement can solve this type of problem, so in this case you'll need the help of an architect.

But assuming that the front entry is visible from the point of arrival, whether this be parking area or street, there are four primary categories to consider. Let's look at each of them in turn.

Path and Place

The path leading up to the stoop or porch, and the front door beyond, is every bit as much a part of the design as the doorway itself. This process of arrival sets expectations for what's on the other side of the door.

The path leading to the front door does not have to be straight, but if it takes too circuitous a path some will abandon it and take a more direct

questions to ask yourself

In evaluating the strengths and weaknesses of your own front entry, there are a number of questions to ask yourself. Some may require you to think about issues you've never considered before. To arrive at a good design solution, however, you must first analyze the problem properly, so be sure to give this exercise the time it deserves.

- *Is the front entry in the right place?*

- *How does the front entry relate to the street, driveway, or pathway?*

- *Is there a pleasing arrival process?*

- *Are there any awkward points along the way?*

- *Does the landscaping provide a welcoming atmosphere for the visitor?*

- *Who uses the entry? Is it used often, rarely, or never? If never, is this something you want to remedy?*

- *Do guests arrive with coats? If so, is there a place to put them?*

- *Is there some sort of cover overhead for someone who is waiting for the door to be answered?*

- *Can you hear the doorbell from outside? (Visitors need to know they've been heard.)*

- *Is there some glass, obscuring or clear, that allows a visitor to see that you are coming to answer the door?*

- *Is there a place to shift gears from outside to inside worlds as you and your guests enter the house?*

- *Can you see into adjacent spaces, or are you in an enclosed space once you enter?*

- *Does the receiving place have access to daylight, or is it lit only by light fixtures?*

- *Is the receiving place a clearly defined space, or is it undifferentiated from the room it opens into?*

- *If the front door delivers you right into a primary living space, is it at one side of the room or in the middle?*

- *Is the receiving place or foyer unnecessarily tall or formal?*

- *Is the receiving place too cramped for comfort?*

- *Does the receiving place make you feel welcomed into the house?*

There are few modifications you can make to the entry process that will have so much functional benefit or bang for the buck as adding some form of shelter above the front door.

THE LONG WAY HOME

Street

Guest parking

Front door is invisible from guest parking area.

route. People generally don't like being forced to be inefficient with their steps. Be sure to make the path wide enough that someone walking its length does not feel cramped, and if there are steps up to the front door, make sure there's a wide enough platform at the top so that he or she can stand comfortably and wait while you come to the door.

Covered Entry

A covered entry not only looks good from the street, but it also provides guests with a pleasant, sheltered place to stand while waiting for the door to be answered. Even if the weather is not an issue, the cover overhead gives the visitor the impression that he or she has already been welcomed by the house. It has extended out to meet the guest, which is instantly reassuring and hospitable.

The roof over the door should ideally extend at least 3 ft. out from the face of the house so there's room to stand completely within its shelter. At its most minimal, such a shelter can be no more than a small lean-to or gable, while in a more expanded form the added roof can be extended across the face of the house to create a front porch. If you select this strategy, be careful not to make the porch too deep from front to back or the front door will get lost in the shadows. A porch that's somewhere between 8 ft. and 12 ft. deep offers room for porch furniture without losing the importance of the door.

Special Front Door

A door that is beautifully crafted or of an unusual dimension or color can also affect a visitor's experience of the house. In my own designs, I have

The genius of this covered entry, carved from a corner of the main house form, is that it welcomes you both from the driveway (pathway on the left) and from the street (pathway on the right).

often hired a craftsman to make a wider-than-usual front door—perhaps 3 ft. 4 in. instead of the usual 3 ft. 0 in. If you are using the existing standard door opening, however, you can forgo the extra width and focus on the character of the door itself. And if your budget is tight, you can take a standard door and add some color to make it uniquely yours. In a way, this door is like the expressive face of the house. It tells guests something about who you are and provides a preview of the more personal interior experience that it conceals.

Receiving Place

The place you step into once the door is opened is another point that makes a big impression. What is revealed and what the space feels like as you enter are critical in shaping your (and your guests') experience of the home's character.

No matter how beautiful the receiving place, if it is dark, the dreariness will be the thing that's remembered. I always try to find a way to introduce more daylight, whether by adding a window, a front door sidelight, or glass in the door itself. Using lighter colors for the walls and ceiling can also help to brighten a dull receiving place, as can some strategically located lighting fixtures. Wall washers and up-lights are my favorites because they use walls and ceilings as big reflectors and bring them to life. The most common solution, a center fixture or chandelier, doesn't work very well because it casts the same level of lighting over everything, which tends to flatten the whole space rather than enliven it.

Front entries are often the most prominent feature on the face of a house. They deserve a solidity equal to their importance, such as supplied here by these generously proportioned columns and the wide frieze board above them.

A single column, a partial wall, and a lowered ceiling create just enough definition for a receiving place in what had been an open corner of the living room.

If there is no receiving place, and you are dumped unceremoniously into a main living space, I would strongly recommend a remodeling of the area to define a receiving place, even if it is small. This can be done by adding a column, a half wall, a lowered ceiling, or ideally all three. Too little definition to the space is almost worse than doing nothing at all because it looks tacked on. But enclose it too much and it becomes isolating and confining. For a receiving place to work well, it has to be integrated into the entire composition of the room. Because this is such a pivotal place in the home's design, it's worth hiring an architect or designer to help you think through the options.

Interior Views

One of the largely overlooked characteristics of the receiving place is its role as orienter to the rest of the house. A well-designed receiving place

A generous gabled roof provides more shelter than the former roof overhang and does a much better job of signaling that this is the main entry. The artfully crafted door adds personality and reinforces the message.

This receiving place is bright, airy, open to the center of the house, and also connected to the life of the street.

gives you a glimpse or two of what is to come as you continue your passage into the house. But if it tells you too much all at once, if you can see everything from the front door, the rest of the house can be a bit of a letdown. It has already revealed all its secrets.

Although you may never have thought much before about the shaping of what can be seen from any particular point in the house, throughout the course of this book, you'll learn that this is a key ingredient of a well-designed house. It is, in many ways, a collection of well-designed views. And the receiving place is where this collection of views begins.

A view can be modified by moving a door or widening an opening between rooms, for example, so as you consider the following types of views, the tools at your disposal are windows, doorways, and framed openings.

Connecting Views

What do you want your guests to see when they first enter your house? Is there a beautiful outdoor view? Which rooms or spaces would you like them to be able to see from here? And where would you like them to go next? The primary view that connects to an adjacent space will be the one guests will be most strongly drawn toward. A remodeling is often needed when the house is sending the wrong signals. Perhaps, like a lot of older houses, it is saying, "Come on into the formal living room," when in fact no one today ever uses that room. Instead, you may want guests to head toward the kitchen and family room. To make that happen, you'll need to play up the view toward that area and reduce the visibility of the formal living room. In general, the wider open the view to a space, and the lighter the space, the more it will draw guests toward it.

(top) Don't forget to consider the view back toward the receiving place. In this case, the openings that offer views from the front door also set up framed views of the entry area.

(above) You don't have to restrict yourself to a single connecting view. A successful receiving place often includes views to three or four adjacent spaces.

light to walk toward

A highly effective way to make a house feel bigger than it actually is, as well as to move people toward the back of the house, is to provide a view along the longest axis. This may be a view from the receiving place to the very back of the house, or it may be a view along the diagonal, from one corner of the house to the other. For this strategy to work as an attractive interior view, you'll need either a window or a lighted painting at the far end of the vista. The brightness will draw people toward it.

same footprint, far better front entry

Turning their unheated entry porch into a heated, interior entry space with a powder room and coat closet wasn't quite as simple as Minneapolis couple Kate and Dean had hoped. They figured on renovating the porch as it stood, in effect filling in the walls under the existing roof. But the old porch was so worn and out-of-kilter, it had to be torn down to the foundation and a new, fully enclosed porch built in its place. Architects Dan Nepp and Rachel Hendrickson were able to design the new entry porch so it looked very nearly like the old one, but with double-hung windows, a proper door, and Craftsman-style details befitting the 1920s house.

The hitch was that the enclosed entry had to look "porch-y," as Dan puts it, because, like the one it replaced, it stands beyond the setback line for the house. So Dan and Rachel combined wide wood pilasters (a fancy word for inset columns) at the corners with ample windows to give the entry a porch-like openness. In the end, a setback variance was approved, based on the "porch quality" of the new entry. And though the newly enclosed entry might stick out beyond the setback line, it doesn't "stick out" from the house visually. That's because Kate and Dean wisely chose to upgrade the housefront at the same time as they enclosed the porch. There's now a seamless charm about the whole place.

doing away with a door swing

When the old three-season entry porch was fully enclosed, the homeowners gained not only an entry hall, coat closet, and powder room but also a more functional sitting area, now that the entry door doesn't swing right into the living room.

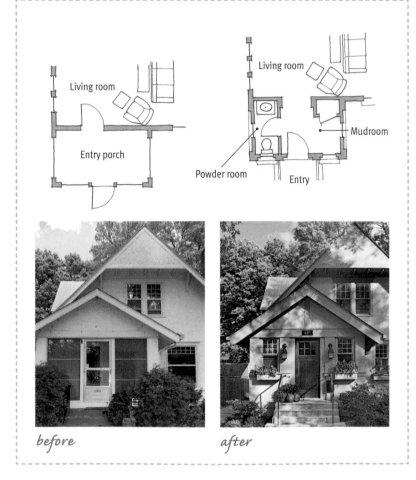

before   *after*

"The porch is modest in scale . . . it fits the house . . . it doesn't outstrip it."
— Dan Nepp, architect

Remodeling the entry porch occasioned a rethinking of the entire exterior color scheme. White on white became a two-toned interplay of stucco and wood trim.

Planter boxes lend the new entry porch and housefront a well-cared-for look.

A solid, Craftsman-style door gives the entry porch substance it never had with the flimsy storm door on the old porch.

A vertical trim piece added to both the entry porch gable and the main gable helps bring old and new together.

(right) A wide, arched opening into the front entry porch takes the place of a door that swung into the living room.

(far right) The entry is simple and functional, with nothing more than what's necessary and nothing less.

front entry as arrival experience

Bill and Lynn called architect Stephen Robinson nearly 20 years ago about the failing basement in their 1960s brick ranch house in Atlanta. So began a series of phased remodeling projects that opened up spaces and improved the flow inside but left the footprint and exterior of the house largely unchanged . . . until this latest phase addressed the front entry.

The new front entry is a masterwork of Not So Big remodeling, employing virtually every concept mentioned earlier in this chapter. Fundamentally, the remodeling moves can be divided in two: those that improve the process of arriving from the driveway, and those that connect the entry to the rest of the interior, making the entry a receiving place, the hub of the house.

The keys to improving the arrival sequence were to take down a brick-walled courtyard that got in the way of a clear entry path; to widen the outside entry area and give it a special door; and to open the entry inside from a narrow hall to a generous square, a true receiving place. The keys to connecting the entry to the rooms beyond were to open up the stairway to the basement so you can see over it, and to use built-ins, lowered ceiling planes, and well-placed openings to set up long views. Stephen aptly calls these connecting views "considered vistas."

a memorable window and door

The remodeled front entry has its own memorable personality, thanks to the bow window, which fits nicely under what had been perhaps too deep an overhang, and a substantial maple door with asymmetrical panels that echo the asymmetry of the entry composition as a whole.

before

after

Recessed lighting amplifies the rhythm of the door and windows while adding warmth.

The sturdy maple door is clearly a singular and special element, with enough substance to signify its importance and draw your eye to its (original) corner location.

The street-address panel adds personality and fits with the look of the door.

A bow window serves as a beacon at night; its curve guides your eye toward the door.

A curved path guides you gracefully to the door; there's no mistaking where to go.

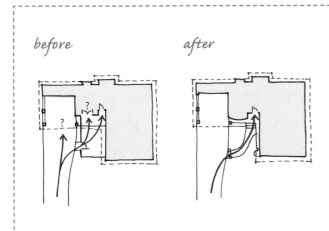

before

after

a clear path to the front door

The original path to the front door took you through a gate into a brick-walled courtyard. Assuming you chose to enter the courtyard and not the carport, you then had another choice to make: enter through a door half-hidden in the corner, or enter through the more prominent French doors. It was at best a confusing arrival sequence. Now the walls and French doors are gone, replaced by a gently curved path that takes you right to the front door, while the curve of the bow window leads your eye to the same place.

a receiving place with connecting views

The original front door opened unceremoniously onto a narrow hallway. A window in the living room did (and still does) provide light to walk toward, but otherwise you confronted a wall just 3 ft. in front of you and a number of uninviting doors. Now you enter into a generous square space that expands across an open stairway and beyond a series of columns. You're in a receiving place, defined by a lowered maple ceiling panel, but you're also treated to connecting views into the dining area, living area, and study. The family room to your left, no longer blocked by the door swing, also beckons.

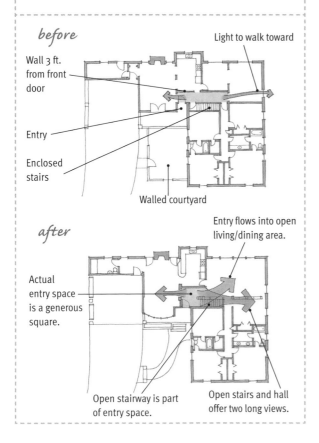

before

Light to walk toward

Wall 3 ft. from front door

Entry

Enclosed stairs

Walled courtyard

after

Entry flows into open living/dining area.

Actual entry space is a generous square.

Open stairway is part of entry space.

Open stairs and hall offer two long views.

The lowered maple ceiling panel defines the entry area.

A maple column and pylon serve as signature elements, signaling the front entry and defining the entry space proper from adjacent spaces.

A lighted painting in the family room serves as light to walk toward.

The open stairway allows in light and reveals a wall for displaying art, adding personality to the entry.

A built-in bookcase adds storage space while serving as a railing and warming up the feel of the entry.

The lowered ceiling plane leads to the spot-lit maple wall panel, a subtle bit of light to walk toward.

An open metal railing creates a connecting view across the floor of the study.

A wide view into the living room extends the entry space deep into the interior.

Open stairs make the basement more accessible and inviting.

signature elements

The square pylon and lowered ceiling plane are signature elements that define the entry area, not only upon arrival but also from adjacent spaces. Seeing them helps you to orient yourself within the house and to unify your experience of it.

"Perhaps the smartest move was opening the formerly walled-off basement stairs, creating a dramatic vista from the entry."
—Stephen Robinson, architect

4. back entries

It's one of those odd patterns of behavior that we generally put all the thought and money into creating a spectacular front entry that gets used only once or twice a year, while the entry we use every day is barely considered in terms of design. But there's absolutely no reason why the back entry can't be both beautiful and practical at the same time.

The issues related to back entries vary from place to place, and particularly from climate zone to climate zone, but there are some fundamental design strategies that can be applied no matter whether you live in a snowy, muddy, or sunny area. Some will require a place for snow gear, others a mudroom, and most a place for backpacks, purses, and briefcases. All can benefit from some consideration of what you see and what you walk through as you enter or exit. And just like its counterpart at the front of the house, the back entry should remind you instantly why you love this place. If it doesn't, however functionally proficient it may be, it's doing only half its job.

We don't usually think of it this way, but the back entry, if it's the one you use to come and go through every day, is the most important entry in the house.

not so big principles

The Process of Entering

Just as in the previous chapter on front entries, you'll want to think carefully about the path, the shelter above the door, the character of the doorway itself, and the place you step into as you enter the house. Although the way these strategies are interpreted will likely be less formal than for the front of the house, they still deserve the same attention and care.

In many back entry redesigns, the biggest problem is a lack of space. Rather than giving up before you've begun because of this, or resorting to adding on right away, there are a couple of strategies that will help you discover some space you didn't know you had.

Alcoves off Circulation

The process of entering, however poorly or well designed, takes place along a circulation route—a path through a series of rooms and spaces linking point A with point B. In the example shown at left on p. 63, point A is the garage and point B is the kitchen. In its existing state it's difficult to imagine how there will be enough room for any of the activity requirements listed in the sidebar on p. 67. But what's not being seen is the additional spatial resource offered by the oversized and under utilized living room. To find the space you need, you often have to look beyond the confines of the apparent problem area.

As you can see in the remodeled plan of the house, a small alcove of space has been carved out of the big living room, giving enough room for coats and shoes on one side and a counter with storage cabinets below for purse, briefcase, keys, and so on, on the other. In addition, by moving

(top) A wide, covered porch creates a sheltered pathway to the back door, just beyond the bench.

(bottom) This mudroom has a place for everything, but it isn't formal or fussy; jackets hang at the ready, and boots are easy to reach.

questions to ask yourself

The goal should be to find ways to make the entry process simultaneously enjoyable and functional. If you do it well, it will make you feel glad to be home every time you return—a benefit that cannot be overstated. As you consider your own back entry to get a sense of its strengths and weaknesses, ask yourself the following questions:

- *Is the connection between the place you enter the property and the back door a pleasant one?*

- *Is the back door sometimes mistaken for the front door by guests?*

- *Is the main access to the back door through the garage? If so, is there any personal or endearing characteristic to the arrival process, or is it typically garage-like, with a standard metal door as the primary connection to the house proper?*

- *Is the back entry sheltered from the elements in any way?*

- *Is there a landing, terrace, or other defined place to stand as you prepare to enter the house?*

- *Is there adequate lighting for nighttime use around the back door and along the path between door and parking area or garage?*

- *Is there any glass in or around the back door that will allow daylight to enter?*

- *As you step inside, what do you see? Is there a way to improve this view either by removing obstacles that limit the view to other parts of the house or by relocating the back entry?*

- *If you enter directly into a utility room such as a laundry, is there a way to rearrange the layout so that the entry process is separated from the utility function?*

- *Is there space to set down the things you bring into the house, such as groceries, purses, and backpacks?*

- *Is there a place for everyone to remove and hang up their winter clothing? Are the hooks at the right heights for the users (i.e., low hooks and cubbies for kids)?*

- *Are there any unusual uses for this back entry that you need to accommodate, such as bicycle storage, pet feeding, or dog kennels?*

- *Is the lighting in the area adequate?*

- *Is there enough daylight available to make the space cheery and welcoming?*

before

after

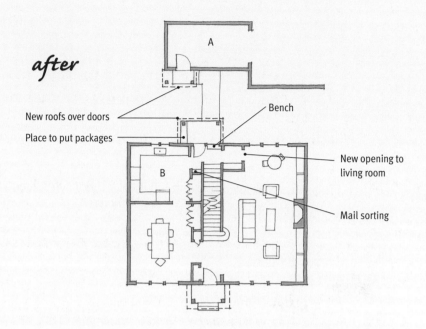

New roofs over doors

Place to put packages

Bench

New opening to living room

Mail sorting

the back door over a couple of feet and by reorganizing the kitchen a bit, a mail-sorting place has been tucked into a tiny nook of space adjacent to a new pantry area. Although this is not a spacious solution, it is one that meets the immediate needs and dramatically improves the utility of the entire main level while simultaneously resolving the back entry problems. Best of all, because the big living room is now both visible and accessible from the kitchen, it is much more likely to be used—an unexpected boon that often results when you tackle a seemingly unrelated remodeling problem.

This is a hypothetical example based on an amalgam of houses I've remodeled in the past, but it shows what's possible when you look for ways to widen the circulation route here and there in order to accommodate functions that require just a little more space than is currently available. As the name of this strategy implies, you are adding a small alcove of space to the circulation route to make it work in a more effective way.

Doing Double Duty

Another strategy you can use to make a little space do more than you thought it could is to have it do double duty—serve two purposes simultaneously. This is an ideal strategy to use when the back door delivers you directly into the laundry room, as happens with a lot of attached garages.

The laundry room is in fact already doing double duty by housing two functions—clothes washing, and moving into and out of the house. But it's not doing either very well. The art of effective double-duty design is to ensure that each function has its own spatial definition. By moving the walkway through the space to one side of the room and giving the laundry functions the rest of the room, thereby making the space an alcove off the walkway rather than the primary focus of the room, you create a spatial hierarchy (see the drawing on p. 64). If it's not possible to move the walkway, an alternative is to conceal the laundry functions behind shades, sliding panels, or folding doors. In this way you can completely separate the two functions visually when the laundry is not in use.

improving a less than lovely laundry

Laundries are often tucked into left-over spaces, as shown here in my own North Carolina house, making it difficult to accommodate any more than the bare necessities. But there *are* creative ways to make even such inadequate spaces work better. By using a front-loading washer and dryer, adding a countertop above for folding space, and some cabinetry and shelving above that, the diminutive laundry became a much more functional and elegant work area.

I bought a standard island top—a 36-in.-wide laminate top with bullnose on both sides—and cut off the back 6 in. to use as a removable shelf at the back of the counter. I concealed the water hookup behind the shelf. To hide the electrical hookups at either end, I made some wood box covers to complete the design—definitely a Not So Big solution to a "not big enough" problem.

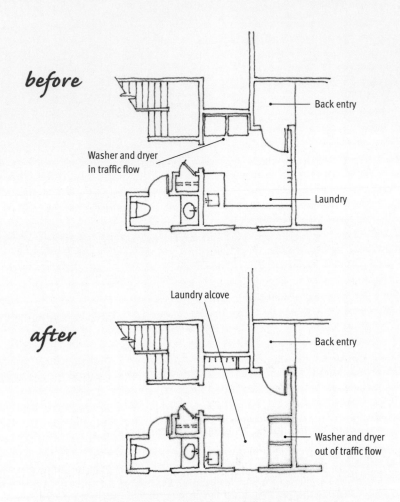

before

Back entry

Washer and dryer in traffic flow

Laundry

after

Laundry alcove

Back entry

Washer and dryer out of traffic flow

By implementing either of these double-duty approaches, when you are walking into or out of the house the hallway is now the dominant function. It is only when you step into the laundry alcove or open up the folding doors or panels that this area becomes the focus.

Long View Through

If there's a way to position the back entry so that the moment you open the door it allows you to see through to a view of the home's interior that you really love, it will make the process of entering far more enjoyable.

Obviously the entryway won't welcome you home if your view is restricted to the laundry room or the mudroom, but if you can see

① Long views from the back entry are just as important as those from the front entry in establishing a connection with the interior.

② **③** The back entry is an experience that begins outside and continues when you open the door. From outside to in, it should be a delight.

A back door in an added breakfast nook (out of photo to the right) clears traffic from the kitchen itself, allowing an unfettered view to the backyard.

through to the main living area, or to an informal eating area that's surrounded by windows with a view beyond to a favorite tree or your flower garden, you'll find that the whole experience of returning home becomes a pleasure instead of a frustration.

Outdoor Focus

There's one other function that a back entry can serve, but it involves a lot of issues related to the kitchen it enters into as well, so for the purposes of this chapter, I'll simply say that a well-designed back entry also has the potential of better connecting the main living spaces to the outdoors and of giving you a beautiful view to look at, whether you are in the process of entering or exiting. If you'd like to read more about this now, skip ahead to chapter 9 (p. 124).

room vs. activity place

It's a common temptation to think about a remodeling in terms of rooms, but if you restrict yourself to room names, you get locked into a limited solution before you've even begun to consider the possibilities. A better approach is to think of the design variables as a list of places for each of the activities you need to accommodate. Take the example of the entry process from a detached garage to the back door. Instead of thinking of specific rooms (garage, back door, mudroom, kitchen), consider the activities that take place there. Your list might then look like this:

- place to step out onto as I close the garage door

- sheltered place to set briefcase and purse as I unlock the door

- place to hang keys and coat and to stash briefcase and purse once I've stepped through the door.

- place to put down and sort the mail

- place to sit, take off shoes, and greet the dogs

- place to enter kitchen

By listing the activities you typically go through in the process of entering, you are much more likely to come up with a design that serves those activities well.

When architects and designers go through this process, they do multiple design solutions rather than continuously work at only one. It's what we call *schematic design*. In doing multiple versions, we discover possibilities for solving the problem at hand that we wouldn't have come up with if we'd stayed with only one solution. What you'll discover as you continue through this book is that the art of good design requires staying flexible and considering many different ways of solving a problem. The first idea that pops into your head is typically not the best. If you get married to that idea right away, it shuts out the possibility of discovering a better solution.

a better, not bigger, way to get inside

After buying a 1920s Bungalow in Newton, Massachusetts, architect Todd Sloane and his wife, Elizabeth, took time to figure out what they could and couldn't do with the house. Along with adding a modest family room with a master bedroom upstairs (described on pp. 268–269), they decided to improve the back entry. They considered replacing the narrow entry porch off the kitchen with a mudroom addition wide enough for a full closet with bifold doors. But property setbacks wouldn't allow it, and neither would their modest budget. Instead, they put their money into the family room and simply enclosed half the back porch, turning it into a mini-mudroom. When you get right down to it, a smaller mudroom does everything a larger one would have done, only better, because it doesn't take up the whole porch and thus cut off the kitchen from the backyard.

A baseboard heater fits neatly under the bench, where it warms shoes as well as the mudroom.

The enclosed mudroom still feels a lot like the open porch it replaced, thanks to ample windows.

The porch's beadboard ceiling and clapboard siding were left in place and simply painted white.

"In the end, it's all about what we had to work with."

— Todd Sloane, architect and owner

The small mudroom preserves half the porch as a covered entry area. Fully enclosing the porch would have eliminated the covered entry and also boxed in the kitchen.

A window to the kitchen is located where the door used to be.

Even the white-painted board that capped the former half-wall of the porch remains; it's visible just below the paired mudroom windows, embedded in the mudroom wall.

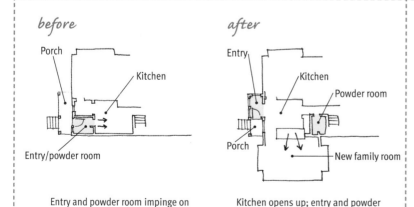

before

Porch

Kitchen

Entry/powder room

Entry and powder room impinge on kitchen . . . and on each other.

after

Entry

Kitchen

Powder room

Porch

New family room

Kitchen opens up; entry and powder room split up.

freeing up the kitchen

The old entry hall took up kitchen space and was often blocked by the powder room door. Turning half the back porch into a mudroom and moving the powder room farther inside not only improved the entry process but also gave space back to the kitchen.

a mudroom takes the heat off a kitchen

As is often the case with mudrooms and back entries, you can't talk about the new mudroom on Mike and Kim's 1940s cottage home in Deerfield, Illinois, without also mentioning the new kitchen. That's because the two spaces were conceived of as part of one remodeling project, and, as planned, they now work together. Mike and Kim called on architect Bud Dietrich to add light to their home, clear up traffic flow in the kitchen, and add a mudroom for family members and the family dog. Adding a few feet, opening up to the dining room, and reorienting the cabinetry improved the kitchen. Adding French doors between the dining room and the existing screened porch took porch circulation out of the kitchen. And that left enough space for a mudroom, connected to the kitchen by an unobtrusive pocket door.

The mix of small roof shapes holds the secret to shaping the roofs of the additions: There's no need to match an exact size or even shape, just the diminutive spirit of the original cottage home.

Remodel

Kitchen

Screened porch

Dining room

Mudroom

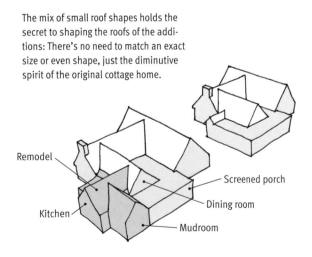

(above) At less than 9 ft. square, the mudroom has space for built-in cubbies, a window, and a door. Its vaulted ceiling makes it feel larger than it actually is.

(left) A glass pocket door allows light from the mudroom to enter the kitchen but not cold air or the mess of coats and boots.

before

after

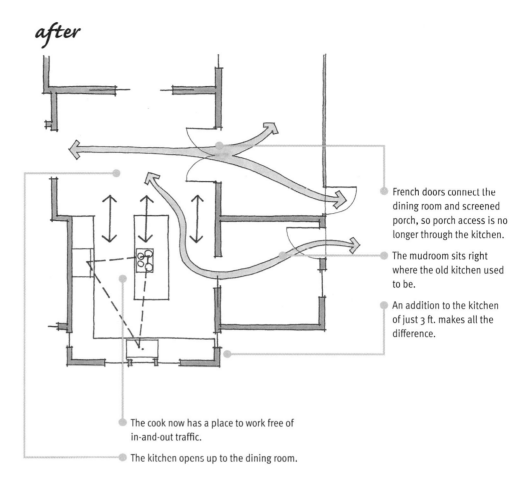

French doors connect the dining room and screened porch, so porch access is no longer through the kitchen.

The mudroom sits right where the old kitchen used to be.

An addition to the kitchen of just 3 ft. makes all the difference.

The way to the backyard or screened porch used to go right through the kitchen "work triangle."

The cook now has a place to work free of in-and-out traffic.

The kitchen opens up to the dining room.

"The mudroom and kitchen echo the vaulted living room, which sold the house to Mike and Kim in the first place."
— Bud Dietrich, architect

It may be just a mudroom, but with its red door, gable end, ocular window, and copper-roofed overhang, it's also a proper entrance.

PART II

Kitchens and Gathering Spaces

5. working within the footprint

The most common problem in many houses, apartments, and condominiums is that the kitchen does not work for the way we live today. In many dwellings, it is either not practical or not possible to increase the size of the space available, so that working within the existing footprint is the only option. But although it may seem a huge limitation, this constraint can be a blessing in disguise. There are hundreds of things you can do to improve what's already there, often resulting in a less expensive but equally effective solution to your aesthetic and functional problems than if you had engaged in a more extensive remodeling. Even if you are assuming you need to do a more significant remodeling, use the ideas here to determine whether your assumption is correct. You may be surprised to discover that you can do a lot more with a lot less than you thought.

Working within the footprint doesn't mean ignoring the other dimensions. Here the kitchen stayed in the same spot, but opened to the adjacent family space across an island. Two playful arches add ceiling height variety and frame views inside and out.

before

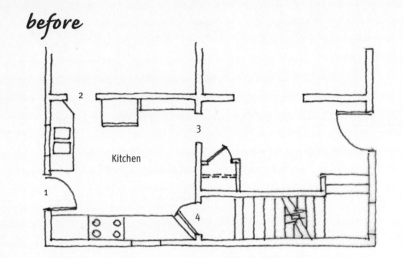

after

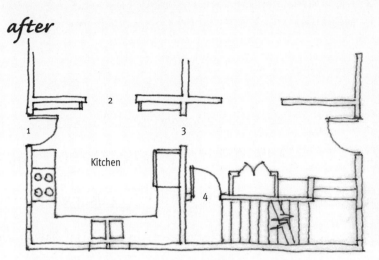

The doors were moved to one side of the room to reduce foot traffic through the kitchen.

Doorway 4 was moved out of the kitchen.

common kitchen problems

Typically the problems that an existing kitchen presents fall into one of the following categories:

• The kitchen is completely isolated from all the other rooms in the house.

• There are too many doors entering the room from too many sides, which turns it into Grand Central Station and makes it very difficult to work in.

• There is insufficient storage area or counter space.

• There is no place to sit down.

• The room is poorly laid out, making it feel cramped and awkward to work in.

• The kitchen is just plain ugly.

When you are staying within the existing footprint, you need to focus on three main things: how to improve the circulation of people through the space so that it doesn't bisect the work area; how to distribute the functions better so they make the best use of the space available; and how to open up the room to adjacent spaces so that it feels less confining. As you address each of these issues, you'll have the opportunity to make the kitchen look more pleasing at the same time.

You already know the things about your kitchen that drive you crazy, but the questions in the list on p. 76 are intended to help you identify some problem areas and some possibilities that are less obvious. By giving each of these questions careful consideration, you may find yourself imagining alternative solutions to your kitchen dilemmas that have never occurred to you before. You can't see the best solutions until you've looked at all the potentials. So use this list to open your mind to the possibilities.

The questions in the list, which will help you to focus on the key remodeling "within the footprint" issues of circulation, function, and connection to adjacent spaces, are by no means the only questions worth asking. As you answer, you may come up with other questions that pertain to your particular likes and dislikes and to your particular kitchen configuration. If the question arises, include it in your list. Your answers to all these questions are there to serve as catalysts for your design solution. Now let's take a look at some Not So Big principles that will give your ideas more form.

questions to ask yourself

- If you have many doorways opening into the kitchen, is there a way to reduce that number and to locate them all to one side of the room?

- Is there a way to open up the kitchen to adjacent living spaces?

- Is the room large enough to include an island?

- Is there a way to improve the work triangle—the inter-relationship between the cooktop, the sink, and the refrigerator?

- Is there a way to rearrange the work surfaces so that there's more unobstructed countertop?

- Is there sufficient layout space to either side of the cooktop and the sink?

- Is the oven located at a height that works for you? If not, do you have 36 in. of linear wall surface for a wall oven?

- Do the larger vertical appliances, such as the refrigera-tor, freezer, and double oven, divide sections of coun-tertop in two? If so, is there a way to locate them at the ends of stretches of counter space instead?

- Do you have at least 36 in. of walking space between countertops? If not, is there a way to increase the distance between countertops to make the room less claustrophobic?

- Do you have more that 48 in. between countertops? If so, would the kitchen work better for you by reducing this distance?

- Is there anywhere for people to sit in or adjacent to the kitchen work area? If not, is there a way to add some as part of your remodeling?

- Do you have sufficient storage space for your needs? If not, is there a way to increase the amount of cabinet or shelving space, or can you add a pantry?

- Do you have a place elsewhere in the house to locate a pantry area for less frequently needed items or for bulk storage?

- If you don't like your existing cabinetry, is there a cre-ative way to change the way the cabinets look? If not, do you have the budget to refinish or replace them?

- Are there other materials and finishes in the room that you dislike? (Keep in mind that if you don't change these, you will most likely still be dissatisfied with the room, even if it functions a lot better.)

- If the kitchen ceiling is tall, is there a way to extend a soffit or shelf above the cabinetry in which to locate task lighting for the countertop below?

- Is there a way to give the kitchen a more integrated look using changes in ceiling height or continuous shelves or soffits?

- Is there a way to add under-cabinet lighting?

- Is there a way to increase the number of windows in the kitchen, to lower the sill height on existing windows, or to remove valances around existing windows so that more natural light can enter?

- Is there a way to create a point of focus for the kitchen, such as a focal tile pattern or a special hood design above the cooktop?

In a small kitchen, it's especially important to keep circulation paths clear of the work triangle, the imaginary lines connecting the sink, cooktop, and refrigerator.

not so big principles

Tailoring to Fit

The most important step you can take in the remodeling of a kitchen, whether it is designed to stay within the confines of the existing space or not, is to rethink its layout so that it fits the way you actually work in it. Unlike almost any other room in the house, the kitchen has to function like a well-oiled machine when it is being used for its primary functions—food prep and cleanup. If it doesn't do this well, no matter how beautiful it is, it will constantly frustrate you.

By beginning this exploration with only the existing footprint to work with, you may well discover that you don't need extra space. You simply need to rethink the way the work surfaces and appliances are located in relation to one another. So no matter what your preconceptions, take the plan for your existing kitchen (see pp. 86–87) and follow the suggestions below to see what's possible within the footprint first. Treat these as a starting place, and recognize that you may well need someone who is trained in kitchen design to help you explore the options further.

Here are the basic rules of thumb I use:

1. **Keep in mind the work triangle.** This imaginary triangle links the centers of the sink, cooktop, and refrigerator and should not exceed 26 ft. in total perimeter. No leg of the triangle should be longer than 9 ft. or shorter than 4 ft. (in some really small kitchens, this may not be possible) and no major traffic pattern should intersect the triangle. This is an excellent rule to adhere to because it will keep your kitchen work area both efficient and functional.

THE WORK TRIANGLE

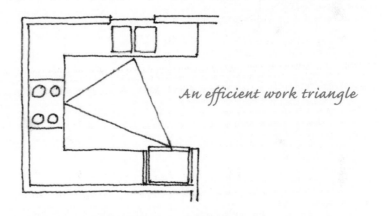

An efficient work triangle

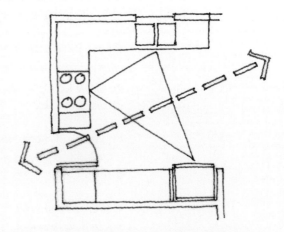

An inefficient work triangle

Avoid circulation that breaks the work triangle.

the 10-inch-deep pantry

A great place to put a pantry is along the edge of a hallway or walkway. By adding just 10 in. to the width of any circulation path in or around the kitchen you'll be building in some of the most usable and least obtrusive storage space that money can buy. The 10-in. depth allows you to accommodate all the typical food storage items, from cereal boxes to flour and sugar containers, and you won't have any of the problems associated with deeper pantries where rarely used items get lost in the back. An elegant door system such as the one shown here can dress up the pantry and make it look more like wall paneling than storage.

PLACING THE APPLIANCES

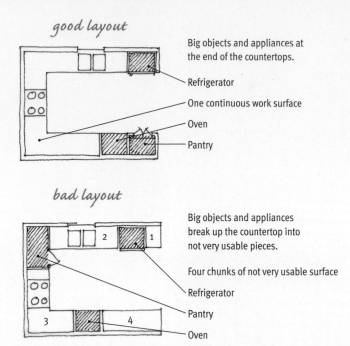

good layout

Big objects and appliances at the end of the countertops.

Refrigerator

One continuous work surface

Oven

Pantry

bad layout

Big objects and appliances break up the countertop into not very usable pieces.

Four chunks of not very usable surface

Refrigerator

Pantry

Oven

2. **Try to get all the doorways on one side of the room.** By doing so you will open up the rest of the room for contiguous countertop and appliance arrangement, you'll minimize the flow of foot traffic through the work space, and you'll open up some longer views from place to place. Although this is not always possible, it makes a huge difference to functionality. (See the drawings on p. 75.)

3. **If a kitchen is 12 ft. wide or wider, consider including an island.** Countertops are typically 2 ft. wide, so if a room is 12 ft. wide, you can add a 2-ft.-wide island in the center and still have 36-in. walkways on either side. (This is what I did in my own kitchen remodeling; see the photos on pp. 11–13.) If you were building a house from scratch, you'd usually make the walkways at least 6 in. wider than this, but in a remodeling the benefit of the island usually outweighs the drawback of the narrow walkways. Don't go less than 36 in. with the walkways though. It'll end up feeling very cramped.

Create an opening or half-wall between the kitchen and any of the adjacent social spaces so that there's a way to see and hear what's going on there without your having to leave the kitchen work area to do so.

4. **Place the vertical objects at the ends of countertops.** Large appliances and vertical pantry cabinets that extend above countertop height can be a challenge to locate because their massiveness stops the flow of the work surface and can end up reducing the effective prep area in the kitchen. By placing them at the end of a wall or countertop run, not in the middle, you'll ensure that the work surface is truly usable.

5. **Select your big appliances early, so you can tailor the design to fit their dimensions.** To accommodate the appliances you want when you are working within the existing footprint, it's important to know their sizes right up front, so you can design with them in mind. Not all major appliances are standard sizes; the difference of a few inches in any direction can make a design either feasible or impossible to implement.

6. **Leave the utility hook-ups where they are (if you can).** If budget is a concern, it's useful to keep in mind that you can keep costs contained by limiting the number of utilities you relocate. Start by assuming you will leave the sink and any gas appliances where they are currently located, and look at the design options that this will allow. Then consider what additional options are opened up when you consider moving one or more of these elements. Sometimes there will be advantages that outweigh the cost savings of leaving them where they are, but many times you'll discover that there are perfectly good solutions that work with the existing locations.

Although there's a lot that's been written about kitchen design, be aware that everyone works in their kitchen a little differently. Listen to the experts by all means, but if you find a rule of thumb or recommendation at odds with the way you work, listen to your own intuition. The most important thing is that it be tailored to fit *you*.

I'm often asked whether it is all right to raise or lower the height of the entire countertop in the kitchen from the standard 36 in. The problem with doing something different than standard is that unless you are staying in the house for the long haul, this is one alteration that can have a serious negative impact on resale.

If you make the countertop higher, you will be precluding any shorter buyers. A lowered countertop presents even more challenges. Not only are there fewer people willing to purchase a house with lower than standard surfaces (bathrooms included), when it comes to kitchen design the lowered height also presents numerous problems for successful integration of appliances. Dishwashers and other below-counter appliances are all made to fit beneath a standard-height countertop, so to integrate them properly becomes a challenge.

Obviously there are circumstances where raising or lowering the countertops is a necessity, but if it's only a vague preference, stick with the standard and raise or lower a section of the kitchen island or peninsula so you have at least one work surface that serves your particular height needs.

Consider creating an interior window or a framed opening to connect the kitchen to surrounding living spaces. Even if the space it opens into is currently a more formal or rarely used room, making this connection also enlivens the room on the other side of the opening.

Connecting Views

One of the simplest and most effective ways to make your kitchen work better for today's more informal lifestyle is to visually connect the room to surrounding living spaces. The challenge is that in order to do so you will often have to give up a small amount of upper cabinetry, and sometimes some lower cabinetry as well. In an already small kitchen, this can seem like a bad idea. But the sacrifice is almost always worth it. The connecting view results in a greatly increased sense of spaciousness, much better communication between rooms, and improved utility and livability.

When a room feels small and confining, it's often hard to imagine that giving up something (like cabinetry) will make it function better. A big part of the problem is that because the room is isolated from the rest of the living space, everyone piles into the kitchen to socialize, which makes the room feel even smaller. By creating an opening between rooms, the socializers are more willing to remain outside the kitchen because they can still see the cook and share in the food prep experience without being in the way.

Ceiling Height Variety

When you are remodeling within the footprint of the existing kitchen, once you've arrived at a layout that works and have identified the potential connecting views, the next challenge is to give the room some personality. If the room is rectangular and has a standard-height ceiling, this can seem like a big challenge, but there are some simple strategies related to the third dimension—the heights of everything—that can make a huge difference.

One of my favorite "tricks" is to extend a soffit—a segment of dropped ceiling—to align with the edge of the lower cabinetry, and then to locate recessed lighting in this soffit to light the countertop below. If the budget can stand it, I'll also add a light cove or plate rail, or both, along the edge of the soffit. This serves both as creative storage and as additional ambient lighting, by using the upper wall and ceiling surfaces as big light reflectors. It adds character to the room and creates a pleasant sense of shelter for the work surfaces below.

If your kitchen already has soffits but they extend only to the front face of the cabinet and stop abruptly with the end of the cabinetry, a common detail in houses built over the past 50 years, you might consider continuing the soffit to the adjacent wall surface to give the room a more elegant look. (You may recall from chapter 1 that this was the strategy I used in my own kitchen.)

Point of Focus

One final strategy for improving an existing kitchen is to give it a point of focus—a place that, because of its design, attracts your attention. Just as a face does for our human form, a point of focus expresses something more about the whole room and gives it a center, even if it isn't literally located along the centerline.

There are many things that can serve as a point of focus, from a composition of tiles above a cooktop, to a beautifully designed kitchen island with hanging lights above, to a favorite piece of artwork, to a window alcove above the kitchen sink. If you can make the focal point visible from other rooms and spaces as well, it will work even better. This simple strategy can improve even the plainest of kitchens, and it doesn't have to be expensive to be successful.

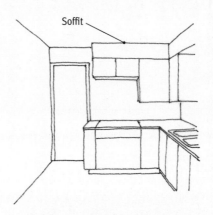
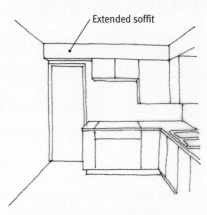

A narrow soffit above the upper cabinetry stops abruptly at the edge of the cabinets.

Continuing the soffit over to the adjacent wall gives a more integrated look.

(top) A focal point as simple as this single decorative tile adds visual punch, and doesn't have to be expensive to be effective.

(bottom) You can use the ceiling as a three-dimensional canvas to give the kitchen its own unique personality: It can be as whimsical and lyrical as you like.

connecting view opens kitchen to dining room

To allow for the new opening between the kitchen and dining room, the old high-backed range had to be replaced with a low slide-in model, a pricey trade-out. Making up for the cost, the granite countertops were left in place, one of the upper cabinets was relocated to the rear wall and the backsplash was made from extra tiles left over from an earlier sink-counter remodel.

Daniel and Sarah's kitchen in Newton, Massachusetts, offers two basic lessons in Not So Big remodeling. First, even a few small moves can make a huge difference. Second, sometimes you have to give up something good to get something better. Daniel and Sarah had remodeled their kitchen just three years before they contacted architect Chris Chu. At issue: no place for their third child's highchair around the built-in corner banquette. The rub: no budget or room for expanding the kitchen footprint and the need to maintain or increase the amount of storage. Chris's solution: to break down the wall between kitchen and dining room, which would replace the built-in banquette as the informal eating area. This meant giving up not just the banquette but also a newer range and microwave, plus the upper cabinets above the range counter. Chris found a spot for cabinets on the back wall by moving a window to the corner, gaining a better view to the backyard in the bargain.

To replace the storage lost by the removal of the cabinets above the range, new cabinets and angled shelves were fitted against the rear wall of the kitchen. The window seat remains in the corner, but custom-built storage drawers were added beneath the seat cushions. The existing radiator remained in place.

The former door opened in line with a single window, not a bad example of *light to walk toward*. The new opening is wider and in line with a pair of windows. The kitchen and dining room now feel more spacious and share more light.

The half wall with columns opens the dining area not only to the range counter just beyond the wall but also to the sink counter and windows beyond.

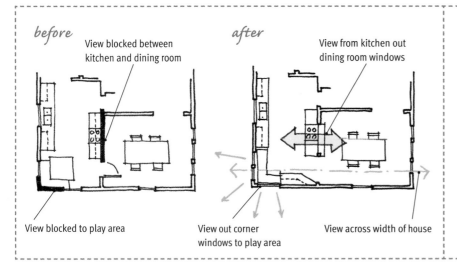

before

View blocked between kitchen and dining room

after

View from kitchen out dining room windows

View blocked to play area

View out corner windows to play area

View across width of house

extending views to the outdoors

The primary goal of the remodeling was to open up the kitchen to the dining room so that the dining table could serve as an informal eating area, replacing the cramped corner banquette. At the same time, the opening between the rooms and new corner windows extended views to the outside.

6. kitchens: borrowing space

If your house is small or the existing kitchen is particularly cramped, you might want to consider borrowing some poorly utilized space from an adjacent room to make the kitchen a little larger. Homeowners often overlook the available area because it seems to be a necessary part of another function, another room. But look again. When you search creatively for some extra square footage, you may have to give up something that's not very important, or relocate something that *is* important but which is not in the ideal location, to gain the space you need.

In this remodel, space was borrowed from the dining room (see plans at right) by claiming its closets for the kitchen. But space was also borrowed from the living room, through the visual connection established by a framed opening over the sink.

BORROWING SPACE FROM THE DINING ROOM

before

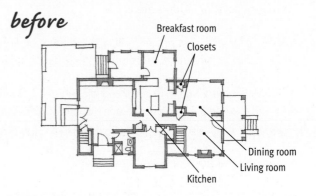

Breakfast room
Closets
Dining room
Living room
Kitchen

after

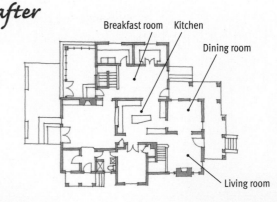

Breakfast room   Kitchen
Dining room
Living room

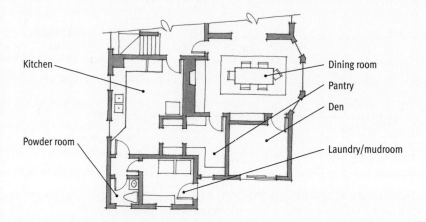

Kitchen

Powder room

Dining room

Pantry

Den

Laundry/mudroom

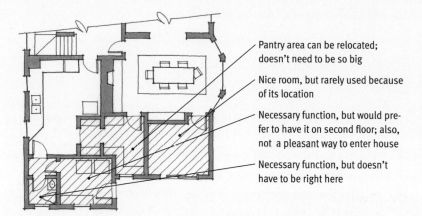

Pantry area can be relocated; doesn't need to be so big

Nice room, but rarely used because of its location

Necessary function, but would prefer to have it on second floor; also, not a pleasant way to enter house

Necessary function, but doesn't have to be right here

Because every situation is different, I'm going to give you a list of possible places where extra square footage may be lurking. As you go through the list, take note of all potential sources of square footage, even if you can't easily see how the various spaces can be reallocated to the kitchen. It's important to stay open-minded and flexible as you consider each of these options. Here's the list:

• Pantry, closets, or storage areas

• Extra large rooms, such as a living room or family room, that can be reduced in size without compromising their functionality

• Necessary functions, such as a powder room, dining area, or back entry, that could be relocated to open up some underutilized square footage on the other side of, or adjacent to, that function

• A room that rarely or never gets used

• Enclosed circulation space, such as a hallway, receiving place, or foyer, that is wider or larger than necessary, and could be opened up to the adjacent kitchen without losing its functionality

By circling on your plan (see the sidebar on p. 86) each of the areas that can offer some additional square footage you'll be identifying the potential boundaries of your kitchen's expanded footprint. You can then use tracing paper, laid over the plan, to try out some different layouts. (Don't draw directly on your measured drawing or it will become very difficult to make heads or tails of in short order. Make yourself several copies of the original.)

If you decide to hire a professional to help you with the design, the architect or designer will make many sketches of possible alternatives before settling on two or three to show you. By keeping an open mind as you evaluate all the options, you're likely to find the very best solution for your remodeling—one that will serve your needs well and increase the value of your home at the same time.

not so big principles

Double-Duty Dining

One of the best opportunities for borrowing adjacent space is to take over an existing dining room. A Not So Big House does not typically need both a formal and informal dining area, yet many homes have both.

making a floor plan of your existing dwelling

To be able to look at alternative design strategies for a specific area, you'll need an accurate plan of the area in question as well as the surrounding areas. If you don't already have a floor plan of your existing house or apartment, here's how to make one.

Using a sheet of grid paper, sketch the layout of the area as best you can. This is just a rough draft onto which you will record dimensions, so it doesn't have to be perfect. Be sure to give the walls some thickness as you draw or you may get confused. Walls are usually $4\frac{1}{2}$ in. thick if they are built with 2x4 studs.

Now measure the dimensions of each space, the length of each wall segment, the width of each door and window, as well as the location and dimensions of each appliance, countertop, and cupboard. Write down your findings as in the drawing at right on the facing page. It's important to write neatly or you will quickly get confused. Use the feet and inches side of your tape, rather than the inches only, and make sure you are doing so consistently. And although it may seem unnecessary, check every dimension twice.

When you have taken as many dimensions as you can find, look for a place from which you can take an overall dimension—one that ties all the small segments you've just taken into one longer run. You can use this to verify that your shorter segments all add up to the right number. Ideally, you will find an overall dimension that runs from side to side and an overall dimension that runs from front to back. By summing all the shorter dimensions that occur along each longer run, you can quickly find errors or missed dimensions.

With all these pieces of data in hand, you are ready to draw up the final version of your plan. Take another sheet of grid paper and pick a scale that you will use to draw up your plan. Architects typically use $\frac{1}{4}$ in. = 1 ft. 0 in., but if the area you are measuring is small, you may want to use $\frac{1}{2}$ in. = 1 ft. 0 in., which will make it easier to see when you're done.

Translate each of your collected dimensions into the scale you've chosen. So, for example, at $\frac{1}{2}$-in. scale, 2 ft. 3 in. will be (2 x $\frac{1}{2}$ in.) + $\frac{1}{4}$ ft. ($\frac{1}{4}$ x $\frac{1}{2}$ in.) = 1 + $\frac{1}{8}$ in. = $1\frac{1}{8}$ in. This process can be simplified significantly if you buy yourself an architectural scale, which has several standard scales marked on its various sides. Be sure to use the correct side of the scale each time you mark a dimension on your paper. Connect up all the dimensions as you go, and you'll see the plan evolving with each line you draw.

If you hire a professional to help you later on, don't be surprised when he or she wants to go through this same process again. Because accurate dimensions are so important, each of the professionals you work with will almost always want to verify dimensions personally. This is how they will be able to ensure that the design they are proposing really works.

layout sketch

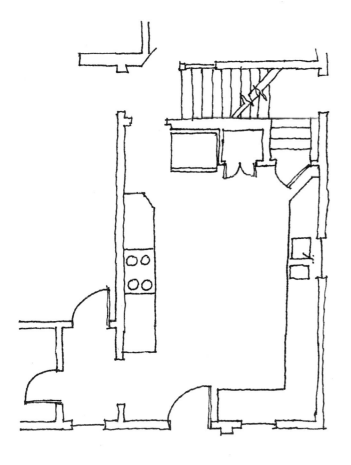

adding dimensions

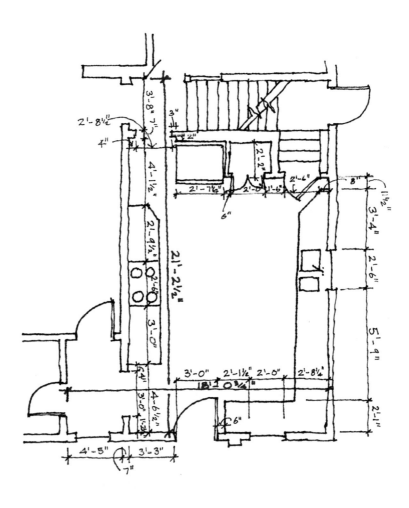

If you're concerned about having more formal dinners take place directly adjacent to the kitchen, there are several ways to limit the view between the two, such as with a raised countertop or with sliding partitions that separate kitchen from dining area.

The informal dining area, if designed properly, can serve both formal and informal functions, and since the formal dining room is typically located adjacent to the kitchen, in many cases this room provides all the additional space that's needed. So unless you take particular pleasure in throwing formal dinner parties that require a separate room, consider eliminating the dining room and dedicating the relinquished space to the kitchen.

Framed Openings

When we think about borrowing space to make a room bigger, we usually assume we are talking about adding square footage. But there's another way that you can borrow space without actually adding to the size. When a room is linked to another visually, so that you can see a substantial or focal part of one room from the other, you'll find that both rooms end up feeling bigger. This can be done by adding framed openings between rooms.

A framed opening is essentially a doorway without its door. This type of opening is most effective when it provides a wide connection between spaces while still differentiating room from room. If you remove all trace of the wall between two rooms, the result is essentially one room instead of two. Paradoxically this feels smaller than when there's still some small visual cue to tell you that the two rooms are separate. The role of the framed opening is to identify room from room, and when used effectively it can make the spaces concerned feel spacious instead of cramped with only the most minor of remodelings.

Creative Storage

Often when an area of the home is dedicated for storage it ends up being poorly used—especially if that storage is too deep to easily reach to the back of—so it's not unusual to find yourself wanting to repurpose some of this underutilized storage space for kitchen floor space. Creative stor-

A framed opening can be a doorway without its door (left photo) or a wide opening defined by a deep beam and just enough wall at either end to support it.

Cabinets placed above the windows in this high-ceilinged kitchen add storage and create deep nooks similar in feel to protruding window bays.

age is a Not So Big principle intended to remind you that not everything that needs to be stored requires prime real estate, and that when something *is* stored in a highly utilized part of the house, it should be the type of storage that can be used and/or appreciated daily.

There's often some square footage languishing in not very well used cupboards, closets, and pantries between rooms in the most heavily trafficked parts of a house. In many older homes, there's a butler's pantry between the kitchen and dining room, for example, that we don't really have much use for today. Often they end up filled with the "good" china—that set you received when you got married or that you inherited from your grandmother, but which never actually gets used. If this sounds familiar, consider borrowing this space for the kitchen expansion and finding a more decorative but less space-consumptive way of exhibiting just a few of the prized dishes within the remodeled space, so that it becomes a form of creative storage.

Although it may seem a bad idea to remove storage area to acquire some additional square footage, a small amount of more creatively designed storage can replace a large amount of poorly designed storage, allowing you to borrow the space you need for your kitchen remodeling *and* have more functional storage space as well.

double-duty dining rescues a cramped kitchen

The kitchen architect Gail Wong remodeled for Mary and Marcus in Seattle is a perfect example of the *double-duty dining* concept described on p. 85. The original kitchen in this 1940s house had all the usual vintage-kitchen culprits: not enough counter space, poor lighting, dated cabinets, and too little storage. And it was cramped, with circulation passing through the work triangle, the refrigerator door swinging into the doorway to the dining room, and a breakfast table that didn't belong. The adjacent dining room also felt cramped. Connected to the kitchen by a narrow doorway, the dining room was a touch aloof and formal.

Like many architects, Gail gives her clients a questionnaire at the outset of a project to discover their likes and dislikes, needs and wants. Mary and Marcus requested more storage, a better view to the backyard, and greater openness between the dining room and kitchen. With a tight budget, adding space was out of the question. The clear move was to break down the wall between kitchen and dining room, do away with the U of counters in favor of an L and an island, and fully allow the dining area to be part of the everyday life of the kitchen. By making the island a *pod of space,* a floor-to-ceiling element within the newly expanded space, Gail achieved the perfect balance of openness and separation between kitchen and dining area.

kitchen island as pod of space

Sometimes a kitchen island just wants to be a countertop floating above base cabinets. But when you're looking for greater separation between the kitchen and what lies beyond the island, consider upper cabinets above the island. Add posts or columns (the ones you see here are for visual effect, not structural reasons), and you've created what I call a *pod of space,* an element that sits within a room and is also, even in a small way, itself a container of space.

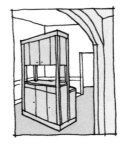 

The TV is positioned on a shelf to be viewable from either the dining area or the kitchen.

This is a sweet archway with fat trim and a classic curve.

The cooking island is paneled to match the wainscoting.

Robust wainscoting matches the height of the back-splash, helping to tie together the dining area and the kitchen beyond.

Only a small doorway connects the dining room to the kitchen.

The trimless archway has a rather dated curve to it.

The window is too low for a good view to the backyard.

A taller casement window brightens the low countertop of the breakfast table.

Beneath the low countertop is room for chair legs and your feet as well as 1-ft.-deep storage cabinets.

telephone station

You don't need much room for a phone station; this space is just 3 ft. wide and a standard 24 in. deep. It has the basics: a place to sit and put your feet, good lighting, and a clear counter surface. It might be preferable for the microwave to be elsewhere, but it fits nicely here; in a Not So Big kitchen, that's what doing double duty is all about.

Little things make a big difference. The new window above the sink is lower to improve the view to the play area in the backyard. The base of the window lines up crisply with the top of the backsplash, which serves beneath the window as a sill. Much-needed electrical outlets are hidden behind a valence at the bottom of the upper cabinetry.

"The cooking island was designed to separate the kitchen and dining area while allowing for a visual connection."

—Gail L. Wong, architect

The old stand-alone range sat blankly against a wall blocking a view to the dining area. The new cooking island maintains a degree of separation but provides a framed view into the dining area beyond. The new upper cabinets add storage and lighted display space as well.

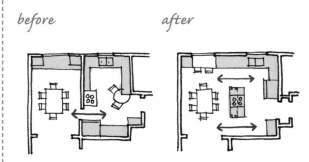

before   after

a classic u-to-island

Taking a conventional U-shaped kitchen cabinet and counter arrangement and opening it into an L-shaped arrangement with an island (whether or not, as here, a wall is also involved) does two things: Most obviously, the new arrangement opens up the kitchen to the adjacent eating area, making the two spaces nearly one. Less obviously, an L and an island create two circulation paths (the red arrows) where there had been just one.

kitchen combined
with dining room
equals informality

There's no such thing as the quintessential Not So Big remodeling project, but Mary Beth and Ed's remodeled kitchen in Pittsboro, North Carolina, comes close. The kitchen had been a box filled with a jumble of cabinets, appliances, and open shelves; the adjacent dining room was another box, appointed with formal furniture that didn't fit the casual way Mary Beth, Ed, and their children actually lived. Architect Sophie Piesse joined the two rooms together by breaking down the wall between them, then gave the new, larger, live-in kitchen colorful charm to match the 1929 farmhouse, charm the old rooms never quite had.

The wall between the rooms wasn't structural, but Sophie placed columns at the end of the new peninsula to define a cooking area to one side and dining and living area to the other. The columns are simple posts with generous base and crown molding that is consistent with the wide moldings in the rest of the house. The other new details are equally modest: basic white subway tile, cheery wall paint, butcher-block countertops, and open shelves. Mary Beth and Ed kept their range, the painted wood ceiling, and the hardwood floors. Their remodel wasn't about trading up as much as it was about opening up.

The long wall painted spring green, a takeoff on Mary Beth's favorite green dishes (on the shelves at right), ties together the formerly separate dining room and kitchen, while complementary yellow walls set off the cooking area within the expanded space. Materials and details had to be affordable, easy to maintain, and suitable for a family with young children.

fun and function

The eating nook is a playful take on the classic booth, with file drawers hidden beneath the benches and a stand-alone table that can be expanded with leaves and added chairs for larger gatherings. One chair is at the ready in the home-office nook.

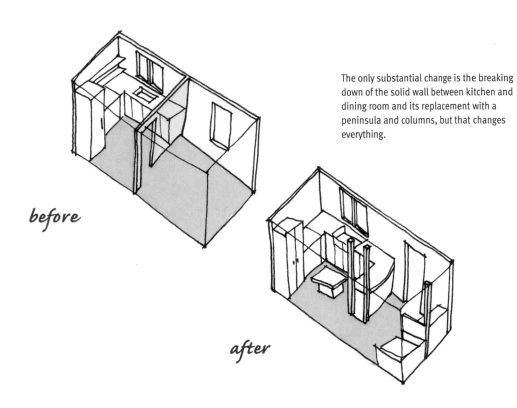

before

after

The only substantial change is the breaking down of the solid wall between kitchen and dining room and its replacement with a peninsula and columns, but that changes everything.

things line up

The height of the wide windowsill was designed to align with the top of the original range, plus a smidge so that the backsplash can be composed of exactly four rows of subway tile to minimize tile cutting.

"You mean I can get rid of that stuff!"
— Mary Beth

(upon realizing she could unload her formal dining room furniture)

The original and remodeled kitchens have the same floor and ceiling and similar open shelving, wood countertops, and white painted cabinets. The difference between old and new is between outdated frumpiness and fresh surfaces, crisp lines, and less visual clutter.

7. kitchens: opening up

In the two previous chapters, we've looked at how to remodel the kitchen by staying within the existing footprint (chapter 5) and by borrowing space from adjacent areas (chapter 6). Now we're going to focus on one overarching objective for any kitchen remodel: To make a house live in a truly Not So Big manner, all the main living spaces in the house need to be visually connected with one another. To make this happen, we need to remove some walls and obstructions to seeing from place to place while still maintaining the individual identities of each activity area or function.

Most people assume this separate identity can only occur with the use of walls, but an unintended consequence of a wall is that the circumscribed activity area also becomes isolated. That's how we used to build when we lived more formally, but it really doesn't work for most households today. So in a Not So Big house or remodeling the differentiation between functions is done with ceiling height changes and with wide openings in the wall surfaces instead. In this way, the emphasis is placed on connections rather than separations.

keys to not so big living

- The kitchen is no longer isolated from the main living and dining areas.
- If formal rooms are used less than a half-dozen times a year, they are repurposed or made to do double duty.
- If there are still formal rooms, they are more connected with the kitchen than before.
- There is a strong visual connection between kitchen and everyday dining and socializing areas.
- The entire composition works as a singular whole while each function maintains its individual identity.

before

Dining room

Kitchen

Living room

Bedroom

Bedroom

after

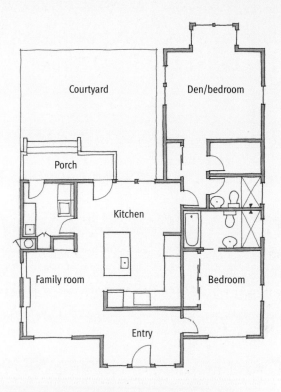

Courtyard

Den/bedroom

Porch

Kitchen

Family room

Bedroom

Entry

The original kitchen was cut off from the living room. The remodeled kitchen opens across an island to the family room, offering a diagonal view to a new fireplace (see the floor plans above).

questions to ask yourself

For any remodeling that involves the removal of walls, you'll need the assistance of a structural engineer to determine what's possible. But for the time being, as you consider each of these questions, assume that you will be able to remove the desired walls and other obstructions, replacing them with beams and columns as needed.

- *Ideally, which walls would be removed or opened up to connect the kitchen with adjacent living spaces?*

- *What potential obstacles prevent you from removing or adding an opening to each of these walls?*

- *If there is a major obstacle, such as a fireplace or built-in, list the pros and cons of keeping versus removing this object.*

- *What plumbing, ductwork, or electrical outlets would need to be relocated if each wall were to be removed?*

- *Are there rooms or functions that you want to keep separate from the rest, such as an away room, laundry room, or powder room?*

- *Are there rooms or functions that you would like the option either to enclose or open depending upon the occasion? If so, which ones are they?*

- *With respect to kitchen layout, is there a better way to organize the cabinetry and appliances in order to open up a wall that would allow you to make a stronger connection with adjacent living spaces? (Here you may want to use some sketch paper and your plan*

from chapter 6 if you are working alone, or to ask your architect or designer for suggestions if you have professional help.)

- *Are there any low-hanging cabinets that are causing unnecessary separation between kitchen and informal dining or living areas?*

- *Do you need to replace the cabinetry to integrate the look of the kitchen with the other living spaces, or can it be reused?*

- *Even if it can be reused, do you want to reuse it, or would you prefer to start from scratch? If so, is this a viable option financially?*

- *If you open up the kitchen to adjacent living spaces, what remodeling will be necessary to these other living areas to tie everything together into a successful overall design?*

If no thought is given to the differentiation of place from place, you end up with the ubiquitous great room—lots of space, but no "there" there, no sense of comfort or intimacy. So in this chapter we'll look at how to open up the floor plan of the main living level but maintain the individual identities of each of its constituent parts.

In each of the case studies and examples used in this chapter, you'll see aspects of what you've learned in the two preceding ones, but now illustrating how these techniques can be woven together into an integral whole—a main level that meets the requirements for Not So Big living.

common problems

The most common obstacle to opening up the floor plan is the presence of a special feature such as a fireplace or built-in buffet that's strategically located on the wall separating kitchen from dining or living room, or some apparently indispensable kitchen cabinetry or appliance (see the photo and plans on p. 102).

Part of the design process entails weighing the benefits of keeping the special feature versus opening up the kitchen. For example, let's say you love the look of an existing living room fireplace that's located on the wall between kitchen and living room, but you never use that room because you can't easily reach it given the separation that's created by the fireplace wall. Keeping the fireplace means you literally never use the 400 sq. ft. of space that would be made available if the fireplace and adjacent wall were removed. It may be hard to part with the fireplace, but it will obviously make a huge improvement to livability.

Alternatively, you might discover through advice from a professional such as an architect or builder that the fireplace only *looks* as though it takes up the whole wall. He or she may inform you that in fact the flue is only 15 in. by 15 in. wide, making it possible to open up the view between kitchen and living room without losing the whole fireplace (see the photo below). The process of evaluating different options, without getting attached to a single solution too early in the process, is one of the key characteristics of a truly effective remodeling.

Often it's possible to open up the kitchen to an adjacent living room without giving up the chimney and fireplace.

before

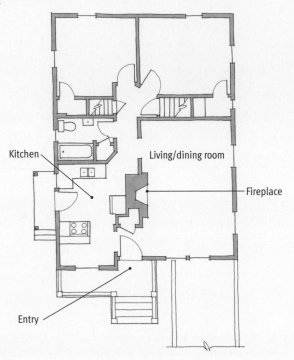

Kitchen

Living/dining room

Fireplace

Entry

after

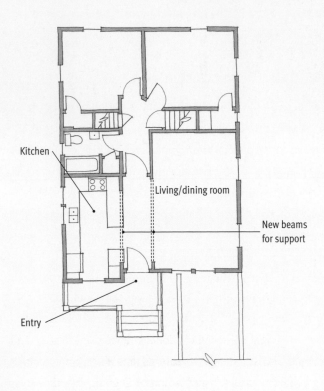

Kitchen

Living/dining room

New beams for support

Entry

A fireplace is a desirable feature, but in this case, removing the chimney was the key to opening up the kitchen to the main living spaces, and to improving circulation. The entry area is now more connected to the living spaces, and the pathway to the back rooms no longer cuts through the kitchen or living room.

(above left) A kitchen work table with stools is an ideal place for casual gathering, just beyond the front entry area.

(above right) When the kitchen can be seen from adjacent living spaces, it becomes a focal gathering place, a magnet for activity.

not so big principles

Focal Gathering Place

In most households these days, the kitchen is the hub of activity, the primary living space. It's where people gather while food is being prepared, where homework is done, where bills get paid, and where both light and serious conversations take place. So in a kitchen remodeling you want to give it greater importance visually than it would have received a few decades ago.

The existing layout of the kitchen may be a challenge in that people are always getting in the way while you are trying to prepare dinner. By opening up the kitchen to other living spaces, you can simultaneously eliminate the frustrations *and* improve the opportunities for socializing.

By making the kitchen visible from other living areas, you also add to its vitality. It becomes a focal gathering place in large part because it can be seen. A light and activity-filled area is a magnet for more activity. So your job in a remodeling project is to encourage the activity but to minimize the movement through the work area. That should be the territory of the cook's alone. There are some rules of thumb for doing this:

- Keep circulation pathways to one side and never through the center.

- Provide seating for onlookers that's close at hand and high enough that they can see the cook.

- Make sure there's a clear line of sight to sitting areas that are farther away from the kitchen area so that conversation can flow freely between the cook and other household members.

- If there's a kitchen appliance that receives regular visits from people other than the cooks, such as a refrigerator or microwave, position it so that it is easily accessible without the need for a walk through the kitchen work area.

- If TV watching is a shared activity of the household and one that occurs while the cook is at work in the kitchen, make sure that the TV is visible to the cook as well.

Diagonal Views

If you think back to your first geometry class, you may recall that in a right-angled triangle, the longest line segment is the hypotenuse—the diagonal line that connects the ends of the vertical and horizontal lines. One of the best ways to make a living area feel spacious even when it is (below and facing page bottom) A raised countertop combined with columns is one of the best ways to open a kitchen to adjacent living spaces while screening the kitchen work surfaces and differentiating one space from the other.

(right) If you know to look for potential diagonal views when considering a kitchen remodeling, you may be able to give the main level of your home a much more spacious look and feel without it having to cost a fortune to accomplish.

quite restricted in size is to open up a diagonal view from one corner to another so that you are able to look along the hypotenuse—the longest view in the house. This makes your eyes and senses believe that there's more space than is actually there—a great way to make less into more.

Differentiation of Parts

When opening up the main living level of a floor plan, it is important to give each activity area its own identity while simultaneously making it an integrated part of the whole. There are various ways to do this; in each case, the objective is to define the activity area and to create a sense of shelter around it.

Raised countertop One of the simplest ways to create a sense of shelter, as well as visual screening for a kitchen work surface, is to add a section of raised countertop between the kitchen and adjacent rooms. The raised area works best when it is 4 in. to 6 in. taller than the rest of the counter-top surfaces. This gives good screening for the work surface and makes a comfortable height for bar-stool seating. A higher raised countertop will make it difficult to feel connected to the cook, thus limiting conversation.

Columns define space Another way to differentiate the kitchen from surrounding areas is to use columns, which are often required structur-ally when a bearing wall has been removed. Although homeowners are often concerned that a column will restrict view between activity places, the amount of obstruction is in fact minimal and the benefit of spatial definition is great. We forget that when a column is in the way of our seeing something, we automatically move our bodies an inch or two in either direction so that there's no obstruction.

(top) A dropped ceiling is an inexpensive way to shelter and define an activity area within a larger space.

(bottom) A soffit is a segment of dropped ceiling that is used to define one room from another or to give a sense of shelter to the area below. It provides a visual cue that this is a separate place from the taller adjacent area.

FLOATING SHELF

A change in floor level and flooring material is a simple but effective way to define one space from another. Here the eating area is a step below the kitchen.

Ceiling height variety   My favorite technique for differentiating place from place is to use changes in the ceiling plane as subtle visual dividers. Because the ceiling is above eye level, defining room from room creates no obstruction at all and yet clearly identifies where one activity area stops and another begins.

When remodeling, it is always less costly to bring ceilings down from their existing height than to raise them, which usually requires reworking the existing structure. People often worry that a lowered ceiling will make the space seem smaller, but this is not the case. Our eyes read the contrast between ceiling heights, with the result that the original ceiling level looks taller than it did without the dropped areas to contrast it with.

To accomplish a lowering of ceiling heights, you can use sections of dropped ceiling, soffits, or floating shelves.

- **Dropped ceilings**—These are places where an entire area of ceiling is dropped to a lower height than the surrounding ceiling. This works well for areas like alcoves and hallways where you are identifying the place as subordinate to, or more intimate than, the adjacent spaces. You can also use the same technique when you have an extra-tall ceiling—9 ft. and up—to give each activity area a separate identity and a clear indication of spatial hierarchy. So, for example, you could make the kitchen and dining area ceilings 8 ft. tall, the living area the full 9 ft., and the window seat and piano alcove 7 ft. tall.

- **Soffits**—When referring to an interior ceiling, a soffit is generally understood to be a narrow linear segment of dropped ceiling surface. We're most familiar with these above kitchen cabinets and bathroom vanities, but you can actually use a soffit wherever you want to give a room more definition. I often draw the parallel between a soffit and the visor or brim of a hat. When you wear a hat, the brim defines the space that is your territory beneath it. Inside a room that has a surrounding soffit, you'll experience much

the same thing. A soffit that divides kitchen from dining area, or dining area from living area, simply delineates where you are moving from one to the other.

- **Floating shelves**—If you prefer a more open feel, you can substitute a floating shelf for the soffit. They both accomplish the same differentiation of activity areas, but the floating shelf offers a surface above for storage, display, or uplighting (see the drawing on the facing page). Frank Lloyd Wright frequently used floating shelves in his designs, giving the resulting interior a lighter, airier feel.

Changes in level or flooring   Another option for defining place from place is to make a change in the flooring material or in the level of the floor. A material change provides a subtle demarcation, while a change in floor height accentuates the movement from one activity area to the next. The addition of a step or two between rooms can be an excellent way to make a clear and markedly pronounced differentiation between rooms (see the photo above).

The problem with a change of level, however, is that it makes movement between rooms impossible for someone in a wheelchair or using a walker, so the application of this type of differentiating feature has become less popular in recent years as we've become more aware of Universal Design practices.

updating becomes an opportunity to open up

The harvest-gold range, original to the 1974 house, might have been reason enough for Martha and David of Chapel Hill, North Carolina, to update their kitchen. But what they wanted even more than new appliances was a kitchen with a feeling of openness and connection to the outdoors. Martha, in particular, had developed an aversion to upper cabinets and soffits, which seemed to impinge on the old kitchen. Architect Sophie Piesse took Martha's concerns to heart with a remodeling scheme that involved a number of Not So Big moves: breaking down a wall between the kitchen and an underused office space, connecting to a back deck with French doors and larger windows, and replacing the bank of upper cabinets with storage under an island and in a wall of pantry cabinets. Sophie suggested a more subtle, reconfigured soffit as a way to hide ductwork from the range hood above the island. Martha and David chose a downdraft range vent instead—but Martha insisted on keeping the soffits after all, which now give the work surfaces just the right amount of definition within the otherwise free-flowing kitchen.

The existing kitchen.

curved island controls circulation

The curve of the island offers a delightful sitting area, with a view into the cook's area and beyond to the backyard. Doing double duty, the same curve helps direct traffic flow between the entry area, dining room, and family room, preserving the kitchen proper for the cook.

before

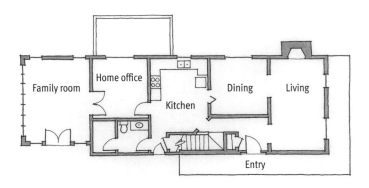

after

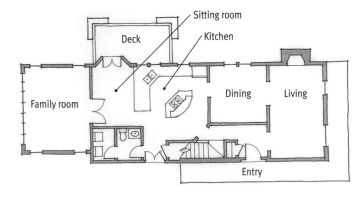

"It's nice to make a kitchen that has many different spaces within it."
— Sophie Piesse, architect

The key to opening up the kitchen was eliminating upper cabinets and removing the wall between the old kitchen and home office, creating a connected sitting area. The bay of windows and glass French doors further connect the sitting area to the back deck. On the run of cabinets between the kitchen and the sitting area, the corner cabinet behind the sink is deep enough for four file drawers, which sit unobtrusively beside the bookshelves.

The view from the kitchen now extends beyond the sitting area and into the family room, where the old aluminum sliding windows were replaced with casements that match those in the kitchen.

The far column is needed to carry the ceiling load where the old wall was removed; the near column is there to balance the look.

A shallow soffit defines the kitchen workspace below.

The new casement windows have divided panes that tie them visually to the house's traditional double-hung windows, while affording someone standing at the counters an unobstructed view.

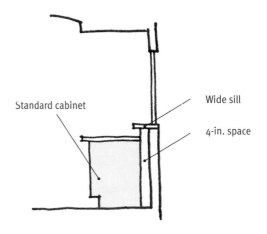

Standard cabinet

Wide sill

4-in. space

Setting standard 24-in.-deep cabinets 4 in. from the wall creates depth for a generous sill and allows for ample counter space in front of the microwave.

To balance costs, the island features Silestone™ composite countertops, while the other countertops are less expensive laminate with a maple edge. The island base is composed of two 30-in. cabinets connected by a curved piece of maple veneer over simple framing. You can see one cabinet door in the photo below.

8. kitchens: bumping out

If none of the remodeling strategies outlined in the three previous chapters can accommodate your kitchen needs, the next step is to consider adding on a little square footage by bumping out a segment of wall by a few feet, perhaps to make room for an eating alcove or to increase the width of the kitchen to allow for a center island. But make sure to start with just the minimum that's needed to attain the functionality required. This will keep costs down, as well as maintain the scale and proportioning of the existing house.

One of the biggest challenges when taking this approach is "right-sizing" the bump-out for its appointed function. I've been involved in many remodelings where the decision has been made early in the design process to add on a small amount of space, only to be frustrated during construction when a well-meaning builder tries to persuade the homeowner that if they are bumping out a few feet, they might as well bump out more—that it won't cost much extra.

Although this may be true sometimes, it doesn't mean that it is necessarily the best solution for the house or the particular problem being solved.

Our default mode today is to go for the bigger solution. More space must mean better space surely but it's just not so. More often than not, more is less: less quality, less character, less functionality. We are so convinced that more is better, in fact, that we often have to be shown over and over again to convince our senses that bigger isn't always better. But to make less into more you have to spend time in the design and construction process to tailor the new space to fit both the existing house and your particular needs. And when it comes to adding on even a small amount of space, this tailoring begins in a surprising place.

listen to your roof

Not only do you need to identify the areas where additional square footage is needed and that are easy to add on to—such as an alcove off an existing kitchen to accommodate an informal eating area, or a kitchen extension such as the one shown in the plans below—but you must also consider what the roof allows you to do. Here's a simple example to give

Bumping out 5 ft. onto the terrace and aligning the kitchen wall with the rest of the house enabled the kitchen to accommodate an oval island. An outdated acrylic bubble skylight was reshaped to echo the curved island below.

before

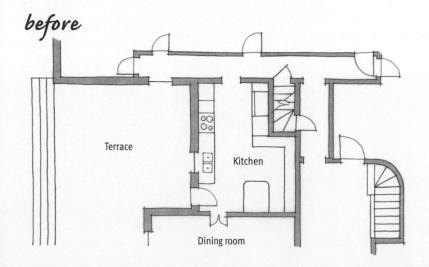

Terrace

Kitchen

Dining room

after

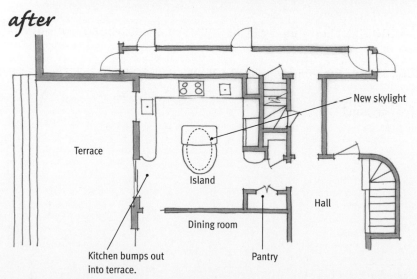

New skylight

Terrace

Island

Hall

Kitchen bumps out into terrace.

Dining room

Pantry

questions to ask yourself

Where do you need additional square footage? (You may want to mark the possible areas on your floor plan.)

- *Is there an area of the floor plan that is too narrow without additional square footage?*

- *Is there an area that would be significantly more functional with additional square footage?*

- *Are there any obvious places to bump out based on the floor plan alone?*

- *Does the roof or level above make this bump-out a possibility? (If you are not sure, you'll need to ask a designer, architect, or remodeler.)*

- *Are there any setback requirements that would require a variance if you were to pursue this bump-out? (If you aren't sure, see "Setbacks" on p. 116.)*

- *What is the minimum size of bump-out that would serve your purposes?*

- *Are there any obvious alignments either in floor plan or related to the roof form that will help determine the size of the bump-out?*

- *Are there any places that are obvious candidates for a bump-out because of an existing condition such as an overhanging second floor?*

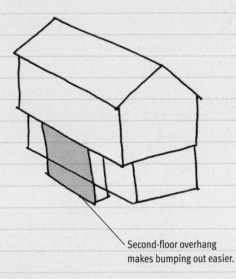

Second-floor overhang
makes bumping out easier.

The cantilevered window seat bump-out in this family room addition adds space, personality, and functionality without expanding the footprint of the new foundation.

you a sense of what I mean. If there is a section of the house that jogs in and then back out again (see the drawing below), the jogged-in area may provide a simple place for additional square footage. You may decide to align the new space with the adjacent walls, or you may decide to bump out a little beyond this surface so that the exterior wall still has some character. But the primary determiner of which solution to pick comes not from the floor plan but from the roof above.

In plan, adding this square footage seems simple enough, but there are situations where it won't work—at least not without some significant roof reconfiguration, which can cost more than it's worth to accomplish. Take a look at the two roof forms below, both covering the same floor plan.

BUMP-OUTS

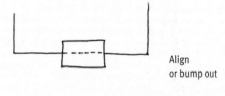

Align
or bump out

bump out

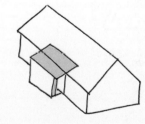

filling in a bump-in

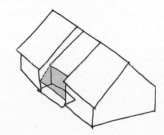

Lean-to roof
over bump-out

setbacks

Every piece of property comes with certain restrictions as to where you can build. One particular type of restriction is called a *setback*, and as its name suggests, it indicates how far back from the front, side, and back property lines you must set your building. When it comes to bumping out or adding on, before you do any planning you need to find out precisely where these setbacks fall in relation to your existing house. This is not something you can eyeball. To obtain a building permit, you will need a survey that confirms that the addition you are planning falls within the allowed building area. Obtaining the survey can save you a lot of headaches later because it will ensure that all the options you are considering are feasible.

A surveyor will also be able to identify any other easements and setbacks that will govern where you can build. If your property is located on a river or lake, for example, there are often setbacks required from scenic easements.

Some jurisdictions allow roof overhangs to protrude into setbacks while others do not, so be sure to check with a local building official if there will be any part of the house intruding into the setback area.

If you can't do what you wanted to because of a setback issue, it is sometimes possible to obtain a "variance" by going through the proper channels. A call to your local building inspections department is the best way to ascertain whether it is worth applying for a variance, and if so, what procedures you'll need to follow. If you are working with an architect, he or she can help you with this process.

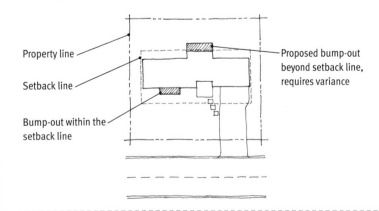

Property line

Setback line

Bump-out within the setback line

Proposed bump-out beyond setback line, requires variance

In the left drawing on p. 115, the addition of the jogged-in square footage is easy to accomplish with no change to the roof form. But to create a bump-out by extending the space beyond this you'd need to add an extra piece of roof, either in the form of a gable or a lean-to. (Notice that the lean-to will need a lower slope to give the full ceiling height of the existing room.)

In the right drawing on p. 115, the addition of the jogged-in area only makes sense if you can live with a lower ceiling height. Otherwise you'll have to do some pretty dramatic roof surgery, which will likely be prohibitive in cost given the small amount of square footage being added. So the roof is the feature that, in both cases, determines the best solution for the addition. In fact, if you have a roof form similar to the right drawing on p. 115, you may decide that there are better and less expensive places to add on.

As you can see, adding a bump-out usually involves more than just filling in or bumping out the walls, so this is definitely an area where you'll benefit from hiring an architect to assist you.

not so big principles

Alcove versus Room Extension

When a bump-out is small, attached to the existing house a bit like a saddlebag on a bicycle, the interior result is an alcove off the main space with its own unique identity. But what makes it an alcove as opposed to an extension of the room? Let's take a look at a built example to see the difference. In the house shown on the facing page, architect Gail Wong bumped out the entire back of the house by 30 in. In this situation, you cannot tell either from inside or outside that there's an addition. But if the bump-out had extended only partway across, it would now appear as an alcove.

EXTENSION VS. ALCOVE

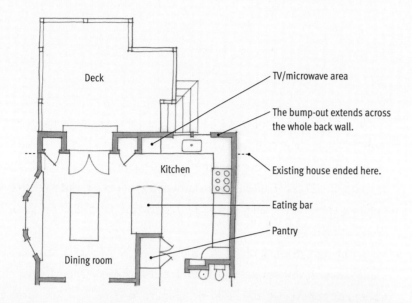

Deck

TV/microwave area

The bump-out extends across the whole back wall.

Kitchen

Existing house ended here.

Eating bar

Pantry

Dining room

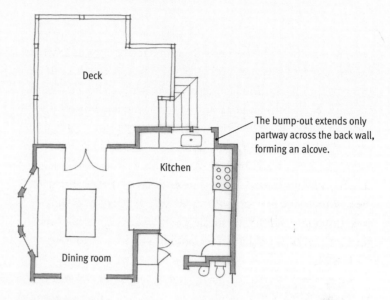

Deck

The bump-out extends only partway across the back wall, forming an alcove.

Kitchen

Dining room

Sometimes a bump-out creates an alcove that reads like added space; in this case, the entire back wall has been extended, so the kitchen still reads as one space—an extension rather than an alcove.

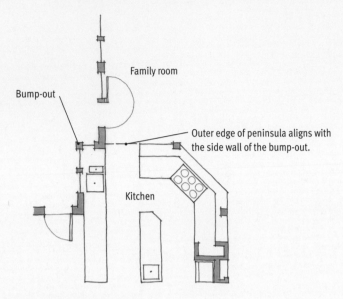

Bump-out

Family room

Outer edge of peninsula aligns with the side wall of the bump-out.

Kitchen

Triple windows centered over the sink in the bumped-out wall of this kitchen provide a focal point for the whole room.

Neither version is better than the other, but the feeling of each is quite different. If you want to draw attention to an area of the kitchen as a separate place—as with an eating area, for example—the alcove that results from a smaller bump-out may add the character you are looking for, while if you want the room to feel like a singular whole, extend the bump-out across the entire width of the room.

Alignments

Whenever you add on, even with something as small as a bump-out, it is important to consider what the walls and windows align with in the remodeled plan, as well as when viewed from the exterior. A bump-out can look like an integrated part of the whole design when it is aligned with adjacent elements, or it can look like an ill-proportioned tack-on if alignments are ignored.

This doesn't mean that you have to line everything up with existing walls. It simply means that you need to consider the other elements in

the composition both inside and out. One of my favorite alignment tricks is to make a 30-in.-deep bump-out, similar to the one shown in the drawing above, so that the kitchen cabinets have a place to nestle into, and the side wall of the bump-out defines the visual end of the kitchen. By aligning this side wall with the outer edge of a peninsula or island the whole room is given an integrated appearance.

Window Composition

An important benefit of any addition or bump-out is that you can give it, and the room it is added onto, an interesting composition of windows that adds personality to the house both inside and out. Whether the windows provide a centered feature for the inside of the room (as shown in the photo at left) or surround the bump-out to create an alcove filled with light and view (see the photo on the facing page), the result is one of newly introduced character created by the patterns and geometry of the various window combinations.

In this bumped-out alcove from the case study to follow, a bank of tall windows slips past the original exterior wall of the kitchen, inviting the eye outward toward the garden.

one kitchen, two bump-outs

Deborah and Geoffrey loved living in their 2,000-sq.-ft. cape in Brookline, Massachusetts, where they maintained a delightful front-yard garden beyond the same low picket fence that graced the house when it was built in 1932. The problem was the small kitchen, which consisted of an L-shaped counter with a single window to the north. Although the kitchen opened to a side terrace, it was cut off from the south-facing sitting room and front-yard garden, blocked by a closet, half-bath, and vestibule. Deborah and Geoffrey called on Boston architect David Amory to make the kitchen larger, brighter, and more open. They also wanted a basement-level carport tucked behind the house.

Setbacks restricted the expansion of the kitchen toward the side yard, so David added a 4-ft.-wide bump-out eating alcove there and then placed a 5½-ft.-wide cooking bump-out over the new carport. In a sense, this cooking bump-out juts into midair. Together the two bump-outs add around 100 sq. ft. to the kitchen without burdening the house with a single, large addition. But the kitchen feels even larger than the extra 100 sq. ft. alone would suggest. That's because David also opened it up within its original footprint, eliminating the closet and vestibule so that space flows around the half-bath (now, in effect, a room within a room), connecting the kitchen at last to the sunny front-yard garden.

Bump-out #2   Bump-out #1

The bump-outs expanded the kitchen without turning it into one big room. The countertop and island define the cooking bump-out; the desk nook and window wall define the eating bump-out. The eating area is further defined by its floorboards and ceiling boards, which run perpendicular to those in the kitchen.

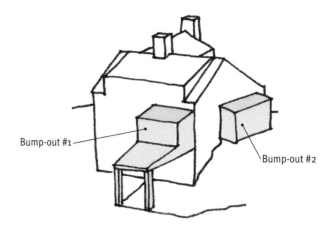

Bump-out #1

Bump-out #2

The expansion of the kitchen involves two bump-outs: a 5½-ft.-wide cooking area above a new carport at the back and a 4-ft.-wide eating area at the side, with a phone desk and a door to a terrace garden.

remodeling with respect

Deborah and Geoffrey's house was designed in 1932 by renowned Boston architect Royal Barry Wills and was awarded the Gold Medal in the Better Homes in America Small House Competition. The top prize was presented to Wills by President Herbert Hoover. *Better Homes & Gardens* featured the house in its July 1933 issue in an article entitled "Trim as a Clipper Ship," praising its "economical layout." The homeowners and architect David Amory were intent on honoring the spirit of Wills's original and on maintaining its trim appearance. The two modest bump-outs do just that.

(above) Here's a great double-duty move: One of the original upper cabinets was removed from the pantry to expand the pantry into an existing under-stair closet; the same cabinet was placed in the kitchen, where it visually ties the updated kitchen to the old pantry, while saving the cost of a new cabinet.

(left) With windows on three full sides, the bump-out in the foreground is essentially a sunroom. The bump-out at the back includes a window on all three sides (one is visible in the far corner), lending the work counter a bright, airy feel.

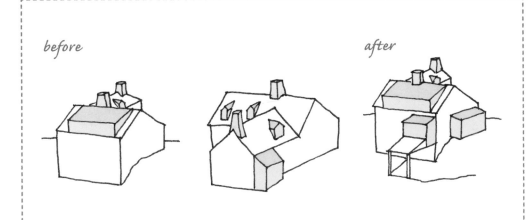

before

after

taking cues from the roof

A simple, gabled Cape Cod roof allows for all manner of appendages so long as they're scaled to the primary roof. In this case, the house already had a number of bump-outs, including a shed dormer at the back and a little "wood closet" that extends from the living room as a continuation of the front gable. In this context, the two new shed-roofed kitchen bump-outs fit right in.

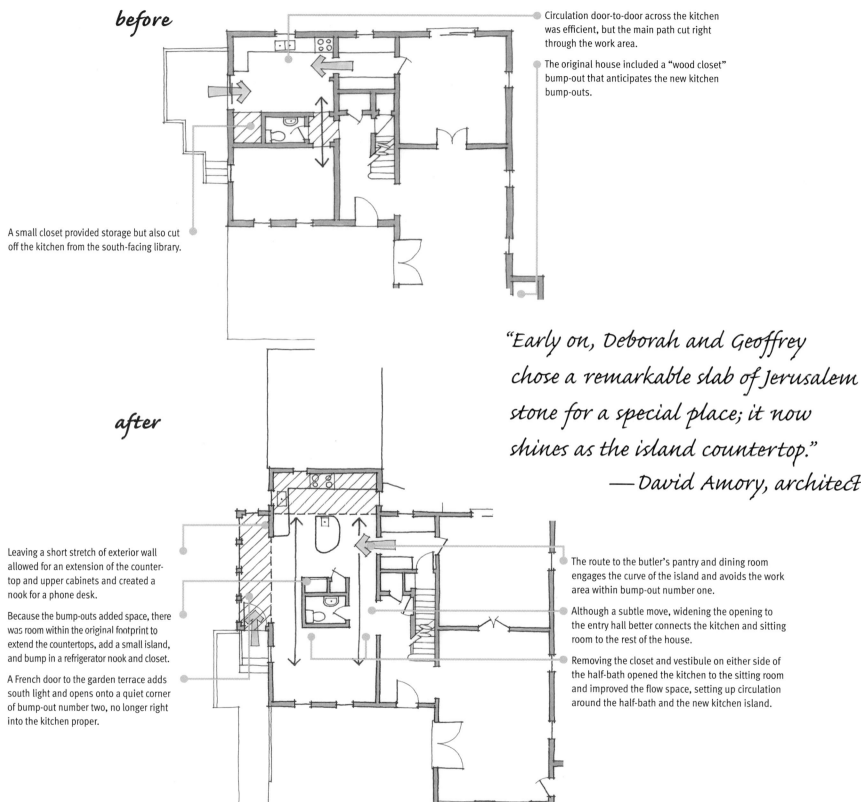

before

Circulation door-to-door across the kitchen was efficient, but the main path cut right through the work area.

The original house included a "wood closet" bump-out that anticipates the new kitchen bump-outs.

A small closet provided storage but also cut off the kitchen from the south-facing library.

"Early on, Deborah and Geoffrey chose a remarkable slab of Jerusalem stone for a special place; it now shines as the island countertop."
—David Amory, architect

after

Leaving a short stretch of exterior wall allowed for an extension of the countertop and upper cabinets and created a nook for a phone desk.

Because the bump-outs added space, there was room within the original footprint to extend the countertops, add a small island, and bump in a refrigerator nook and closet.

A French door to the garden terrace adds south light and opens onto a quiet corner of bump-out number two, no longer right into the kitchen proper.

The route to the butler's pantry and dining room engages the curve of the island and avoids the work area within bump-out number one.

Although a subtle move, widening the opening to the entry hall better connects the kitchen and sitting room to the rest of the house.

Removing the closet and vestibule on either side of the half-bath opened the kitchen to the sitting room and improved the flow space, setting up circulation around the half-bath and the new kitchen island.

9. relocating the kitchen

Sometimes, in spite of all your best efforts to work within the footprint, open up the kitchen, or bump out a wall, you just have to accept that there's simply something wrong with the location of your kitchen. If you find yourself dissatisfied with all the options contemplated to date, it's time to consider relocating the entire room to a different part of the house.

Although this is almost always more expensive than leaving the kitchen in its current location because of the utility connections that must be moved, it can sometimes be well worth the extra money. If it makes you happier in the house for the long term, and if it allows all the main living spaces to work better together, it's definitely worth considering.

It doesn't necessarily take much of a move to make a dramatic improvement in livability. Simply relocating the kitchen into the space currently occupied by an adjacent formal dining room, for example, can change the kitchen's character from introverted and disconnected from outdoor living to extroverted and interwoven with the surrounding landscape and garden as well as with other interior spaces. In such a situation, the entire experience of living in the house is changed. The remodeled kitchen and associated living space seem significantly larger and airier despite the fact that no actual square footage has been added. It has simply been reapportioned. That's clearly money well spent.

cost control

Before considering relocating the kitchen, keep in mind that this strategy should be contemplated only after the previous options have been studied and evaluated. The most common reason for the escalation of costs in a remodeling project is that the most expensive solutions are considered first rather than last. By looking carefully at all the strategies in the preceding chapters first, you'll be certain that you are making the best use of the money you have available.

before

Dining

Laundry

Kitchen

Family room

Living room

Porch

after

Kitchen

Mudroom

Laundry

Dining

Family room

Mail center

Living room

Porch

Swapping the locations of the kitchen and dining room sometimes makes perfect sense. After the switch, this kitchen is connected directly to the backyard and to a reconfigured mudroom, powder room, and laundry area. The dining room now adjoins the living room and family room as well as the kitchen; it serves equally as an eating area and a space for family projects.

questions to ask yourself

You can use your answers to these questions to help you generate alternative schematic designs. So, for example, if your primary frustration with the kitchen's current location is that you can't expand the room as much as you would like because of a lack of adjacent space, consider moving the room to a part of the house that is already larger, such as a rarely used formal living room or dining room, and see what happens.

- *Why are you dissatisfied with the current location of the kitchen?*

- *Are there physical obstacles, such as walls, chimneys, or built-ins, that are preventing you from opening up the room as much as you would like?*

- *Does the existing kitchen have a limited connection to the garden or outdoors?*

- *Is there limited area in which to expand the kitchen as much as you would like?*

- *Is the current kitchen location too far from other frequently used parts in and around the house, such as the garage, backyard, screened porch, back entry, or main living area?*

- *Is the current kitchen located on the opposite side of the house from the direction you'd like it to be facing?*

- *Is the current kitchen far from an outside wall of the house, making it dark, isolated, or uninspiring?*

Once you've generated a few relocation options, make a list of the pros and cons of each and compare them in order to assess which one offers the most advantages.

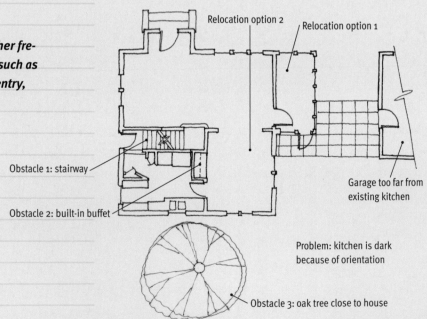

Relocation option 2

Relocation option 1

Obstacle 1: stairway

Obstacle 2: built-in buffet

Garage too far from existing kitchen

Problem: kitchen is dark because of orientation

Obstacle 3: oak tree close to house

imagining the possibilities

The idea of moving the kitchen can be somewhat daunting. How do you know where to put it if not where it is right now? The best place to start playing around with different alternatives for kitchen locations is with the same floor plan of your existing spaces that you learned to draw in chapter 6.

Once again you'll want to take the floor plan that you measured out on grid paper and place a sheet of tracing paper over the top of it. You'll use this tracing paper to play with options. Try not to get married to any particular solution for a while. Consider it your job simply to try out all manner of alternatives, using as many fresh sheets of tracing paper as you need.

Just as in any field, brainstorming works best when there are no limits. So give yourself permission to imagine anything, however crazy the idea may seem. Although you'll discard most of the crazy notions, they'll help you to think outside the box and may open your eyes to something obvious that wouldn't have occurred to you otherwise.

Don't forget about the room you are vacating: It is part of the design solution, too, and It must work well or you are simply trading one set of problems for a new one. If you can't make a solution that works, put that piece of tracing paper aside and try another option. Not all attempts at

Floor-to-ceiling sliding glass doors not only connect the kitchen to the outdoors but also allow views through the kitchen to the backyard from adjacent spaces farther within the house.

The sculpture and wind chimes, aligned with the window above the kitchen sink, are as much a part of the kitchen's design as the placement of the sink itself.

a solution will result in a design you'll like. That's the nature of the process. So rather than get frustrated, simply move on. If you think of it as playing rather than trying to figure out the perfect solution, you'll come up with better options, and you'll enjoy the entire process.

not so big principles

Outdoor Focus

One of the most important features for a kitchen is to be connected to the outdoors. In many older houses the kitchen is almost completely separated from the garden or backyard, making the room where most indoor living takes place seem isolated and depressing, regardless of its size. Because we are so deeply affected by light and view, it is important to make the connection to the surrounding landscape a high priority in any kitchen remodeling.

Identify which part of your property you'd most like to be able to see from the kitchen. If possible, make the connection not only one of view but also one that allows you to move from inside to outside by providing a door—French, terrace, or sliding—so that you can see through it (see the photos on p. 127).

Make the view that you see from inside the kitchen a part of the design solution. Place the windows so that the window sill is low to the countertop to maximize view, and consider the placement of plantings, paths, and objects that can be seen in the garden from within the house.

For example, when I moved into my house in Raleigh, I aligned a beautiful piece of sculpture with the window above the kitchen sink. The sculpture was placed at the base of a tree at the far side of the dry creek bed that runs across our property. I also hung some spectacular wind chimes from the same tree (see the photo at left). So when I stand at the sink, I am looking directly at something beautiful, something that gives order to the natural world beyond the boundaries of the house. This is as much a part of the kitchen's design as the placement of the sink itself because it is something that brings me constant enjoyment.

Window Positioning

There are few things that can have as much impact on the character of a room as the position of the windows. Most people assume that the place for a window is in the middle of the wall, but there are many other ways to place windows, each giving a different quality of light to the room. Let's look at each option in turn.

Adjacent to a perpendicular wall Placing a window in this manner turns the entire perpendicular wall into a big light reflector, which bathes the whole room in light even if the window is small. I often use this technique adjacent to upper cabinets or a wall of pantry shelves, so that the surface of the cabinets serves as the reflector (as shown in the bottom photo on the facing page). There are few techniques that work so well to make a small space seem larger.

(left) A wall of windows from countertop to ceiling dramatically expands the kitchen outward.

(below) A window placed adjacent a bank of upper cabinets turns this kitchen wall into a light reflector.

Cabinets to either side of the sink create the effect of a deep-set window bay while bouncing light into the room.

dramatically increase the room's connection to the outdoors and make the space seem much larger than it actually is. This is because our eyes read the outdoor area as part of the room (as shown in the top photo on p. 129). The less visual obstruction there is, the more powerful this effect will be.

Deep-set windows If wall space is at a premium and you can't give up much of it for additional window area, consider making the windows appear to be deep-set by flanking the window frame with upper cabinets, painted or stained a light color (see the photo at left). This will bounce more daylight into the room, and in so doing, make the room appear larger and cheerier. When direct sunlight is introduced into a room in this way, it can make the whole room radiant.

Corner windows Perhaps the strongest connection of all with the surrounding landscape can be made with corner windows. Because our eyes expect to see structure at the corner of a room, when that corner is all glass, we are fooled into believing that the room extends out into the garden, and we feel a sense of freedom and boundarylessness.

Openability

One other consideration that's useful either when relocating a kitchen or when opening up a kitchen to adjacent spaces is to make it possible either to open or close the room to surrounding spaces with the use of sliding partitions. This solves one of the biggest concerns for people who are used to having a separate kitchen, namely that all the kitchen mess will be visible for all to see. With the addition of sliding panels, the kitchen can be hidden from view when desired.

From ceiling to countertop Another way to increase the sense of connection to the outdoors is to minimize one's awareness of the window frame—to make it appear that there's no separation between you and the outdoors. You can do this by taking the windowsill all the way down to countertop height and the window head all the way up to the ceiling surface.

A wall of windows Even if it isn't practical to make the windows extend from ceiling to countertop, a wall that's devoted mostly to windows can

Opening up the corner of a room gives the impression that the house continues beyond the boundaries of the exterior wall. If you add a soffit above and cabinetry to either side, as here, you also create the impression of a deep-set window, bouncing more light into the kitchen and creating a wonderful place to work.

kitchen becomes library, library becomes kitchen

Need a bigger kitchen? Perhaps you already have one . . . in the guise of another room in your house. Such was the case for John and his wife Melinda in Washington, D.C. The kitchen in their 1922 house was way too small for two avid cooks; it served as a main route between the front and back of the house; and, thanks to a previous owner's ill-conceived remodeling, it had no door at all to the dining room. The dining room, for its part, was too large to feel comfortable, and the library was too sunny for books. Each of the rooms was charming in its way yet not quite right.

Architect Ralph Cunningham realized that most of the problems of size, flow, and function could be solved with one swift move: Put the library in the small space that had been the kitchen and the kitchen in the large, sunny room that had been the library. Here, it could become a true family kitchen, with a spot for casual dining and a big view out to the backyard garden. To this bold move, Ralph added a number of smaller moves that made the rooms work better both individually and together. For instance, turning a few feet of dining room into a fat wall added storage space to the kitchen so it could remain more open, while shortening the dining room so it would feel cozier. In this house, trading spaces and paying attention to little details added usefulness and delight, without adding square feet.

"A few swift moves, both bold and subtle, can dramatically improve the spatial configuration of a house."
—Ralph Cunningham, architect

The old kitchen was shoehorned into a small space just off the back entry vestibule, which was also the path from the kitchen to the library. Now the library occupies the old kitchen space, and the kitchen is at the back in the former library space.

Architect Ralph Cunningham designed the kitchen to look like a room with the same generous, vintage character as the other rooms in the house, rather than like a sleek, contemporary kitchen. To this end, wall cabinets are kept to a minimum, and the cabinetry was designed to feel like furniture pieces set within the tall, beamed room. If the old kitchen felt like a cramped afterthought, the new kitchen feels like the bright, open heart of the house, a family gathering place, connected to the backyard garden.

before

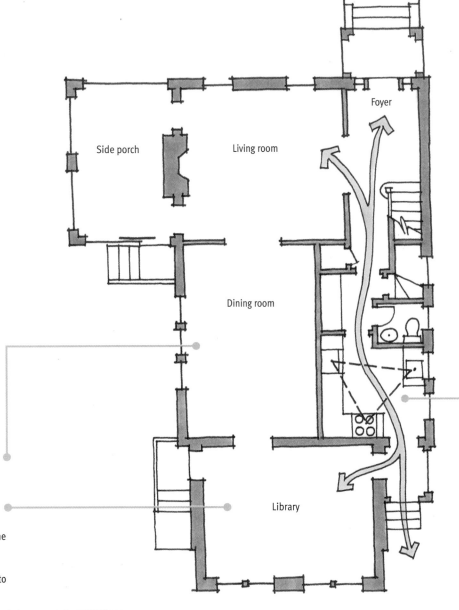

Side porch

Living room

Foyer

Dining room

Library

The main circulation route between the front foyer and stairs and the backyard and library went right through the center of the kitchen and the "work triangle" that should be the cook's realm. Doorways in opposite corners left too little room for countertops.

The dining room felt too big to be comfortable, especially when compared with the adjacent living room and library.

The library was in a poorly enclosed back porch, in need of an upgrade even if its function didn't change. It faced south to the backyard, but its modest windows didn't take full advantage of the sun and view (even though they allowed too much light to reach the books).

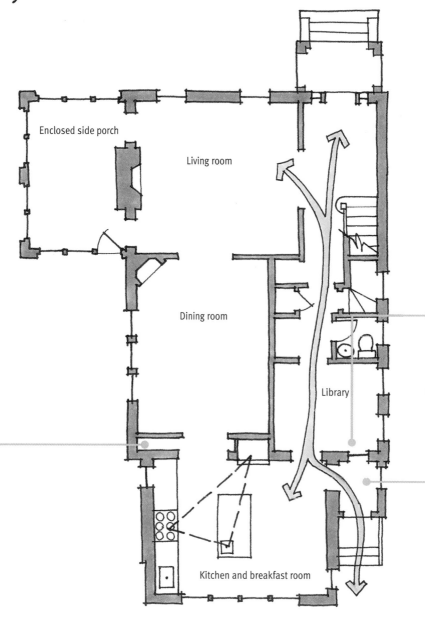

after

Enclosed side porch

Living room

Dining room

Library

Kitchen and breakfast room

Creating a fat wall between the kitchen and dining room by thickening an existing wall shortened the dining room, giving it more intimate proportions. It also provided a hidden, slide-out pantry, as well as a place to tuck away the refrigerator, allowing the kitchen to remain open and airy.

In place of the doorway to the old kitchen is a hand-carved Indian screen called a *jalee,* one of John and his wife's prized possessions, through which you glimpse the back entry vestibule (see the top photo on p. 132).

Problem areas like the back entry, which spilled right into the heart of the kitchen, became opportunities. Now upon entering from the backyard, you turn into a corner of the new kitchen devoted to circulation. You're in line with a window at the far end of the kitchen that draws you forward.

turning
to face
the light

The kitchen in Lisa and Theo's Tudor Revival house outside Boston was large enough, but it was dark and outdated. The path from the back door to the rest of the house went right through the middle of it. And though the kitchen opened to a family room, the counters faced the opposite direction, forcing the cook to turn his or her back to the breakfast table and sitting area.

Lisa and Theo asked architect David Amory to update the kitchen, add natural light, and improve the connection to the family room and garden. David decided to reorient the kitchen toward the family room, while shifting the mudroom to the north wall, where the kitchen counter had been. David's solution is a great example of how even a slight kitchen relocation can make a dramatic improvement. The shift involves the mudroom as well as the kitchen and yet it's not a room swap; it's a dance of spaces, a kitchen and mudroom do-si-do.

The mudroom and adjoining pantry now serve as a pathway from the back door to the front of the house, so you don't have to walk through the kitchen if you don't want to. But the dramatic change is in the kitchen, which opens across a generous island to face a bank of tall windows that runs the full length of the combined kitchen/family room and wraps around the south end, drawing the garden into the bright, open space.

The kitchen now faces the family room across a cooking and prep island. Tall windows bring in light and open out to a garden view. Painted wood ceiling battens align with the window mullions, tying the room together and leading the eye out to the garden.

"Not only did the kitchen point in the wrong direction, but the family room didn't take advantage of the wonderful garden views. The rooms needed an about-face."
— David Amory, architect

kitchen and mudroom do-si-do

The kitchen shifted south, closer to the family room and garden views, while the mudroom shifted north. As the arrows show, the kitchen and family room are now more fully engaged with each other, the mudroom now tucked away from the family room.

Some of the beams above the kitchen are structural; rather than have them appear randomly placed, architect David Amory added a few more to make a pattern. He further animated the kitchen with his trademark curves: maple brackets supporting the island countertop and a curved side to the painted maple phone desk in the foreground, fashioned from full-size templates David drew by hand on site.

(right) Giving up a potential cabinet for a corner window paid back in a greater sense of openness, more light on the countertop, and a view to the rear entry stoop. Limiting the number of cabinets was the key to giving the kitchen its open feel.

(far right) The extra-deep 8-in. windowsills are there to conceal the radiators below, but they also add substance to the base of the window wall and they're perfect for display.

The mudroom and pantry are not just service spaces; they're part of a welcoming entry sequence that begins on a veranda covered with akebia and clematis. None of this would have been possible if the kitchen had stayed in its original place.

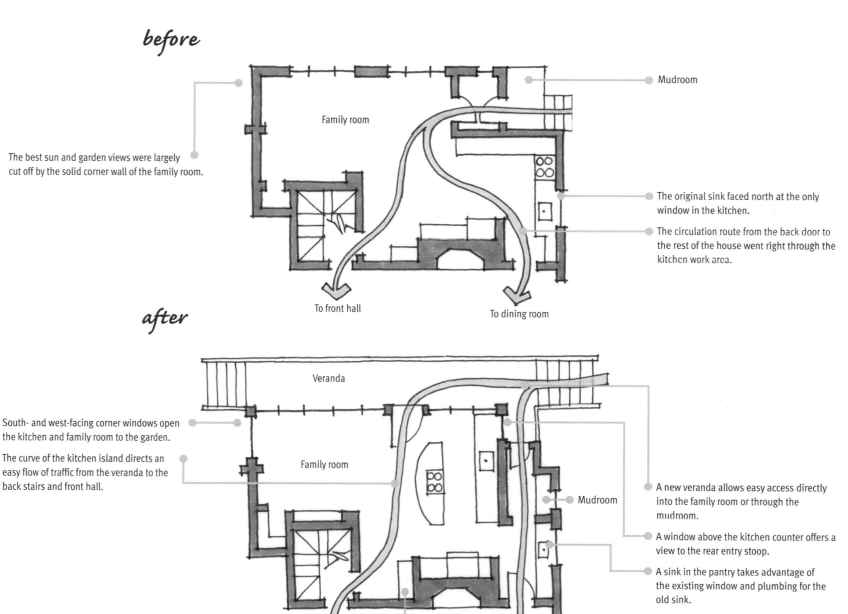

before

The best sun and garden views were largely cut off by the solid corner wall of the family room.

Family room

Mudroom

The original sink faced north at the only window in the kitchen.

The circulation route from the back door to the rest of the house went right through the kitchen work area.

To front hall

To dining room

after

South- and west-facing corner windows open the kitchen and family room to the garden.

The curve of the kitchen island directs an easy flow of traffic from the veranda to the back stairs and front hall.

Veranda

Family room

Mudroom

A new veranda allows easy access directly into the family room or through the mudroom.

A window above the kitchen counter offers a view to the rear entry stoop.

A sink in the pantry takes advantage of the existing window and plumbing for the old sink.

Direct access to the house from the back door now bypasses the kitchen.

To front hall

Phone desk

To dining room

10. kitchens: adding on

For many homeowners contemplating a kitchen remodel, the starting assumption is that they'll have to add on. But as I hope you're coming to understand, there are often much less dramatic strategies that can offer you just as much additional square footage to live in at a significantly lower cost. Although it is conceptually simple, it takes a lot of labor and materials to break through an exterior wall, add foundation and roof, and extend the existing structure outward.

That said, there are of course a number of occasions when adding on *is* the best answer. Perhaps the house is small and there is no way to borrow space from adjacent areas. Or you want the kitchen to expand out into the garden to bring in more light and view. Or perhaps you want an informal kitchen eating area and there's simply no place to put it. In all these situations a small addition may be what's required.

A long kitchen was opened up inside and connected to the back-yard garden by the addition of just a few feet across the rear wall of the house.

The existing roof can help you decide where to add on and what shape to make it. This simple two-story gabled addition grows naturally out of the slightly taller two-story gabled roof that shelters the main house. The new roof is in the same family of forms and helps give the back elevation a much more interesting face than it had previously.

listening to your roof—again

In chapter 8 we discussed bumping out, which is essentially a very small addition, and we looked at the importance of paying attention to your roof. When adding on in a more extensive way, the roof is equally important. By understanding what that roof will readily allow you to do, you can make the added space look like a natural part of the house so that it doesn't shriek "I'm an addition" to the neighbors.

The drawings on p. 142 show four of the most common roof situations when considering adding on—a two-story gable, a one-story gable, a two-story hip, and a one-story hip—along with a few addition options for each. Obviously, this set of drawings does not depict every possible option, but it is designed to give you pointers for finding solutions for your own roof situation. If your house has a combination of roof forms or is more complicated than those shown, you should contact an architect or residential designer.

not so big principles

3D Composition

One of the most challenging aspects of any design project is crafting a pleasing composition. When you are designing in three dimensions, you have to think about what each face of the house will look like, what it will look like when seen from all the different angles it is visible from, and what it will both look and feel like on the inside. And when you are adding on, you also have to consider how the new will blend with the old, so that when you are done it looks like one house with one unified character.

Given the potential complexity, it's always a good idea to hire an architect who is used to working with remodelings to help you when it comes to adding on. The quality and character of the overall composition can have a huge impact on the value of your house. A well-proportioned addition can greatly enhance the value of your home, while a poorly proportioned addition can actually reduce the home's value, even though both additions may cost exactly the same amount.

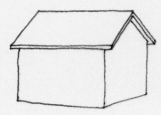

Two story with gable roof

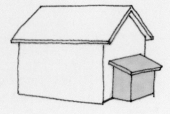

Two-story gable with lean-to bump-out

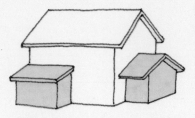

Two-story gable with lean-to bump-out and gable addition

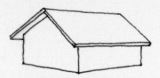

One story with gable roof

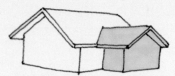

One-story gable with gable addition

One-story gable with gable addition and lean-to bump-out

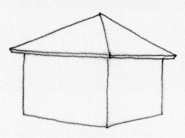

Two story with hip roof

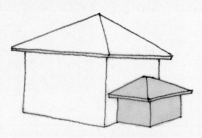

Two-story hip with hip-roofed addition

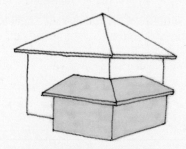

Two-story hip with wrap-around hip-roofed addition

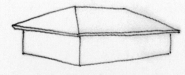

One story with hip roof

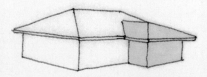

One-story hip with hip-roofed addition

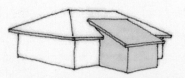

One-story hip with lean-to addition

Quality, Quantity, Cost

Early in my professional career, I discovered that you have to determine which two of the following three variables—quality, quantity, and cost—are most important to you. Because remodeling is an inexact science and prices fluctuate as much as the cost of a barrel of oil, if you are unwilling to allow one variable to "float," that is to remain indeterminate, you simply cannot build.

Most of the people I've worked with over the years have a very specific objective in mind when they add on. They may be adamant about their addition's quality, for example. They may want to make sure the house still fits into the scale of the neighborhood once they're done. Alternatively, they may want their house to look and feel bigger in order to better fit in with the neighbors. Or they may have a limited budget beyond which it really doesn't make sense to add on. When it comes to remodeling, the values of other houses in the neighborhood are often more of a definer of budget than the amount you can personally afford.

a word about complexity

In general, the more complex the shape of the addition, the more expensive it is likely to be. So if you are proposing to build an addition with lots of different roof forms and lots of indents in the floor plan, be prepared for the cost to be substantially more than one with a simple sloped roof and basic rectangular footprint.

Though a more complex structure may be visually more appealing, be aware of the cost implications of your decision. If you are uncertain about the difference between one solution and another, check with an architect or remodeling contractor whom you can trust. Whenever I'm designing an addition, I attempt to keep the structure fairly simple and keep the complexity that can add character for the finishing of the interior, where it will affect the homeowners' lives more directly.

Adding a second story may be highly desirable from a standpoint of square footage, but it won't be a smart investment unless there are houses of a similar scale in the neighborhood. When the addition is done as gracefully as shown here, the charm and character of the home are maintained and the cost of the addition is readily recoupable within just a few years time, should a move become necessary.

questions to ask yourself

- *From an interior layout standpoint, where would you like to add on space?*

- *Are there any property setback requirements that would prevent you from adding on in any direction that you are considering? (See the sidebar on p. 116 to read more about setbacks.)*

- *Does the location of your preferred addition have reasonable roof solutions? If not, are there better locations from a roof solution standpoint?*

- *Could your needs be accommodated by placing the addition where the roof most readily allows?*

- *How much additional square footage will give you the best spatial solution? (Remember here that less is more in most instances, even though the cost per square foot of space may well be higher.)*

- *When you place this amount of square footage in the desired location and put a roof on it, does the new addition look in proportion to the existing house?*

- *If the roof looks too large, is there another way to arrange the addition so that the roof shape and scale is more in keeping with the proportions of the existing house?*

- *Is there more than one way to roof the addition you are considering? Try finding three or four solutions, and then picking your favorite.*

The smaller roof of this addition reinforces the shape of the original roof, and the whole complements the existing house.

This bulky addition off the front of the house bears no stylistic resemblance to the original.

Small additions are often more expensive per square foot than large additions, but they can provide well-tailored space without overwhelming the original house.

One factor that may be a surprise when adding on is that the smaller the addition, the more it costs per square foot of added space. This is because the primary cost of adding on lies in the exterior envelope—the part that's keeping the outdoors *out*. No matter how few square feet you add on, by breaking through the existing exterior wall and remaking the weather barrier, you have to deal with all the materials and details that go into that weather-tight coat, from insulation, to vapor and air barriers, to windows, to flashing, to roofing. There are lots and lots of critical

details that must be thought through and carefully executed, whether you are adding on 10, 100, or 1,000 sq. ft.

Builders will often use this piece of information to encourage their customers to add on more space than they really need. The argument makes eminently good sense if the goal is primarily one of square footage. But if it's not—if what you are looking for is well-tailored space that fits with the existing house—this can be poor advice. I've seen many people add on more space than they really want, spending only slightly more than they would have if they'd right-sized the addition, but come to find that the end result is out of proportion with their needs as well as with the rest of the house.

This is obviously what we are trying to avoid with a Not So Big remodeling. So despite the allure of more for less, stay focused on the amount of space you really need, rather than what's possible. This is how starter castles and really ugly oversized additions come into being.

So, if you are determined to have your addition built to a high level of quality in design and craftsmanship, and if you have a defined budget, then the variable you must allow to float is that of quantity. If on the other hand, you know you need to add on a particular quantity of space and you have a limited budget, then be prepared with a list of lesser materials selections that can be substituted for the ones you'd prefer, in case the bids come in too high (a not unusual occurrence). And if you have both a quantity and quality that you are determined to meet, then be prepared to let your budget float until after the bidding and negotiation process is complete.

The modest addition of a breakfast area that doubles as a back entry provides much-needed family space and frees up the once-cramped kitchen for cooking.

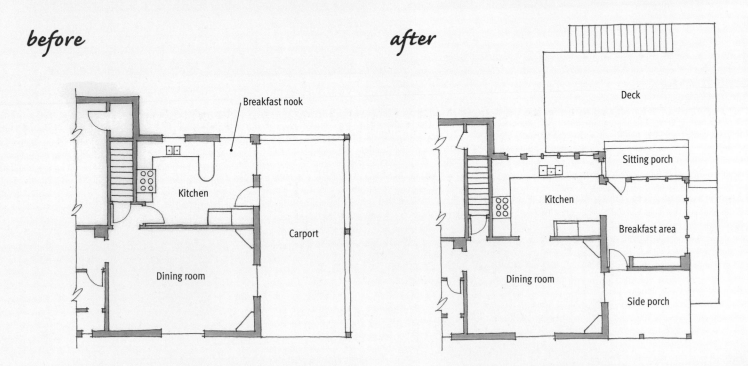

before

Breakfast nook

Kitchen

Carport

Dining room

after

Deck

Sitting porch

Kitchen

Breakfast area

Dining room

Side porch

Match Existing

This innocuous-sounding phrase is often used on a set of blueprints or construction drawings to indicate that the new materials and details used should look similar to the old. The problem is that the phrase is wide open to interpretation. Very detail-oriented remodelers will read it as a directive to make new and old indistinguishable from one another, while others will interpret it as meaning "generally similar." The difference in cost between these two approaches to the same note on a drawing can be enormous.

Before sending the drawings for your remodeling out for bids, make sure that you clarify in writing what "match existing" means to you. For example, if in your existing house you have double-hung windows with an unusual division of glass, do you want to match that pattern exactly, or are you comfortable with a pattern that is readily available as a standard product? Do you want the somewhat complicated profile of the trim around the exterior of your existing house to be replicated in the addition, or are you willing to accept a flat trim of the same width in its stead? Do you want copper downspouts like the rest of the house, or will you be satisfied with aluminum?

Making it clear what you mean can save a heap of grief and frustration during construction when, all too often, homeowners discover that there's a world of difference between what they meant and what is being provided by their contractor.

Matching the existing house can mean picking up on details, such as fascia boards and roof brackets, and keeping to the overall spirit of the original; it does not have to mean slavishly repeating the old.

change the kitchen, change everything

The existing house felt a bit truncated on the south side (the left side in the photo below); the original builder perhaps put up the archway to help balance the housefront from the street. The addition adds further visual weight and complexity while serving as a counterpoint to the front entry gable.

Here's a remodel in St. Paul, Minnesota, that began as a simple kitchen upgrade, grew to involve a modest addition, and wound up transforming the entire house and how it's lived in. And yet, with just an additional 320 sq. ft., it's still a Not So Big remodel. Cathy, a professor at a nearby university, had been in the house for 25 years when she decided it was time for a new kitchen. She called architect Paul Buum, and they sat down together around a cleared-off corner of the table in the dining room, which Cathy used as her office. Paul could see that in this small house, which had no eat-in kitchen, there clearly wasn't room for both dining and office work in one space.

He encouraged Cathy to think beyond the kitchen to how she really used the house. It wasn't long before they agreed that the kitchen belonged on the south side, connected to the garden and closer to the driveway and garage. A small addition to the south would solve many problems at once: Cathy would get a new, sunny kitchen; she'd have a proper mudroom; she'd gain an office space on the north side, where the kitchen used to be; and she'd get her dining room back. There would even be room to sneak in a full bath beside the office, so the office could one day become a bedroom should Cathy decide to live on one floor.

"Cathy would have been happy just having a new kitchen, but now she has a whole new house."
—Paul Buum, architect

As the site plan shows, the new mudroom puts the everyday entry much closer to the garage than the front door, which had been the only way in.

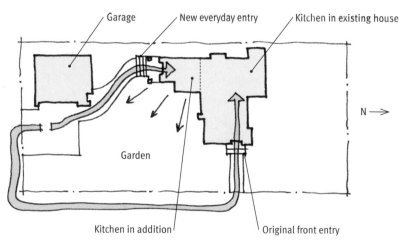

The kitchen is about as small as it can be, just 200 sq. ft., but it opens up to the sunny southeast garden. For the first time in 25 years, Kathy can step into her kitchen and enjoy morning light.

a plan for living on one level

The main goal of the remodeling was to put a new kitchen on the sunny side of the house and turn the old kitchen into a home office. At the same time, the seeds for single-floor living were sewn: A full bath allows the office to be converted into a bedroom. A floor pan and plumbing in the mudroom closet allow for a stacked washer and dryer.

Lining up the mudroom door with a circulation path through the kitchen extends the kitchen beyond its walls. Grandchildren can run freely back and forth while Cathy works in the kitchen U (to the left in the photo).

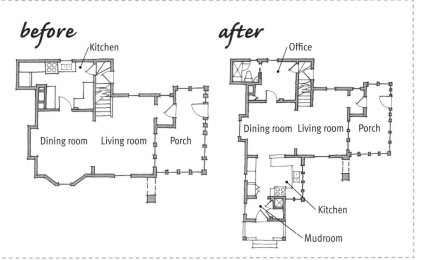

before

Kitchen

Dining room   Living room   Porch

after

Office

Dining room   Living room   Porch

Kitchen

Mudroom

(facing page) Corner windows capture morning light and gently thrust the kitchen into the garden. A bank of windows means fewer upper cabinets, a storage problem solved by floor-to-ceiling pantry cabinets (see the far right photo).

The wide opening with a half-wall allows light from the kitchen windows to reach the dining room and gives each space both identity and openness.

On the wall opposite the kitchen workspace, the refrigerator and a deep pantry cabinet create room for a bill-paying nook.

11. kitchens as catalyst

Although the impetus for a remodeling project is often an ill-functioning kitchen, the fact that you are even considering tearing up the very heart of the house invariably precipitates the desire to fix, expand, or otherwise improve a number of other rooms in the house as well. If your budget is limited, you need to stay aware of this propensity for "project creep"—the inclusion of other parts of the house into an initially small and self-contained kitchen remodeling. But in this chapter, we're going to assume that your budget allows for improvements to other parts of the house as well, and take a look at the possibilities for significantly improving the surrounding areas.

We've seen how borrowing space, opening up some walls, and relocating the kitchen all require that other parts of the house be remodeled at the same time. But what if you use the kitchen remodeling as a reason to remodel or add on in a more comprehensive way? Does the kitchen remodeling inspire you to update the whole look and feel of the main level perhaps—weaving all the rooms and spaces together with an integrated aesthetic? Or are there some spaces missing from your current house that can't be found simply by reorganizing the existing layout—things like an in-home office, a main floor bathroom, or a mudroom/pet room? A kitchen often becomes the catalyst for this kind of rethinking of a larger segment of the main level, and when it's done well, it can make the house feel like an entirely new place.

A kitchen remodeling project can be an opportunity to remodel and better integrate adjacent living spaces as well.

not so big principles

Theme and Variations

The first step in creating a new, more integrated look for the affected areas of the interior is to select an aesthetic—a style, if you like that word better—that will weave the parts into a singular whole. I call this giving the space a "theme and variations," much as a piece of music starts with a recognizable theme tune and then has variations on that theme as the piece continues. You'll select a visual or spatial theme to work with, and then use that theme to create variations throughout the rooms and spaces you remodel.

We'll look at a number of common techniques for adding a theme and variations, but don't feel limited to only these options. They are simply examples to get you thinking, and you'll find other possibilities in the case studies for this and other chapters as well.

The third dimension One of my favorite ways to give a remodeling a spatial theme is to vary the ceiling height, using lowered ceilings over subordinate spaces such as hallways, alcoves, and smaller rooms, and higher ceilings over the more important rooms. Lowering small sections of ceiling gives a spatial variety that is very appealing visually and has the added advantage of making the whole composition seem larger than it actually is—an illusion resulting from the contrast between the lower and higher ceiling heights.

In addition to the examples shown here, you may want to look back at chapter 1 to see how I used this technique in my own remodeling to add some spatial variety while integrating the look and feel of the whole.

Lowering small sections of ceiling, above a countertop or over a hallway, for instance, adds spatial variety and makes the full-height spaces seem that much larger.

questions to ask yourself

- Are there any adjacent areas that you'd like to remodel at the same time you are tackling the kitchen?

- Which rooms will you be able to see into once your kitchen remodeling is complete?

- Would you like to make any of these surrounding areas match the style and character of the new kitchen?

- What are these spaces lacking? List the shortcomings of each.

- Consider using ceiling height and framed openings rather than walls to delineate one activity place from the next.

- If you plan to add on, refer to chapter 10 for questions to ask yourself in order to find an appropriate location for the addition.

- Some common additions and revampings that happen simultaneously with a kitchen remodeling are:

  - Family room

  - Mudroom/pet room

  - Laundry

  - Powder room

  - Full main-floor bathroom

  - Pantry

  - In-home office

  - Rethinking of existing dining and living rooms

  - Informal eating area

In Sarah's home in Raleigh, running a headband throughout the house provides a connecting theme. In the guest bathroom, the base of the sloped ceiling is used as the height of the top of the new trim band, making the trim depth the height of the distance between the shower tile and the ceiling.

Headbands and beltlines Another effective approach is to add a continuous beltline, such as a chair rail or wainscoting, or a continuous headband, such as a trim line connecting the tops of all the doors and windows. If the house has a more traditional feel, you can also use a crown molding at the top of the wall, where it meets the ceiling.

The advantage of a beltline or headband is that it makes the ceiling height appear taller than it actually is. It works because our eye reads the beltline or headband as a divider; by accentuating the difference between the lower section of wall surface and the upper section, we imagine that there is more there to look at . . . and more translates into taller. You can intensify this effect by making the area below the line a darker color than the area above.

There is no right way to introduce a beltline or headband, by the way, and no one width that is better than another. You can be quite playful with the application of these bands and create a delightful ambiance, ranging anywhere from classic to contemporary.

Color When it comes to tying a house together, the repeated use of a particular color or colors can add significant personality at minimal cost. In general, the darker or more intense the color applied, the more importance and weight that surface will appear to have. So use a stronger color on the walls and surfaces you want to draw the most attention to and a quieter color for surfaces that you want to downplay.

Thick walls Many architects and designers use a technique that we refer to as "thick walls" to give an integrated look while adding spatial definition and significant storage to a home's interior. Typically interior walls are 4 in. thick. These are perfectly adequate for most structural and room division purposes, but they aren't usually all that inspiring. Wherever an opening is punched through a wall with more depth to it, or where a wall

When applying color for variation, use a strong color on walls and surfaces you want to draw attention to.

the headband

Adding a headband doesn't have to entail a lot of work. In my own home, I wanted the benefit of the headband without all the extra work and expense of replacing existing trim. So instead of removing the existing window trim and adding a headband that also doubles as the upper piece of trim casing, I simply ran the new trim band directly above the existing window casing. The new trim is cherry and only 2¼ in. wide. It could have been even narrower and still done the trick.

I then applied paint below the trim band but not above, which fools the eye into believing that the room is taller and more spacious than it really is.

inset is added in a thick wall, you create the appearance of both solidity and integrity. Thickness gives a wall a sense of permanence, most likely the result of our collective memory of when walls were made of stone, mud bricks, or the like.

Because thickness is such a notable feature, when a thick wall runs from one end of the house to the other or connects one part of the house to another as in the example shown on the facing page, the entire composition is then perceived as a whole. So the addition of a thick wall is an excellent way of imparting a new and unified character to the home without having to make changes to all the rooms and spaces it links together. Just the thick wall element alone can provide the integration if it is done well.

Library walls One common way to add thickness to an existing wall is to cover the surface with bookshelves. (I often refer to bookshelves as thick wallpaper.) There are few things more visually stimulating or more useful. The technique is most effective when the shelves extend from floor to ceiling and from wall to wall. That way your eye believes that the whole wall has depth and thickness and is thus more permanent.

THICK WALL REMODELING

before

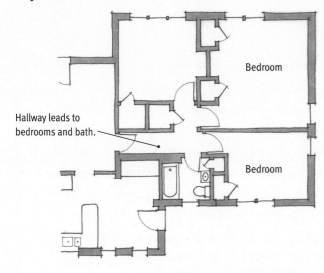

Hallway leads to bedrooms and bath.

Bedroom

Bedroom

after

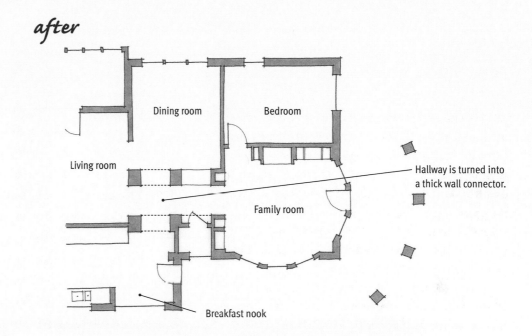

Dining room

Bedroom

Living room

Hallway is turned into a thick wall connector.

Family room

Breakfast nook

Thick walls, whether "library walls" of built-out bookshelves (far left) or beefed up columns (left, and floor plans above), impart a unified character to a series of spaces.

everything in its place

When Minneapolis home-owners James and Wendi first approached architect Steve Nordgaard of TEA$_2$ Architects, they requested a kitchen addition with an eating area and perhaps a family room. They also wanted to improve the character of their outdated and not entirely faithful Mediterranean-style house. After a quick budget check, however, James and Wendi realized they couldn't afford to add on. Steve realized they didn't need to. The house already had enough square footage. But the way it was laid out—its plan—made much of that space inefficient and hard to live in. The powder room was placed where the kitchen belonged; the breakfast table was in what made more sense as a service area; and the living room was long enough for two seating areas, but it was difficult to furnish even one. Correcting these and other fundamental plan issues would prove the perfect opportunity to give the house a full infusion of Mediterranean flair.

The formerly closed-off kitchen now opens to the dining room. Thick Douglas fir beams tie the spaces together, while a pair of deep plaster beams define a transition zone between the two rooms. Both the wood beams and the plaster work represent variations on the Mediterranean theme of the house.

where to put the TV?

The narrowness of the living room was turned into an advantage when it came to finding a place for the TV. Arranging sofas in the center of the room allowed a view to the existing fireplace on the outside wall and to the TV on the opposite wall. Conveniently, the opposite wall was a fat wall—the back side of the pantry. Stealing a little depth from the pantry created an inset for the TV. The plaster wall itself is thick enough to house a paneled wood pocket door, which conceals the TV as it adds Mediterranean character.

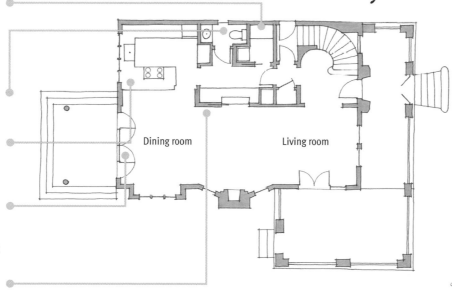

before

The breakfast area lacked natural light. Its redundancy as a place to eat (in addition to the dining room) represented an opportunity to repurpose the space.

The back door opened right into a narrow leg of the kitchen. The door was replaced by a bank of windows over the sink counter, a better use of the wall facing the backyard.

The powder room lacked privacy, blocked the dining room–kitchen connection, and intruded on the kitchen, leaving it an awkward L-shaped space.

Dining room

Living room

after

Because the powder room is no larger than it needs to be, there's enough space for a laundry room. Notice how the zigzag wall between powder room and laundry room allows for maximum functionality with minimum open floor area.

The new powder room is tucked out of the way, beyond a short vestibule off the new service hall.

The wide peninsula counter has room for three stools, whereas the old counter had room for just two. This helps make up for the lack of a breakfast table.

The deep bay in the dining room was replaced by four French doors, bringing daylight closer to the dining table and allowing the backyard to be reached without going through the kitchen.

An inset within the *thick walls* (plus a little extra depth borrowed from the pantry fat wall) houses a flat-screen TV, which can be hidden by a large sliding panel door.

Dining room

Living room

"*From the front entry, you have to walk all the way into the kitchen before you see the ovens and refrigerator. So it feels less kitchen-y.*"

—Steve Nordgaard, architect

The rhythm of the wood beams ties together the dining room and dual sitting areas of the living room. The beams actually play up the long dimension of the unified space, adding drama.

variations on a Zen theme

For San Francisco homeowner Mitch, the idea was to start with a very small house so that even on a limited budget he could afford thoughtful design and quality natural materials. He found a 700-sq.-ft. row house that fit the bill, but it was far from the meditative sanctuary he was looking-ing for. So he asked architect Mark Brand to cast an air of Zen calm about the entire house, which isn't as daunting as it sounds, given that the sum of the house consisted of a kitchen, a bath, a living room, and two bedrooms, all on one floor above a street-level garage. To achieve a harmonious feeling, Mark unified the spaces with a fir *headband*. The trim combines with shoji-like sliding glass-panel doors and quiet colors to replicate the qualities of traditional Japanese post-and-beam architecture, with a nod toward modernist simplicity.

Mark's other overarching move was to focus the interior spaces on a small backyard Japanese garden, created by landscape designer Lisa Charpontier. Simple details, minimal furnishings, and the ever-present garden just outside lend Mitch's home a quality of peace and tranquility, as well as a sense of spaciousness far greater than its diminutive footprint would suggest.

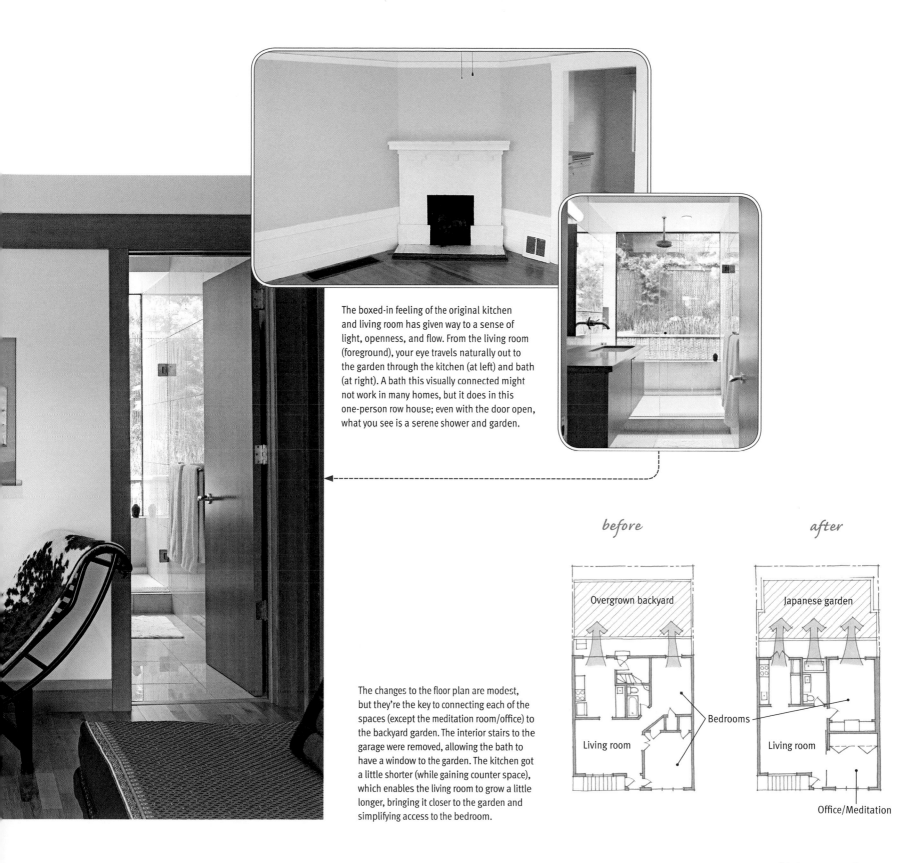

The boxed-in feeling of the original kitchen and living room has given way to a sense of light, openness, and flow. From the living room (foreground), your eye travels naturally out to the garden through the kitchen (at left) and bath (at right). A bath this visually connected might not work in many homes, but it does in this one-person row house; even with the door open, what you see is a serene shower and garden.

The changes to the floor plan are modest, but they're the key to connecting each of the spaces (except the meditation room/office) to the backyard garden. The interior stairs to the garage were removed, allowing the bath to have a window to the garden. The kitchen got a little shorter (while gaining counter space), which enables the living room to grow a little longer, bringing it closer to the garden and simplifying access to the bedroom.

before

after

Overgrown backyard

Japanese garden

Bedrooms

Living room

Living room

Office/Meditation

❶ The galley kitchen—perfect for a single homeowner—seems to extend beyond the glass doors into the backyard garden.

❷ A continuous band of fir trim, a *headband,* connects the tops of the doors and windows. Vertical trim combines with the headband and window trim to give the bedroom the quality of a traditional Japanese post-and-beam house.

❸ ❹ Sliding glass doors—a modernist interpretation of rice-paper shoji screens—open into a bedroom converted into a meditation space. Within the space, bifold doors open to reveal a home-office nook.

❺ The Japanese garden, raised above the basement garage level, functions as a small outdoor room and—of equal importance—as an extension of interior spaces.

"*We wanted to be as authentically Japanese as possible, but importing Hinoki wood was too expensive. So we used Douglas fir, which isn't all that different.*"
—Mark Brand, architect

double-duty window glass

This budget-conscious remodeling includes one splurge: several thousand dollars for switchable privacy glass in the bath. The window has a layer of plastic laminated between layers of glass. The plastic is milky white until a small electric current lines up its molecules so that it becomes clear. It's an incredibly elegant way to switch from garden view to privacy, without giving up daylight.

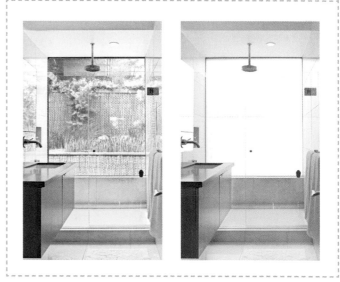

12. living spaces

Although living spaces usually don't have as many specific needs and functional requirements as a kitchen, we frequently overlook some layout basics that can make a room work much more effectively. A very common frustration, for example, is the apparent collision of focal points—the fireplace, the TV, and the view. We assume that we must orient the furniture around just one of these focal points, and then can't decide which one that should be. But there's another way of looking at this problem. Ask yourself how you look at each of these features. A fireplace isn't generally something you watch for hours, as you do a TV screen. Neither is a view, unless it is a particularly dramatic panorama. So you can design the seating arrangement to focus on the TV, letting the fireplace play second fiddle and allowing the view to wrap around the seating more like a warm embrace than a focus.

Though the fireplace occupies the center of the wall, the TV has been positioned so that it is the primary focus of the seating arrangement.

Although this is a specific example of a particular dilemma, it illustrates a way of thinking that is useful in many aspects of design. The process is this:

1. Determine what the apparent dilemma is. (In the given example it was that all three items are things we want to look at, often simultaneously.)

2. Identify how each item is perceived, what its particular requirements are for proper appreciation. (The TV is watched directly with eyes trained upon it, while the fireplace and the view are glanced at from time to time.)

3. Look for a solution that is not based on either/or thinking, but rather on both/and reasoning. (In our example we could arrive at the solution by asking ourselves, "How can I see and appreciate all three at the same time?")

Many living spaces are difficult to furnish because the room is an awkward shape—perhaps it is too long and thin or has a circulation route that cuts right through its center. As you begin to think about how to make this space more conducive to comfort, take a look at the obstacles to feeling settled (see "Questions to Ask Yourself" on p. 166).

not so big principles

Interior Views

One of the most important aspects of a well-functioning living space is that it be visible from several other gathering places in the house—such as the kitchen, eating area, and away room. Why is this important? Because when a space is visible it gains in vitality. It's what will make the living area into the focal gathering place you want it to be. (See chapter 7, for more on focal gathering places.) In fact, the more places it can be seen from, the more alive it will feel.

The views between spaces, when thoughtfully designed to be engaging from a number of different perspectives, can transform an otherwise plain house into something that delights you wherever you look. It

Visual layering, created by framing the view between spaces, helps the whole interior to feel larger than its actual square footage would suggest.

questions to ask yourself

- Is there an easy way to arrange furniture in the main living area?

- If the arrangement of the room is a problem, is this because of the particular furniture you own, or is it a characteristic of the shape of the space?

- Does the space have an obvious focal point, or does it feel haphazard and lack a clear center?

- Is there a major circulation pathway directly through the living space that cuts the sitting area in two?

- If so, is there a way to relocate a door or framed opening to redirect the passage through the space? Alternatively, can you relocate the furniture so that the sitting area isn't divided by the passage through the space?

- Is the living area too tall to feel comfortable when just one or two people are sitting there?

- Is there a way to lower a segment of ceiling or add a floating shelf around the edge of the room to give a sense of shelter to the seating area?

- Can you add a darker color or wood finish to the tall ceiling surface to give it some visual weight? Alternatively, is there a way to lower the ceiling throughout the space?

- Is there an acoustical problem with the space? Does it sound too noisy? If so, is the room wide open to many other spaces?

- Is there a way to add some spatial layering (see "Not So Big Principles" beginning on p. 165) to help break up the openness without reducing visibility?

- Is there a way to introduce some softer surfaces that will better absorb sound, such as carpet, rugs, drapes, and fabric?

- Does the living space feel dark or dreary?

- Is there a way to add some windows to let in more light and view?

- Is there a way to add some focal points or visual weight with color?

- Can you add some light fixtures to reflect light off walls, ceilings, or particular pieces of artwork?

- Does the living space feel isolated from the other living spaces? If so, take a look at chapters 7 and 11 for ideas to connect it with surrounding spaces.

- Is there a way to make the living space visible from other major congregating areas in the house?

doesn't have to be expensive to accomplish, and often it doesn't even require any wall moving. What it takes is an eye for composition. By using the entire living area with its adjacent spaces as a three-dimensional canvas, you can create your own spatial and visual music. The view from each of the adjacent areas can be thought of as a separate canvas, a separate interior view. And by designing each of the interior views to work on their own as well as collectively, you'll create a space that is lovely to look at from every angle.

For example, as you sit at your kitchen table and look into the living area, what do you see? How can you make it come alive? Are there walls you want to accentuate, a strategically located painting that could be hung and then highlighted, or a new window that could be added to invite you in?

There are a number of simple strategies for adding this kind of visual vitality. Let's take a look at a couple of the most effective ones.

Focal Wall

Although we normally think of paint as a decorating tool rather than a remodeling strategy, a deep color can give more expression and shape to a space in a highly effective yet inexpensive way. A surface becomes the focus of a room when it has visual weight, which makes it appear heavier or denser than the surrounding surfaces. Obviously a material such as stone or wood will do this, but so, surprisingly, will a simple coat of a contrasting paint color.

One of my favorite strategies for giving a bland room a little more character is to paint a wall or ceiling surface with a saturated color. As you'll see in the examples throughout this chapter, you don't have to restrict yourself to just one color either. The combination of complementary colors used on different kinds of surfaces can add an entirely new dimension to a space. Although there's nothing wrong with leaving everything white, give yourself permission to experiment and try a little color. You'll be amazed at how much the space seems to change shape and come to life. (See case study 20 on p. 172 for a great example of the power of paint.)

Painting a wall with a strong, saturated color creates a focal point, adding dimension and character to a space.

light coves and wall-washing soffits

You can turn your walls and ceilings into light reflectors with two very simply Not So Big moves that are often installed in conjunction with one another. A plywood soffit houses recessed lighting at one end of this living area, creating a bright focal point for some artwork while simultaneously sheltering the seating below. Along the other walls of the room a trim line is projected out from the wall by 2 in., and a lighting strip of small halogen bulbs is hidden behind it, bouncing light off the wall surface and ceiling above.

Reflecting Surfaces

Any light-colored wall or ceiling can be used as a reflecting surface to bounce light around within the living area to enliven the space. In chapter 9 we talked about window positioning and about locating windows adjacent to a perpendicular wall so that they reflect daylight deep into the living space. In just the same way, you can use artificial lighting pointed at any wall or ceiling surface to accomplish a similar effect.

A strategically placed pin spot light, or a wall or floor sconce that bounces light off the ceiling, can have a huge effect on the brightness and cheeriness of the room. These kinds of lights function very differently from the ubiquitous recessed down lights which, as their name suggests, point toward the floor. Since floors are usually covered with furniture and rugs and are usually darker in color, they reflect very little light. But a light-colored wall surface functions very differently, providing two kinds of lighting simultaneously—a focal point of light for a painting or other highlighted feature, and a more diffuse ambient lighting that brightens the whole room.

Layering

Many living spaces are simply too amorphous to feel comfortable in. There's plenty of room for more than one activity area, but there's no "there" there. To make such a space more appealing, you may need to add a little spatial definition by including a feature such as a framed opening, an implied wall, or an area of lowered or implied ceiling to differentiate one place from the next without obstructing the view between them. This kind of visual layering can completely change the appearance and appeal of an otherwise undistinguished rectangular room.

Use each feature consistently. You can, for example, lower ceilings over subordinate spaces, and let the more important main living space

Spatial layering is achieved subtly in this family room addition through a change in floor level from that of the existing house down to grade level.

Adding even a modest framed opening can dramatically change the feel and functionality of a large, undifferentiated space. Here, the ceiling beam and columns help define discrete dining and sitting areas within a still open space.

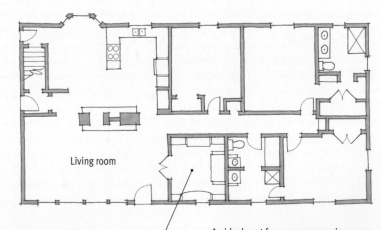

LOCATING AN AWAY ROOM

Living room

Guest bedroom converted to away room

An ideal spot for an away room is a room that's immediately adjacent to the main living space, such as a rarely used formal dining room or, as here, a guest bedroom. Moving the door from the hallway to the living room wall connects the away room directly with the living area.

retain the full height of ceiling available. Or you can add a framed opening to designate where one activity area stops and the next one begins. When used with discernment, this technique for adding character can also make a small space seem significantly larger than it really is because our eyes now perceive several places where before they perceived just one. Just as punctuation helps us to extract the full meaning of a sentence, spatial layering serves the same function for our eyes, separating the space we're looking at into bite-sized pieces without obscuring the experience of the whole.

The Away Room

In most homes today, there is a lot of noise-generating equipment that affects everyone who is home when it's in use. For example, when the TV is on in the family room or main living area, it is difficult to do anything other than listen to what is being broadcast. If children are playing a video game, the airwaves are filled with the sounds of the game, and there's no escaping the noise because they're in the family room, which is open to the kitchen. In both these situations, it's not the activity of TV watching or video game playing that's the problem, but the fact that everyone in the vicinity is subject to its acoustical dominance.

What's needed is a room that allows household members to remain visually in contact but which eliminates noise pollution. An away room is a space that either contains the noise generation or separates its users

Well-crafted doors turn a space off the dining room into an away room while adding visual interest to both spaces.

from the noise from adjacent living space. Ideally, it is close to the main living area and serves as an acoustically separate retreat place that's still visually and/or psychologically connected with the main gathering area in the house.

In size it is best kept relatively small and cozy—perhaps 11 x 13 or thereabouts—and ideally it should be designed both to contain a noise source, such as a television or stereo, as well as to isolate external noise from within the space. In this way it can be used for a wide variety of purposes.

If more houses were equipped with this small but useful room, I'm convinced that many people would be satisfied with less square footage. We often end up making our houses larger in an effort to get away from each other's unwanted noise. There's a simpler solution. It's called a door. And a door that's made of glass, allowing view without the sound, gives connectedness but eliminates the irritation.

shaping space with color

Marie chose her apartment in Raleigh, North Carolina, because she liked its loft and the quality of light. She also appreciated the manager's offer to paint one wall with an accent color. But she didn't like any of the color choices. Fortunately, the manager agreed to let Marie choose her own, so long as she bought the paint. Marie settled on six favorites, including a deep red, a burnt orange, and a rustic oak. She spent around $250 for paint and supplies, and took just a couple of days to paint, helped by five or six friends as they could spare the time.

The key to keeping the project from taking too long or costing too much was to paint only accent walls, not the whole apartment. By introducing strong colors to the dominant forms in the apartment—three angled walls, the hearth, a wall inset— Marie dramatically changed the character of her home, and she did it on the cheap. You could say painting is just decorating, but because Marie expressed form and accentuated space with color, the paint became something more.

Remodeling is an attitude; it's about making space—and life— feel different; sometimes paint is all it takes.

The apartment was interesting spatially, but with everything painted white, you could hardly tell. A thoughtfully chosen palette of six colors (four seen here) transformed the space by bringing out existing spatial aspects. Notice how the deep red draws your eye to the angled wall and front door and how two colors of paint help express the two layers of walls in the loft.

The hearth is a dominant form, so it wants to stand out. Subtle colors would have worked, but these deeper colors really allow the hearth to make a strong statement. The short angled wall at the far corner of the dining room offers a refrain.

"I like a clutter-free look, but the apartment felt like a plain white box. Paint gave it a personal flavor, and I didn't have to buy a lot of stuff."
—Marie, homeowner

The wall niche was a nice idea, but without the paint it fell flat. Painting it a strong color brought some drama to the room, making much more of its very simple form.

The deep red paint accenting the wall opposite the entry door is a marvelous example of doing more with less. The strong color brings out the angular form of the wall, anchors the living space, and leads your eye out the French door to the balcony. Marie says it makes her feel good just to see that red color when she comes home.

opening up without adding on

Often a Not So Big remodeling solution is right there in your house, waiting to be discovered. Such was the case with Jim and Mary's 1,300-sq.-ft. ranch in Ann Arbor, Michigan. They called on architect Michael Klement to add a fireplace, introduce daylight, and create a greater sense of spaciousness in their cozy but nondescript postwar home. Climbing into the 18-in. space of Jim and Mary's shallow attic, Michael discovered two layers of roof framing already in place, which gave him the idea to add a rooftop light monitor. By extending the upper roof rafters forward, Michael made room for a west-facing, trapezoidal window. Opening up the ceiling allowed light from the window to filter down through the existing rafters and fall across the walls.

The exposed rafters themselves add drama and soft shadows. But the light-filled opening does more than illuminate the living room and adjacent spaces below. Just as important, it serves as a counterpoint to the new fireplace, which reads as a freestanding, sculptural object bathed in light. The fireplace gains visual punch by slipping between the rafters as it rises up through the ceiling opening.

A sculptural fireplace rising up through an open ceiling is now the focal point of the living room that had been little more than a dead corner. The floating granite hearthstone and the notch cut into the fireplace surround contribute to the sculptural effect. Opening up the wall around the fireplace allows the adjacent spaces to enjoy the light and drama of changes made above the living room.

The new roof peak and windows together are known as a "monitor," and just like the monitor on top of George Washington's Mount Vernon, this one lets light into the middle of the house while adding a flourish to the roofline. The monitor feels right because it's an honest expression of what's going on inside; it's not something tacked on to the roof for looks only.

"Before drawing anything, I like to show up in coveralls and have a look around, spend some time learning the language of the house."
—Michael R. Klement, architect

shine a light

A skylight might have been the simplest way to introduce light into the middle of the house, but the vertical window within the extended roof is more playful and more interesting visually. A skylight often lets in too much direct sunlight. The vertical window allows even bright sunlight to wash down the high wall behind the fireplace and diffuse softly into the rooms below.

No light

Too direct

Diffuse

13. basements

If you are fortunate enough to live in an area of the country that requires a basement, you have a tremendous spatial resource at your disposal that those in warmer climes do not. Remodeling a basement is in the true spirit of Not So Big—taking an existing unused space and making it useful without adding a single square foot of new space. Although most lower levels border on dungeon-like tombs for unwanted junk, there's no reason this below-grade square footage can't be made just as appealing as its main- and upper-level counterparts. With so many activities seeking a home within the footprint of the existing house, this undeveloped space can become anything from a spacious home office to a child's playroom paradise.

The problem is that we typically think of a basement as cheap throwaway space during the original construction process, so this lower level never gets the design attention it deserves.

A window to walk toward dramatically improves the experience of stepping down to a basement.

Adding shutters below a small, high window gives the illusion that the window is much bigger.

common issues with basements

In really old houses, there's often insufficient headroom in the basement to turn the area into living space, there may be no floor slab, and there may also be moisture issues, though these are not restricted to century-old homes. If you have any of these problems, it's best to call in a professional to help determine whether it's possible to reclaim the space and, if so, at what cost.

Newer basements typically have a different set of challenges. Apart from the lack of finish, they come with a whole host of other concerns, from miscellaneous low-flying ductwork, to long, skinny spaces more reminiscent of a train car than a house, to a veritable forest of columns. Frequently there is little or no natural light, and where there are windows, they are high up on the wall with a sill height that only emphasizes the jailhouse quality. Add to this the process of descent from brightly lit main-level space to the dingy pits of despair at the bottom of the stairway, and you have a pretty clear idea of why we avoid dealing with the basement, let alone explore its potentials.

However, none of these issues is insurmountable. All it takes is the application of a few rules of thumb and a little thoughtful design to transform this sow's ear into a silk purse.

1. Add light to walk toward on the way down

A big part of a basement's unattractiveness relates to the way you enter the space. If you descend into darkness, you'll never like the space at the bottom, no matter how beautiful it is once you get there. So the first rule of thumb is to add a lighted painting, or better yet a window on the wall in front of you, at each turn in the stairs. The most important light of all is the one at the very bottom. Make sure that as you make this final descent you are walking toward either a window or a well-lit space.

2. Add windows with lower sill heights

The second major factor in that undesirable basement feel is the location of the windows. If all the daylight enters at the top of the wall, and the windowsills are 4 ft. or more from the floor, you can't easily see out, which tends to make you feel cooped up and closed in. There are ways to disguise the windows to make them look bigger than they really are, which can resolve the problem. In one remodeling I did years ago, we put shutters below the small, high windows, giving the appearance that they descended to 2 ft. 6 in. off the floor (see the drawing above).

Sometimes it is possible to add bigger windows that come closer to the floor by putting in window wells or by adding new windows and doors in exposed above-grade wall surfaces. The best kind of added window well is one that is big enough to allow you to put plantings there

Taking the concept of a window well further, an excavated patio added above-grade character to this basement and is a wonderful outdoor space in its own right.

or a small rock garden—something beautiful to look at that allows the eye to see more than a couple of feet out. In case study 23 on p. 188, there is one beautiful example of this strategy, a project that by adding a little space transforms the basement into an area that is experienced as above grade and is just as nice as any space on the levels above.

3. Identify the obstacles and determine if any can be moved

When you first look at your basement in contemplating a remodeling, you may be overwhelmed by all the structural and mechanical challenges that face you. Rather than give up before you've started though, take a piece of grid paper and draw up the existing situation, as you learned to do in chapter 6 (see "Making a Floor Plan of Your Existing Dwelling" on pp. 86-87). With this plan, you'll be able to see the obstacles all on one piece of paper. Be sure to indicate where there are features overhead that are lower than 8 ft. You'll need to pay special attention to these.

Such things as ductwork, pipes, and beams all need to be accommodated in your design, and if you think about them integrally with the rest of the floor plan, you'll find that you can make an apparent obstacle into a design asset. One of the surprising benefits of remodeling versus building new is that the idiosyncrasies of the existing space serve as catalysts for making the design both more personal and more interesting.

4. Identify potential activity places

Once you have your plan in hand and an understanding of which obstacles can be moved and which must remain (you may need an architect or structural engineer to assist you in determining this), you've got the raw material for your schematic design phase. Just as you did when looking for ways to borrow space from other spots in the house back in chapter 6, here too you'll want to take some tracing paper, lay a sheet over your existing basement plan, and play around with some options.

Ask yourself what you would like to be able to accommodate that you don't have room for on other levels of the house. Common choices include an in-home office, den, hobby room, kids' play space, or exercise space. Make a few schemes that offer different solutions to the layout of the space. As you plan, don't forget about the basement's usual function as storage repository, but recognize that by organizing that storage space you can often reduce the area required.

5. Differentiate place from place

With the selected activity areas settled upon, the next design challenge is to make a clear distinction between areas. You can make this distinction using ceiling height, columns, walls, and even a change of floor level if you have the headroom.

Often in a basement space the ceiling heights have to vary anyway in order to disguise the ductwork and plumbing. Instead of simply wrapping the offending ductwork in a drywall "beam," consider lowering a section of ceiling to form an alcove, or extend the lowered area to give a shape to the activity area in question. (See "Differentiation of Parts" on p. 181.) Or if there is a column in the space, find a way to make it into a spatially defining feature.

The lowered soffit in this basement family room adds character and shapes space while concealing the ductwork that once made a mess of the ceiling.

6. Use finishes similar to those on the main and upper levels

If you want the basement space to feel comfortable, you must use finishes that are of equivalent quality and character to the above-ground levels. It may cost a little more to make the lower level as pleasing and comfortable as main-level space, but over the long haul this added investment will more than pay for itself, both in how you use the space and in resale value. In short, don't cut corners just because it's below grade.

7. Add lighting to bring the space to life

Lighting is even more important below grade than on other levels because you generally have limited access to daylight. But when artificial lighting is done well, especially when the space is used primarily in the evening hours, you won't even notice the limited daylight.

As we discussed in chapter 12, you can use walls and ceilings as reflecting surfaces to bounce light around in the space. And by using a few strategically located spot lights for special pieces of artwork, such as a painting, sculpture, or vase, you'll bring some light-intensity variation into the space, which tends to give it added vitality.

not so big principles

Place of Quiet (and sometimes not so quiet) Remove

In the last chapter, we discussed the concept of an Away Room—a space that's adjacent to the main living area but that can be acoustically separated when desired. A basement retreat takes the Away Room concept a step further, providing a space that's more removed from the main living area and other household activities. As such, a basement retreat is the ideal hangout spot for teenage children and their friends, at the same time allowing parents to coexist in the house without feeling overwhelmed by the teenage invasion.

As another example, the basement retreat may be the perfect place for a family member to listen to music without disturbing the rest of the

Finishes and lighting equivalent to those used above grade keep this basement family room from feeling like second-class space.

ceiling plan

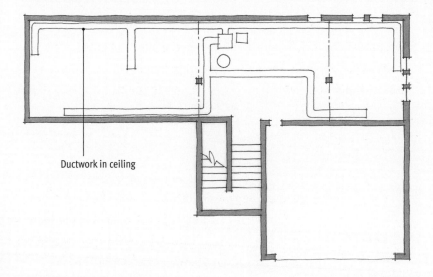

Ductwork in ceiling

floor plan

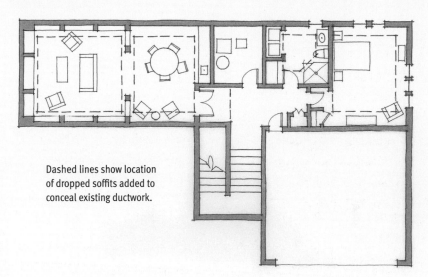

Dashed lines show location of dropped soffits added to conceal existing ductwork.

family. As you contemplate how you might use your basement, consider creating a multipurpose away space that can double both as a place in which to make and contain noise, as well as to provide isolation from noise and activity from other levels of the house.

Differentiation of Parts: Soffits and Dropped Ceilings

A dropped ceiling, or soffit, is a wonderful and inexpensive way to define an activity place in a basement, and it can often do double duty to conceal some of the beams, ductwork, and plumbing that clutter up the space at the same time (see the drawings above and on p. 185). Rather than simply boxing around those elements, take a look at the possibilities if you were to extend a lowered ceiling plane to an adjacent wall to differentiate one activity area from another. It's typically best to avoid slicing through a space with a single drywall box beam because it will

make the room feel chopped up, but lowering one end of a room, or lowering the edges of a space, can provide some wonderful spatial variety.

Where a duct or beam descends lower than 7 ft., you should check with a local code official before assuming you can use the space beneath as living space. Although such an area can be made into a comfortable alcove, there are situations where code requirements preclude this.

Columns

As we discussed in chapter 7, columns can be made into attractive features of a space. Depending upon where the column falls, you may want to add a second one, or a series of columns even, to help define the activity areas. If a column is situated in the middle of a sitting area, however, it's best to redesign the space, or move the column (if possible).

child caves

In almost every basement, there's some leftover space that no one can quite figure out what to do with. These can be used for storage, of course, but another option is to convert them into "child caves," spaces sized just right for a child's body.

When designing a child cave, I like to work directly with the child who will use it. On one remodeling project, I got very direct input from a 5-year-old girl: "I want my secret room to have a green door with a round top and a diamond window in it." And that's exactly what she got. It was her pride and joy.

DROPPED SOFFITS: DO'S AND DON'TS

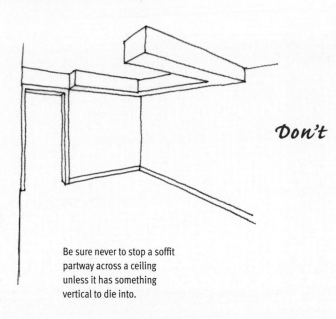

Don't

Be sure never to stop a soffit partway across a ceiling unless it has something vertical to die into.

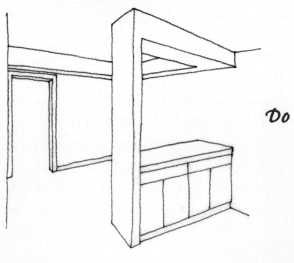

Do

(right) Light from above, bouncing off the reflecting surface of the paneled wall, adds ambience to the basement space below.

(below) It's hard to believe this remodeled family room was once a partially above-ground basement.

Columns are wonderful differentiators when they fall at the natural division between spaces, but when they sit in the middle of an activity area, they can be a serious intrusion.

Often in a basement space the column is no more than a steel pipe, which looks very skinny and flimsy, even though in fact it is more than up to the structural task it is being put to. To make it look appropriately proportioned though, you may want to fur it out to 6 in. to 8 in. square. The most important feature of a column (beyond its structural integrity, of course) is that it look appropriately proportioned to the space.

lose the columns, save the basement

Builder Paul Vassallo and his wife, Jeremy, were attracted to their house in Seattle in part because its basement had the potential to be good, cheap space for their three active boys, a haven from rainy weather. Both Paul and Jeremy have an eye for design and detail. To that, Paul adds decades of building experience, so he could look at the basement as it was—poorly placed columns, exposed joists, dingy paint—and see what was possible. Understanding what can actually be built is especially critical in a basement remodeling, which often requires structural alterations and modifications to plumbing, wiring, and ductwork. These were just the sort of changes Paul and Jeremy employed, along with some clever built-in cabinet work. The result is a spacious family room that's perfect for TV, games, projects, and the occasional bout of roughhousing. What's extraordinary isn't so much the look of the family room—which is very nice, indeed—but how deftly each obstacle the basement presented has been turned into an opportunity.

"If the ceiling is low, skip crown molding and use a narrow baseboard, or the room will appear even shorter than it is."
—Paul Vassallo, homeowner and builder

With the columns gone, the existing beam (now reinforced with steel channels and trimmed out with wood) is about as unobtrusive as it can be.

An existing concrete lip has become a narrow display shelf and a natural stopping point for the wainscot paneling.

The valance above the new built-in cabinets hides ductwork and also establishes a trim line that continues around the room. The depth of the valance was set to match the depth of the ceiling beam.

Cleaning up a basement ceiling

It's not unusual for a basement ceiling to include exposed floor joists with ductwork, plumbing, and wiring suspended below them. Often a beam or two run below the joists as well. And then there are columns.

If you remove a column, then you have to beef up the beam it supported. In this case, C-shaped steel channels were bolted to either side of the wood beam, making it, in effect, an I-beam. The entire assembly was then trimmed out in wood, so, in the end, it looks like a thick wood beam.

Ductwork can be a big obstacle to finishing a basement ceiling (and to gaining much-needed headroom). In this basement, it was possible to place the supply air ducts within the joists.

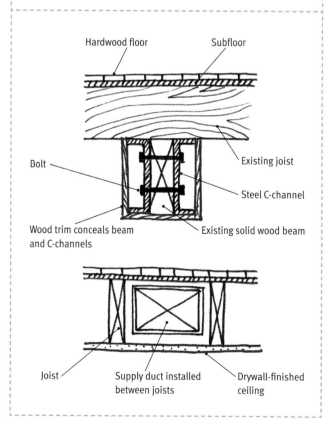

Hardwood floor

Subfloor

Bolt

Existing joist

Steel C-channel

Wood trim conceals beam and C-channels

Existing solid wood beam

Joist

Supply duct installed between joists

Drywall-finished ceiling

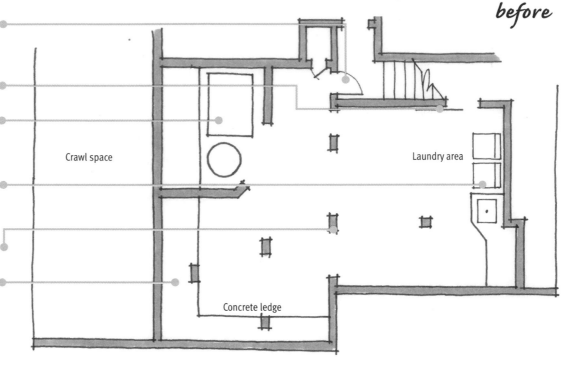

A narrow door at the entry to the basement impeded access without adding much privacy beyond that provided by a door at the top of the stairs.

A sliding door to an under-stair storage area required the entire wall to be kept clear.

The gas furnace and hot-water heater sat on the floor in a dedicated furnace room that took space away from the main basement area.

A laundry area at the far end of the basement took up prime real estate and was at the absolute farthest point from the bedrooms on the second floor.

Four columns chopped up the main basement area without defining space in a useful way.

A 41-in.-high concrete ledge wrapped around two sides of the basement, presenting either an obstacle or an opportunity, depending on how you looked at it.

Crawl space

Laundry area

Concrete ledge

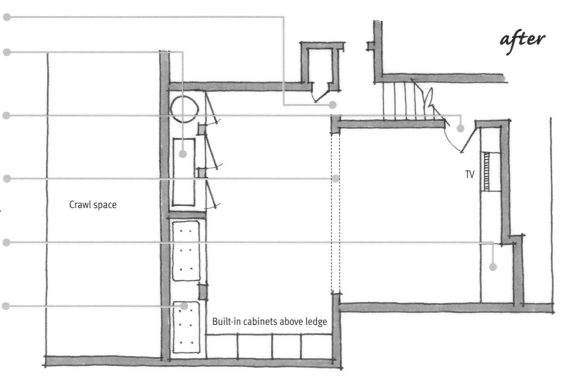

after

The door to the basement was removed, improving circulation at this narrow spot.

A smaller, high-efficiency furnace and hot-water heater fit on top of the existing ledge, allowing the furnace room to become, in effect, a furnace cabinet.

A trapezoidal door under the stairs is cut from the wall paneling so it blends in. Because it swings open, the wall beside it no longer needs to be kept clear.

The columns have been removed, freeing up the main space. The remaining beam, trimmed out in wood, neatly define two areas.

The washer and dryer have been relocated to a large bath near the bedrooms upstairs, replaced by built-in cabinets for media and games.

One leg of the concrete ledge has been outfitted with custom-fitted cushions as a kid cubby. Above the other leg, cabinets were built in.

Crawl space

TV

Built-in cabinets above ledge

Spatially, a valance makes sense here because it provides shelter overhead that defines the kid cubbies as cozy places apart from the main space. In this case, the valance also conceals an existing heating duct. It's a classic double-duty remodeling move.

A wide concrete ledge becomes the perfect platform for kid cubbies to either side of an existing column.

These built-in cabinets take advantage of the existing contours of the basement. A deep pocket in one corner is just the spot for a small refrigerator under the counter and a dart board in a cabinet above.

basement stairs

In a basement remodeling, stairs represent an opportunity. Bring in daylight if you can. If you can't, as in this case, you can detail the stairs as carefully as the basement itself. Here, the paneling and display ledge anticipate those in the room below.

light-filled basement getaway

Marjorie and Tim's modest Craftsman house in Seattle had all the space they needed except a place for leisure activities like watching movies or doing yoga. Their partially above-grade basement was dark and uninviting, but it was dry. So they contacted architect Laura Kraft to help them turn the basement into a family room. Laura showed them how excavating the earth outside the rear wall of the basement would result in a brightly lit room and an attractive outdoor entertaining area. A small addition would ease circulation and allow for a dedicated yoga space as well as a media room. Excavating the crawl space would make up for lost storage space. Marjorie and Tim accepted Laura's design, and they're glad they did. Not only do they have two sweet new rooms but also a significantly more valuable house. The yoga room, which counts as a legal bedroom, and the bath Laura squeezed into the basement have turned a two-bedroom, one-bath house into a three-bedroom, two-bath house.

adding 174 sq. ft. changed everything . . . and nothing

Excavating along the rear wall of the house and adding just 174 sq. ft. completely transformed the basement. The homeowners now have a sunny yoga room, a media room, a second full bath, and a finished laundry area. At the same time, the addition dramatically improved the rear elevation of the house, which had been a flat, largely blank face. And because the scale and detailing of the addition are sensitive to the original, the house's Craftsman nature hasn't changed; rather, it has been improved.

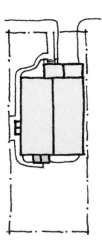
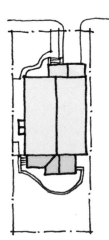

before *after*

"A walk-out basement was more expensive, but only incrementally so, because we were already breaking through the foundation wall into the yard to make the stair run meet code."

—Laura Kraft, architect

French doors that open out to a sunken patio, three windows, and a glass door combined with generous roof overhangs and sturdy brackets lend the addition the appearance of a little Craftsman house, not of a walk-out basement. Indoor-outdoor living is ensured.

It's amazing how well color works here to differentiate layers of space, beginning with the green of the yoga room, moving to the red of the hall, and ending with the yellow of the stairway. Add the play of light, and there's nothing at all basement-like about this scene. Note how the inset bookshelves take advantage of the thickness of what had been the exterior wall of the basement.

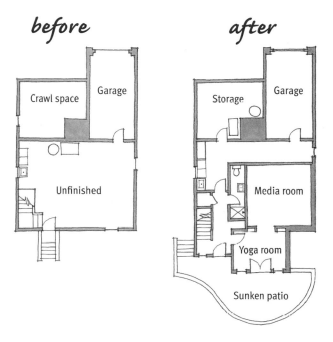

before

after

Crawl space | Garage

Unfinished

Storage | Garage

Media room

Yoga room

Sunken patio

With a few deft moves—excavating along the rear wall, converting the crawl space to full height, and adding a little space—the basement has been transformed from one catchall space to a set of spaces, each in just the right spot: storage at the back, near the garage; a full bath slipped in, near plumbing for the laundry area; a media room (top left photo), where a lack of windows is an asset; a yoga room (bottom left photo) flooded with light and open to the patio; and circulation space that connects the garage and laundry area to the upstairs without crossing either activity room. The laundry chute was wisely left in place.

PART III

Baths and Personal Spaces

14. powder rooms

No room in the house has as much impact per square foot as a powder room. It may be small, but it is certainly not unimportant. If you allow yourself to treat a powder room as an opportunity to express some personality, it can become a real jewel—a place that household members can enjoy every day, as well as a spot for guests to feel well taken care of.

In the case studies that follow, you'll see three powder rooms of the jewel-like variety, but here I want to focus on some of the more practical concerns that often get overlooked but are at least as important as the character of the space.

Avoid making the powder room much taller than the room's longest dimension. Tall ceilings are great for inspiring a sense of awe and for emphasizing the diminutive scale of the human body in relation to the space, but that's not usually the goal in a powder room.

A beltline of trim at the height of the existing windowsill draws attention downward, reducing the apparent height of a small powder room.

Typically, the biggest concern when adding a powder room is where to place it so that it is convenient but acoustically separate from the main living spaces. If outdoor activities such as gardening or kids playing require easy access to a toilet and hand-washing area, the ideal placement is usually toward the back of the house, close to the rear entry door. But in most cases, powder rooms that are included in the original design for the home are located close to the front entry—ideal for guests' use but not always where residents would choose for their everyday needs.

So when you are remodeling, give some careful consideration to the room's primary users—for most households the family members themselves. Unless you do a lot of formal entertaining and wish to keep guests away from the informal areas of the house, design for your own needs and recognize that the guests will typically be friends who are already familiar with and welcome in the more family-oriented parts of the house.

not so big principles

Beltlines

A small room, especially one in which you are often sitting down, tends to emphasize the room's height. The addition of a beltline, either at sink or counter height or a foot or two above, will bring the attention down to the lower part of the room. To establish the height of the beltline you can use almost any feature of the room, from a windowsill (see the photo at right) to a backsplash (as I used in my own remodeling, see p. 15). If you prefer, you can simply place it where it looks best to your eye. There's really no correct height, but in most cases the room's character is improved with the introduction of such a line.

One of the least expensive approaches when introducing a beltline is to use a piece of flat casing (of any width), which can either be painted to match other trimwork in the house or left natural or stained. Alternatively, you can create a beltline using a favorite tile, either finishing the wall below the beltline in tile as well, or adding a narrow band of trim both above and below the tile and then painting the wall below this combination a darker color—one of my favorite details to dress up a powder room.

common issues with powder rooms

There are a number of practical issues to keep in mind when locating and designing a powder room:

- *No one likes to look directly at the toilet when the door to the powder room is open, so lay out the room in such a way that the toilet is hidden until you enter (see the drawings at bottom right).*

- *If an existing in-swinging door makes the room feel too tight to enter easily, consider remodeling the room to include a sliding door (if budget and configuration allow). You can also swing the door outward—not usually ideal but an improvement over an in-swinging door.*

- *Make sure the powder room does not open directly off a main living space such as the kitchen or family living area. This will ensure at least a modicum of privacy to the user.*

- *If space allows, place the powder room far enough from the main living and kitchen areas that there is no sound audible between spaces.*

- *Avoid making the powder room much taller than the room's longest dimension. A small space that is very tall can feel like an elevator shaft—not a comfortable place to stand in, let alone sit.*

- *Avoid using an absorbent floor surface. Harder surfaces that are easy to clean are always preferable in bathroom locations. If you want carpet underfoot, add a rug that can be removed and cleaned from time to time.*

- *Lighting is important in a powder room. It should ideally be adjustable so that it can provide a pleasant ambience, but it can also be made brighter if necessary for cleaning, application of make-up, and so on.*

- *Make sure that the mirror supplied is at an appropriate height so that all users can see themselves without straining. If there are small children in the house, it may also be a good idea to supply a step stool or a pull-out drawer/step that allows them to easily reach the sink and also see themselves in the mirror.*

- *Make sure there's a place for an extra roll of toilet paper to be stored within easy reach (an amazingly frequent oversight!). Also make sure there's a spot to hang or place a hand towel close to the sink.*

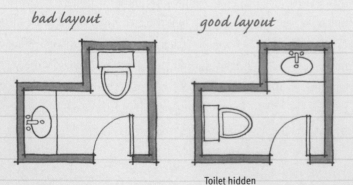

bad layout   good layout

Toilet hidden

Tailored to Fit

If you are really pressed for space, a powder room can be truly tiny. As long as you have 24-in. clearance in front of the toilet bowl and 30 in. of width where the toilet is located, all other dimensions are up to you. (Check with your local code official regarding these minimums as there are slight variations between codes. The numbers given here are from the Uniform Plumbing Code, or UPC.) In recent years many manufacturers have caught on to the need for smaller sinks for hand washing so there are more options to choose from. My favorite, because of its diminutive size and corner installation capabilities, is a unit from American Standard® that requires just 11 in. of wall space from each corner. Although the resulting powder room can feel a bit like an airline toilet compartment, it's definitely better than not having one at all.

For comfort, an elongated toilet bowl is certainly an improvement over the standard models, if you have the space. Although in diminutive bathrooms this may not be an option, the elongated bowl, which is usually around 3 in. longer than a standard toilet, can make an enormous difference for everyday utility.

Acoustical Privacy

There's one other consideration about powder rooms that should not be overlooked: There are significant differences of opinion between men and women about the best location for this room. Women seem to prefer it closer to the main living areas than men. Something very obvious explains the difference in preference. Because men typically stand when using the facility, the sounds are louder, causing a greater sense of discomfort about being heard. Female use is a quieter activity by nature.

(top) A beltline of flat casing (with beadboard wainscoting below) ties the powder room to the rest of the house.

(right) A tile beltline with a dark painted wall below is an easy way to dress up a powder room.

universal design

It's not unusual for a powder room remodeling to be done specifi-
cally for a friend or relative who is mobility impaired. When we are
aware of the special needs of someone we love, we tend to notice
the accessibility inadequacies of our own home more and often
use this as the impetus to make improvements. But since every
house will almost certainly need to provide for someone who is
either using a walker or on crutches at some point in its life span,
it's well worth considering adding some or all of the following
features, no matter why you are remodeling:

- 34-in.-wide door minimum; door should be out-swinging or
  sliding, not in-swinging

- Lever handles on door if out-swinging type

- Single-handle or lever-style faucet

If the room is also to be wheelchair accessible, provide knee
space beneath the sink or use a pedestal or wall-mounted sink. The
room in this instance should be a minimum of 5 ft. by 5 ft. for ease
of maneuvering.

If noise is a potential issue, a bathroom fan that makes sufficient
noise to cover the sounds of water may be a good solution. But if you
really want the men of the house to be completely comfortable, a more
distant location from living and eating areas will work best. And if you
are building a new powder room from scratch, it definitely helps with
noise reduction to fill the wall cavities with insulation.

POWDER ROOM CLEARANCE

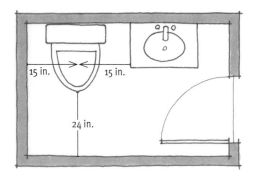

15 in.   15 in.

24 in.

corner-pocket micro move

Although architect Kurt Lavenson and his wife, designer Lesly Avedisian, often work on large, elaborate projects, they consider themselves minimalists. When they turned to the tiny space under the stairs in their own 1920s house in Oakland, they intended to practice what they preach. Under the stairs already was a full (if tiny) bath, with a commode and sink used by guests as a powder room. Kurt and Lesly focused their attention on an 18-in. by 18-in. pocket of space beside the shower. They removed a rusty metal sink and a medicine cabinet with flaking silver and proceeded to outfit the little corner with the charm of the diminutive bathrooms on vintage European trains.

They chose nice but mid-priced fixtures and plumbing components and didn't try to hide them. Nearly all the items are standard, from the mirror to the faucet to the sink. The exception—albeit a modest one—is the custom stainless-steel countertop bracket that supports the sink. (The bracket almost had to be custom because the corner is so out of square.) For guests, the corner sink is a delightful surprise that puts a smile on their faces. Kurt says the corner remodeling gets more comments from visitors than some of his projects that are 100 times its size.

Tucked behind a door under the stairs is just enough space for a Hobbit-sized sink that stops visitors in their tracks. It's not the quantity that counts but the quality. In fact, people often delight in the diminutive.

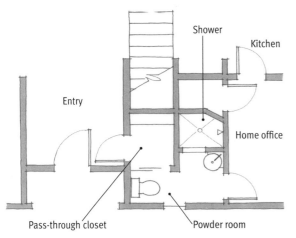

Guests reach the powder room from the entry hall through an arched door that mimics the front door in miniature. They pass through a closet space and open a pocket door to discover the little sink. So they're doubly surprised: first, that there's a powder room at all beyond the closet, and then with the Lilliputian scale of the vanity area.

less space, more detail

A larger window adds more light and a greater sense of space. The custom-made, Japanese-inspired translucent screen simply fits to the inside of the window frame.

The simple detail of a vertical trim piece extending past the adjoining horizontal trim piece is repeated in the toilet-paper holder, ceiling light, and window casing.

The idea behind the remodeling of Bob and Sue's 1950s ranch in North Oaks, Minnesota, was to reconfigure existing space rather than add on. At the bedroom end of the house, architect Kelly Davis of SALA Architects revitalized the master bath and turned an extra bedroom into a generous area for a Japanese soak tub. So it wasn't hard for empty nesters Bob and Sue to justify converting the full bath just outside the master suite to a powder room. Giving up the bathtub would mean gaining storage. But more than that, the smaller remaining space is better suited to the modest purpose of a powder room. Its diminutiveness actually amplifies the quality of its fine materials and craftsmanship, making a little gem of a space, perfect for Bob, Sue, returning children, or guests.

"The smaller the space, the more you have to rely on detail. Wherever the eye goes, you want to find something pleasurable and delightful."
—Kelly Davis, architect

downsizing a full bath to a powder room

For these empty nesters, extra storage was more important than a second full bath.

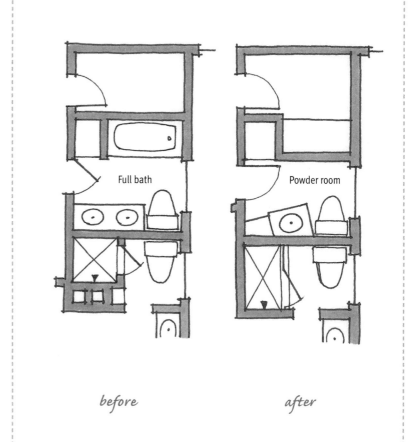

Full bath

Powder room

before

after

The clerestory allows the powder room to share light with an adjacent full bath without compromising privacy.

A lantern-like ceiling light fits the Japanese theme and blends with the cherry trim.

The darker wood header beam is a little piece of the old running through the new, placing the powder room under the unifying slope of the roof.

A cherry-trimmed horizontal valance provides intimate shelter above the vanity and commode, creating a little *ceiling height variety* even in this small space.

Alkco® incandescent tube lights incorporated into the vertical trim cast a warm glow on either side of the vanity mirror.

The most important detail in the powder room for expanding its apparent spaciousness is the large mirror, which abuts trim pieces yet appears as a transparent extension of space, not as a framed mirror hung on the wall.

The tapered vanity is narrow at the doorway but wider where it blocks the commode and supports the vessel sink. The sink appears as a delicate object, in keeping with the Japanese nature of the room.

powder room as artful expression

In chapter 10, we looked at a kitchen remodeling by designer Jamie Wolf (see the photos on p. 140), who transformed a whole string of rooms by adding a narrow band of space across the rear wall of the house (a remodeling move we like to call "The Jamie"). In the original house, a Colonial in Bloomfield, Connecticut, the powder room and an adjoining steam room were conveniently positioned off a back hall. But the two little spaces also cut off the kitchen from the dining room and a study. Homeowners Gwen and Malcolm wanted a larger kitchen and much more openness, but the powder room and steam room stood in the way. Fortunately, Gwen and Malcolm took Jamie's advice to relocate these two rooms. It was a gutsy decision, but it freed up the entire back of the house. And it gave Jamie an opportunity to create a new powder room that expresses a lot about Gwen and Malcolm and helps integrate the addition with the existing house, inside and out.

"Even though it's a tiny, little room, all sorts of exciting things are going on as you open the door."

—Jamie Wolf, designer

(above) In a space that's just 6 ft. 4 in. by 4 ft. 5 in., three small niches that are fit into the wall subtly add depth, while providing places to display artful objects.

(right) A powder room offers a small but powerful (because it's compressed) opportunity to express your personality. Homeowner Gwen is a Swede with an affinity for the American Southwest, a blend that comes through in the colors, materials, and textures of the powder room. It might be too much for the whole house—and too expensive—but for a powder room, it works perfectly.

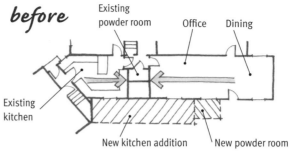

before

Existing powder room   Office   Dining

Existing kitchen

New kitchen addition   New powder room

after

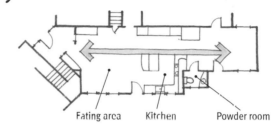

Fating area   Kitchen   Powder room

Relocating the powder room to an addition was the key to opening up the spaces at the back of the house. The new location isn't quite as discreet as the old, but the powder room has gained a window with a private garden view, and costs were kept in check because it shares a plumbing wall with the kitchen.

impact on the outside

Because this new powder room was part of an addition, it represented an opportunity to impact the exterior as well as the interior. In fact, the powder room—which appears on the outside as a small, green cube at the end of the long, red kitchen extension— is essential to the playful, easy way the new fits with the old. Its change-up color breaks down the mass of the addition, and its stepped-back form leads your eye from the garden to the French door to the dining room.

15. bathrooms

Bathrooms are a common catalyst

for a remodeling. Sometimes the work is confined to the
bathroom itself, while other times the project expands
to include adjacent bedrooms and hallways—especially
if the objective is to improve the quality and character
of a master suite (see chapter 19). Although the primary
objectives of a bathroom remodeling seem obvious—to
reduce crampedness, to improve the character, or to add
a function—there are some simple rules of thumb that can
make the money available stretch further and add the most
value and character possible. These are as follows:

This remodeled bath occupies the same space
as the original bath, but it has been reconfigured for greater privacy from adjacent spaces.

- Before you begin, identify which parts of the existing bathroom, if any, can be saved—for example, tile work, half-walls, and window and door casings.

- Use all the tools at your disposal to make the room look and feel larger—mirrors, reflected light, clear glass shower partitions, ceiling height variety, and eliminating or reducing the heights of any walls that make the space feel too confined.

- Where possible, identify ways to introduce natural light—glass block or frosted-glass windows, skylights, and solar tubes.

- Check sight lines to determine if any fixtures would be more functional or less objectionable if relocated to a different wall—toilets are the usual offenders here.

- Don't overspend on the bathroom jewelry (like faucets and fixtures) if you have a limited budget. Instead, use the money you have available to enhance the overall design with color, mirrors, lighting, cabinetry, and tile.

saving what works

Although we often assume we need to change everything about a room, upgrading the look and feel of a less-than-glorious bathroom may be all that's needed for significant improvement. And it's a lot less expensive than a more elaborate remodeling that requires lots of demolition work and reconstruction.

Sometimes you can simply hide what you don't like about the existing bathroom. For example, if you have some really unattractive tile work, the usual solution is to tear it out and start over. But that can mean a lot of demolition work and taking out sinks, toilets, showers, and so on to remove all the old tile. One innovative alternative is to add attractive built-ins above or on top of the offending tile. In the example at the bottom right, the tile is still visible but the wall of elegant cubbies and

(top) Adding mirrors to opposite walls and replacing a solid wall with a frameless glass partition help open and enlarge this otherwise small bathroom.

(bottom) Sometimes you can hide what you don't like, as here, by concealing old tile with new shelving.

questions to ask yourself

- What bothers you most about the bathroom/s you are planning to remodel?

- Do you want to keep or salvage any of the fixtures and faucets?

- Do you want to save any of the existing tile work?

- Are there too many doorways or doors into the room?

- Do the door swings make the room feel even smaller than it actually is?

- Is there a way to remove a door, or to turn it into a sliding door if you still want the separation?

- How much separation between bathroom functions do you want? Is a half-wall sufficient, or do you want a full wall?

- Do you want the toilet in its own compartment, or can it be a part of the whole room?

- If the shower enclosure is cramped, is there a way to make it bigger by borrowing from adjacent spaces?

- Do you need a second sink? Do you have a second sink that doesn't get used?

- Do you have enough storage for towels and linens close at hand?

- Do you have enough room for towel bars and robe hooks?

- What kind of lighting do you prefer?

- Are there walls that can be partially or entirely mirrored above sink height to increase the apparent spaciousness of the room?

- Is there enough natural light in the room? If not, is there a way to add windows or a skylight?

- Would you like to use a special tile (or tiles) as a feature to give the room its own unique character?

- Are there any particular fixtures or faucets that will help establish the size and character of the room?

before

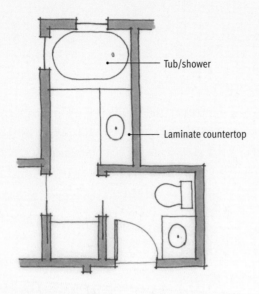

Tub/shower

Laminate countertop

after

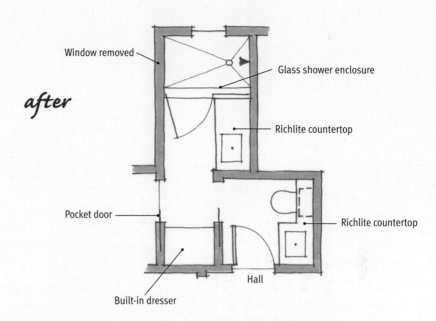

Window removed

Glass shower enclosure

Richlite countertop

Pocket door

Richlite countertop

Built-in dresser

Hall

the new lighting provide a completely different focus for the room. Adding this kind of built-in is a lot less expensive than replacing the tile, and the strategy adds more character as well.

It can be expensive to relocate plumbing, so look carefully at what fixtures really need to be moved to meet your expectations for a better bathroom. You can use the same schematic design process that we discussed in chapter 6 (see p. 86) to evaluate options. For example, you could start by assuming that you'll keep all the plumbing fixtures in their existing positions, and see what you can do with existing ceilings, walls, and finishes to make the room feel larger. If that seems too limiting, consider moving just the sink, for example, or adding a second sink. Then draw an option where perhaps you move the tub, or exchange a tub/shower combo for a larger shower only, as in the example above.

personal preferences

Families tend to develop their own unique patterns related to bathroom use, and there is no one right way to design. Some households are much less concerned about personal privacy than others. For example, some people prefer not to have a door on a master bathroom, while others would find such a thing inconceivable. Some families all use one bathroom in the mornings, no matter how many bathrooms there are in the house, while other families really need one bathroom for each person.

Because bathrooms are among the most expensive rooms in the house, I ask homeowners to carefully consider their own personal patterns and preferences, and then determine the best strategy for their particular situation. If budget is an issue, or if you really don't enjoy

cleaning, I strongly recommend adopting a strategy of "not so many bathrooms." For the typical household, one or two really nicely designed bathrooms are almost always better for livability than three or four ho-hum bathrooms. Most of us really like to go through our routine of daily ablutions in a space that is commodious and a delight to be in.

not so big principles

Reflecting Surfaces

No other room in the house benefits more from the use of reflecting surfaces than the bathroom. If you know how to use mirrors intelligently, you can more than double the apparent size of the room without adding a single square foot of space.

Everyone understands, of course, that mirrors reflect, but to give the illusion of more space you need to extend the mirrored surface all the way to the adjacent perpendicular wall or ceiling surface—or both. If the mirror is used more as an object hung on a wall, similar to the way you would hang a painting, the effect is different. It can still add character, but it doesn't necessarily make the room feel larger. When a bathroom is fairly spacious or if it has a more period feel, then this more limited use of mirror is quite appropriate.

❶ The reflecting surface of a wall-to-wall, countertop-to-ceiling mirror doubles the apparent size of this bath.

❷ Including open storage and display areas can add some much needed character to an otherwise bland bathroom. Although they won't always look as tidy as the ones shown here, they still provide containment for all the stuff.

❸ Framed mirrors maintain a period feel, but the two together create enough reflecting surface to make the bath feel larger and brighter.

Nooks and Crannies

Bathrooms are often overflowing with bottles of shampoo, jars and tubes of cream, powders, towels and face cloths, and so on. And usually there aren't enough places to put them. Because many of these items are in use every day, people tend to leave them out on the counter so that there is little room left to maneuver in without knocking things over. (Of course, photos for books and magazines never show this reality.) This situation can be designed for, however, by providing a number of open shelves, as well as niches in the tiled surfaces that are close to the places where all this stuff is needed—typically the sink and shower areas (see the top right photo on p. 209).

Pattern and Geometry

When a bathroom is small and the budget is limited, few details can provide as much additional flair as some strategically placed tile. Because most bathroom floors are tiled anyway, with a little forethought you can add character at almost no additional cost. If you are planning to align a feature tile pattern with a particular fixture like the toilet in the photo below left, make sure to discuss your design intentions carefully with the tile setter. Although the desire for alignment may be obvious to you, it isn't automatically so for someone else.

When it comes to tile designs, no matter which surface you are applying it to—floor, wall, or shower enclosure—there are almost no limits to what's possible. You can be very conservative in your choices, or you can go wild. You can use one single expensive feature tile in a field of less costly tiles, or you can spend a small fortune buying the most expensive tiles in the store. Either way the results can be fabulous or they can be grotesque. It's all a matter of design, and no amount of expensive tile can ensure *that*.

(left) Natural slate cut and set in a field of smaller tiles creates a beautiful design for this otherwise simple shower stall, providing a focal surface for the whole bathroom.

(far left) If you intend a floor pattern to align with the center of a plumbing fixture, or to be equidistant from the side walls of a room, be sure to talk to the tile layer before he or she begins. A misalignment here will be a constant reminder of that missed communication.

Doing Double Duty

Sometimes when you are remodeling a bathroom, the goal is to make the room do double duty—perhaps as both a guest powder room and everyday kids' bathroom, or as a room that can be used by more than one person at the same time. In these situations, you may want to partition functions. I'm not usually a fan of providing more than one door into a bathroom because it can be very confusing—especially for guests, as they try to figure out which door or doors they should lock.

If it is necessary to divide up the room though, place the toilet in a compartment with only one door. The sink area most readily lends itself to a two-door configuration, though again for guests, you may need to tell them that it is OK for them to lock both doors when they are using the sink.

SHARED BATHROOM

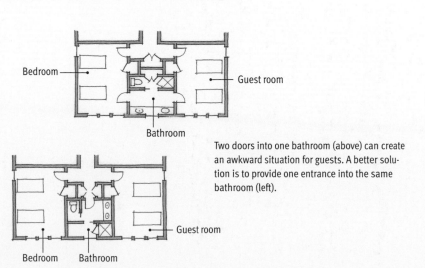

Two doors into one bathroom (above) can create an awkward situation for guests. A better solution is to provide one entrance into the same bathroom (left).

kids and tubs

Whether or not you need or use a bathtub yourself, it's always a good idea to have at least one tub in the house for resale purposes. Young children are rarely bathed in a shower, and sometimes the elderly also prefer a bath to a shower. In addition to the standard-depth tub, many people also like to include a deeper soaking tub or jetted tub. These are not usually appropriate for bathing very young children. But as kids get a bit older, they will almost always become the primary users of the deeper tubs, so if you don't want kids in your master bathroom, place the soaking tub in a different bathroom! I've had many a parent tell me that they've never actually used the whirlpool tub themselves, because they've never had the time, but that their kids use it as a sort of indoor entertainment center. So much for a peaceful haven for adults. That's the dream but seldom the reality.

fitting in a bath and a half

Kari and Patrick's one-and-a-half-story Bungalow in Alexandria, Virginia, had plenty of charm upstairs within the roof but minimal closet space and just one, dated bath. The young couple asked architect Liz Craver Leonard to help them create a master suite with its own bath and walk-in closet and to add a second bath for guests. But their budget would not allow for changes to the footprint or significant alterations to the roof. With space limited, Kari and Patrick had a choice: either a full guest bath or an expansive walk-in closet but not both. They chose the closet, and Liz came up with a clever, cost-effective way to turn the existing bath into a tandem full bath and half-bath. To gain just a little bit of floor space and headroom, Liz expanded two existing arched dormers into one larger shed dormer, a Not So Big remodeling move in tune with the Bungalow spirit.

"In a bath remodel, put your money into things you're going to touch, like the faucet handles."
—Elizabeth Craver Leonard, architect

connect the dormers

Expanding two dormers into one longer dormer added headroom, which made more of the existing floor usable. Just as important was removing the narrow closet (enabling access to the bath from the master bedroom) and replacing it with a walk-in closet.

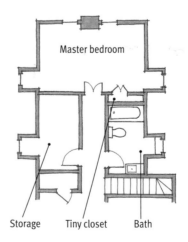

Master bedroom

Storage   Tiny closet   Bath

Master bedroom

Walk-in closet   Half-bath   Bath

before   *after*

The full bath connected to a half-bath functions most of the time as a large master bath with two commodes and his and her sinks. When there are houseguests, a pocket door separates the two rooms, and the half-bath can be entered from the hall.

same room, more space

Although the fixtures are in the same place as before, the remodeled bath feels more open.

Lisa and Ken worked with architect Russell Hamlet to remodel both baths in their 1920s cottage home on Bainbridge Island, Washington. You can see the upstairs bath on pp. 208–209. Like the upstairs bath, the downstairs one is a pure upgrade—a trade-out of materials, fixtures, and finishes, without changes to the floor plan or the location of the fixtures. And yet it shows how much can be accomplished without moving walls or adding space. The remodeled bath feels much larger than the old, when, by volume, it's actually a bit smaller. That's because Russell lowered the ceiling from 9 ft. to 8 ft. at the high point of its graceful arc. Beyond new fixtures and upgraded materials, the magic of this bath is in its craftsmanship and small details: an arched mirror that echoes the curve of the ceiling; a tub seat with a heat register below; curved sconces; and crisp vent slots in the ceiling.

after

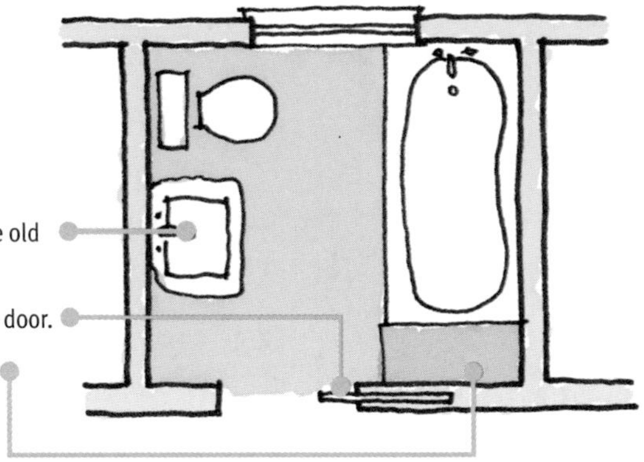

The pedestal sink is less bulky than the old vanity cabinet.

A pocket door replaced the in-swinging door.

A low tub seat replaced a tall cabinet.

"Given the room's infrequent use as a full bath, we equipped the tub with a handheld sprayer and eliminated the shower enclosure, making the room feel more open."

—Russell Hamlet, architect

In place of a space-hogging tall cabinet is a tub seat of earth-friendly Richlite®. The seat and a grab bar make for easily accessible bathing now and in the future.

An arched ceiling of bleached cedar boards adds boatlike character and gives the small room more pleasing proportions. Wainscoting of shimmery blue glass-mosaic tiles adds color and continuity, while a carefully sealed cork floor adds warmth underfoot.

extra bedroom converted to Japanese bath

In the previous chapter (pp. 200–201), we looked at the remodeled powder room in Bob and Sue's 1950s ranch in North Oaks, Minnesota. We mentioned that architect Kelly Davis of SALA Architects also turned an extra bedroom into a Japanese bath and integrated it into the master suite. It's a classic example of *borrowing space*. The master suite already had a full bath with a shower, so the entire adjacent bedroom could be dedicated to bathing. With a Japanese-style soak tub set within a raised wooden platform, the former bedroom is now quite literally a bath room. The gain is twofold. The bedroom-turned-bath is a quiet retreat in its own right. And the original master bedroom feels more spacious because it extends into the bath area, beyond a double-sided, see-through fireplace—one side facing the bed, the other side facing the bath. Bob and Sue's Japanese bath represents a new kind of personal space empty nesters can create for themselves, even in a Not So Big house.

Glass above a *fat wall* separates the bath from a home office beyond, while allowing the rooms to share light.

A Japanese-style translucent screen adds ambience in the bath and glows warmly in the hall as you walk toward the master bedroom.

The fat wall allows enough depth for two small niches, each with a grained cherry back and a simple "puck" light, the sort you buy for under kitchen cabinets.

The tub deck is plumb-colored, honed granite.

Several types of wood—the white oak step, cherry paneling and trim, and the Douglas fir beams of the original house—blend easily, lending the bath visual harmony.

"Neither Bob nor Sue had been to Japan, but they valued bathing as a ritual. The idea was to imply a Japanese aesthetic without getting carried away."

—Kelly Davis, architect

The existing ceiling beam can now be seen as continuing from bath to bedroom, unifying the two spaces.

The double-sided fireplace is a *pod of space*, both containing space in the cabinet niches and sitting within the master suite space, where it separates the Japanese bath from the bedroom beyond without closing it off.

The Japanese bath has connecting views to the bedroom through a slot window to the left of the fireplace, around the fireplace to the right, and through the firebox itself.

The step is necessary to reach the tub, but it also adds to the spatial experience of bathing.

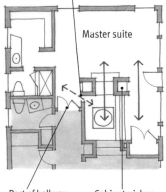

before

Master bedroom

after

Slot window

Master suite

Part of hallway incorporated into the master suite

Cabinet niches and fireplace form a "pod of space" between bath and bedroom.

(before) The original master suite was little more than a bedroom with a bath attached to it.

(after) In the new master suite, space flows between the sleeping area and a former bedroom turned into a Japanese bath.

16. home offices

With more and more people working part time out of the home and with some using their home as their only work place, the in-home office has evolved from being a nice room to have if there's enough space to something that is, in many cases, an absolute necessity. This puts a whole new spin on a room that used to be relegated to a rarely used guest bedroom or a corner of the basement. When you spend over half your waking hours in your home office, it had better be a pleasant place to be, or you're likely to go crazy. It is well worth spending the time and effort prior to remodeling to determine exactly what your needs are.

Attics can be challenging office spaces if they have low headroom and limited wall surface, yet even knee walls can be turned into effective storage areas, and a small attic space can be relatively inexpensive to finish into a room.

finding a quiet place for the office

If your priority is quiet space where you can be alone and undisturbed for long periods of time, you'll need a place that is well away from the activity hubs of the house. This is especially important when there are young children in the house. Before you select the best spot for a home office requiring a quiet environment, do a thorough assessment of how noise travels throughout the house. You may find a space that is visually separate but discover that you still have noise to contend with. For example, a spare bedroom on the second floor may seem ideal, but not if it is situated directly above the family room where the TV is on frequently.

Good spots for quiet offices can be any of the following:

- **A room off the master bedroom.** The advantage of this location is that you have to enter the private territory of the bedroom to access the office so it's more private than most other locations. The disadvantage is that it is in a zone of the house that is designated for sleeping and resting. For some, including the office here is not a good marriage of activities.

- **A converted attic.** This space is usually secluded because it is far from other household activities, but an attic can be an odd shape, with little flat wall surface and a lot of low headroom. This can give the space personality but can be a challenge in terms of functionality. Also, if the stairway is tight or very steep, it can be difficult to get things up and down, and the attic is inaccessible to anyone who is mobility impaired.

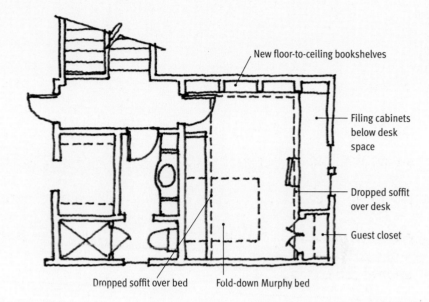

New floor-to-ceiling bookshelves

Filing cabinets below desk space

Dropped soffit over desk

Guest closet

Dropped soffit over bed

Fold-down Murphy bed

- **An unused spare bedroom.** The advantage of this room is that it usually requires little remodeling and has an existing door to separate it acoustically from the rest of the house. But a remodeled spare bedroom may not feel separate *enough* from the rest of the house, and it may still feel like a bedroom, making it seem like only a temporary solution.

- **A rarely used guest bedroom.** Converting this room makes better use of a space that normally sits unused. However, when there are guests, it requires some cleaning up and vacating of the room for the duration of their stay. And layout can be tricky if the room includes a Murphy bed or fold-out couch.

- **An unused living or dining room.** These rooms are usually close to the main entry, making them ideal spots if clients or business associates come to the house often. On the other hand, these rooms are also typically close to the kitchen, the main hub of household activity, so acoustical separation can be a challenge.

questions to ask yourself

Because so many different functions are accommodated by today's home offices, here are some questions to help you determine what you really need:

- *Do you or another household member currently work (for your livelihood) at home?*

- *If not currently, are you or any other household member likely to work at home in the future?*

- *Is there more than one person in the household who works at home? If so, do you need separate offices or one shared space?*

- *Would you prefer to have some separation between the house and the in-home office?*

- *Will there ever be employees or clients coming to the house? If so, how will they enter?*

- *If you are likely to have visitors to your office, do you need a waiting area, do you need the room to be close to a powder room, and do you need other partitioning to separate the workplace from the home space?*

- *How do you plan to use the office, and what functions do you need to be able to accommodate?*

- *What time of day are you likely to use the room?*

- *Do you need good daylighting, or can the office be in a space with little or no access to daylight?*

- *Do you have any special equipment, furniture, filing cabinets, and so forth, that need to be accommodated?*

- *Do you have any particular items you'd like to store or display there—such as books, artwork, safes, etc.?*

- *Do you want to include a comfortable chair or couch?*

- *Which of the following qualities and characteristics do you prefer?*

  - *Quiet*

  - *Close to other household activities*

  - *Close to other family members but acoustically separate*

  - *Visually isolated but acoustically connected*

  - *Both visually and acoustically separated*

  - *Far from the kitchen and the temptations of the refrigerator*

  - *Well day-lit*

  - *With a pleasant view*

  - *Well organized*

  - *Spacious*

  - *Cozy*

  - *Comfortable*

  - *Spare*

This in-home office, which is open to newly added living and dining areas, is differentiated from the more social areas by the loft overhead. When quiet is required the sliding doors between the existing kitchen and the new living spaces can be closed to create some acoustical separation.

- **A corner of the basement.** There's usually plenty of space in a basement to spread out into (with a little cleaning up, that is), but the available space can be dull, dark, and uninviting, requiring more remodeling to make it attractive than any of the other options.

- **A room above or adjacent to the garage.** This location usually feels distinctly separate from the house, giving the experience of "leaving" for work, even though the commute is only a few paces long. On the negative side, since garages are usually uninsulated and unconditioned, there is more remodeling work necessary to prepare the space for year-round habitation.

placing the home office close to a main activity area

If you prefer to be closer to other household members while you work, the challenges are quite different. In these situations, acoustics and visibility are typically not the concern. The biggest challenge may be finding the space, so it will be useful to refer back to chapter 6 again, to help you find ways of borrowing space from other activity areas.

Often, when you want the office close to the main living area, the primary goal is to be able to work while other household members do other things, like watch television or converse. The desire is to have the option of participating if you want to. So, for example, while paying bills in the office, you might want to join in a conversation every once in a while, or you might want to be able to look up and see the TV screen if there's something you're interested in. Give particular consideration to rooms that are currently seldom used. They may be able to double as an office space. Formal living rooms are particularly adept at serving this dual role, or at being completely converted to a home office function.

An unused bedroom has been converted into a comfortable office, connected to the living space by a glass partition that maintains acoustical privacy.

Another popular solution is to create an office alcove that can be opened or closed as desired using sliding or swinging doors. The approach here can be similar to the one discussed in "Away Rooms" on p. 171, and in fact some away rooms will also double as an in-home office when needed.

not so big principles

Gateways

There's a psychological aspect to creating a workplace within the territory of the house. If your commute to work is no more than a few paces away from the room you ate breakfast in, it's important to give your home office a clear sense of separation from the rest of the house, even if that designation is no more than a door. Your objective should be to make the transition feel like a gateway to a new realm.

There are a number of ways to do this. The simplest is to make it look and feel like a different type of entryway than all the other doors in the house. You could use a special door, or you could make the trim around the doorway look more like an exterior entryway than an interior one. Or you could literally make the doorway surround into a completely unique expression of entry. I did this once, many years ago, in one of my first remodelings, by adding a tile frieze above the entry point into the office (as shown in the drawing on the facing page). There was no questioning when moving through this portal that you were entering an area that distinguished itself from the rest of the house. Although this may seem like an insignificant decorating trick, the psychological impact can be great. Once you've entered, you know you are at work, and you are more likely to stay there for the remainder of the work day than when this kind of designation is absent.

Enclosure

There is a real art to making a space that can be closed off from the rest of the house without it feeling confined. If a room is small, like a spare bedroom, for example, you may need to do a little additional remodeling

The Away Room we saw in chapter 12 doubles as a home office. Sliding doors enable the office to share in the life of the house or retreat from it.

GATEWAY TO THE OFFICE

to really make it work as an in-home office. If you do no more than move your office furniture into the space and get to work, you'll likely find that it's difficult to close the door without feeling shut in. By adding an architectural element that adds some breathing room, such as a transom window above the door, a band of high windows opening into the hallway beyond, or some added windows to the outside, you'll feel far less confined even though the actual square footage you are occupying hasn't changed at all.

Another way to increase the sense of space is to add a balcony, however small, so that from time to time you can step out onto it and feel that you are standing "outside." What you accomplish by adding any one of these small features is a sense of release from an otherwise enclosed space. It is the appearance of added space that makes the difference.

make it beautiful and commodious

No matter where your home office ends up, make sure you pay as much attention to making it an enjoyable place to be as you would for any other main living space. We spend much of our lives working in places that are tolerable but certainly not delightful. And yet when we are delighted by the place where we work, our quality of life improves, along with the quality of our output, simply because we are in a better state of mind as we work.

It doesn't have to be expensively designed or decorated. But the little things that make you feel good about being in the space, such as well-crafted built-ins or extra windows to connect you to your surroundings, can be valuable assets for both productivity and enjoyment. The collection of tea cups and wooden boxes shown here finds a home in a sitting alcove in my home office.

Creative Storage

When space is tight, you may have to be innovative in how you store everything that has to be accommodated. With each item that you know you'll need a place for, ask yourself:

- What type of storage would best accommodate it? (shelving, closet space, wall cabinets, counter space, drawers, file cabinets, cubbies, display space, hanging space)

- What are the dimensions of the item/s?

- Is there an obvious place that could house this shape of storage?

- What will be the impact to the rest of the office in adding this kind of storage space?

- Does this suggest any modifications to your initial ideas about location?

- Are there any other creative ways to house the item/s?

One common worry when a room is already small is that to add built-ins will only make it feel smaller. But this is not usually the case, especially if you are able to use the existing windows to reflect more light into the room as a result. This can happen whenever you surround a window with shelving, or when you add a countertop surface or bookshelf directly below a window. The added surface becomes a light reflector. A wall of bookshelves, for example, reduces the width of the room by 10 in. but

(right) In a porch turned into a home office, walls of windows and a long wall of bookshelves more than make up for limited floor area.

(far right) If you are working with an attic area with sloped ceilings, don't forget that there is some unused space in the eaves, which can be used for drawers, flat files, shelves, or low cupboards.

Bookshelves that couldn't fit within this home office are easy to access from the adjacent space, where translucent doors add visual interest whether open or closed.

adds a huge amount of storage space and lots of character. The net effect is a room that looks and feels bigger.

And when space is tight, you don't have to make things perfectly accessible at all times. It's OK to put some occasionally used items in storage space that requires a little shifting of furniture to access it.

17. a place of your own

There's a space that's missing from most houses and apartments that can make a huge difference to your sense of well-being if you'll give yourself permission to create one. I call this missing space a Place of Your Own, or *Poyo* for short. In many ways, a Poyo is the crossover place between a Not So Big House and a Not So Big Life as it is both about space and about time. By making a place where you can express more of your inner nature and your unexplored passions, you are taking an important step in integrating a Not So Big sensibility into the way you live, and not just the way you design your home.

A Poyo can be small—no bigger than an alcove, a window seat, or the corner of a room if that's all you have to work with. Just like everything else related to Not So Big, size is, paradoxically, not the real issue. There is a wide variety of interpretations of what a Poyo can be. For some, their Poyo is oriented around a specific passion or hobby, while for others it is more ambiguous—a place simply to be and to engage the interests of the moment. In *The Not So Big Life,* I describe the process of giving myself permission to create a Poyo in my original Not So Big House in St. Paul, Minnesota (see the top photo on p. 236) and the resulting shifts that occurred as I began to use that space, both for writing and for meditating.

What makes a Poyo function best is the sense of personal ownership of the space. So if a Poyo is to work as a place for personal expression or for engaging a hobby or unexplored passion, it is difficult to make the space do double duty with anything else.

It was quite a revelation to discover how much creativity bubbled to the surface when given the space to do so. In the years that followed, I helped many of my clients to create similar spaces in their own homes, and each person reported new and unexpected developments in their creative life.

You don't have to wait until you know you have the time available to use a Poyo. In fact it seems to work the other way around. If you make the space, the time will present itself.

where to put a Poyo

One of the most important features of a Poyo is that it should be relatively out of the way and private so that when you are using the space other household members know to leave you alone. As with a home office, a quiet place is also a plus, so the same locations are worth considering: Attics, basements, a room above the garage, or a small room or alcove off the master bedroom all seem to work well. Unlike an in-home office though, the space doesn't have to be as functionally oriented. In some cases, it can even have restricted head height without creating a problem. If you'll be sitting down in it most of the time anyway, and it's only for your own use, it can be whatever shape and size you feel comfortable in.

A Poyo is best when it includes some whimsy and is especially meaningful to you personally. My current place of my own, for example, is painted a color that I know my husband would never choose, but which I really like a lot (see the photo on p. 237). And the room is filled with personal treasures collected over a life time that have no meaning for any-

one but me. If the room were anywhere else in the house, and if it were considered a shared space, I would simply put all these treasures away.

not so big concepts to keep in mind

Creating an Alcove

If you'd like to have a Poyo but can't find a suitable spot, it's time to try a little outside-the-box thinking. There may be space available that you can't see because it's currently part of an existing room. When we look at each of the rooms in a house, condo, or apartment, we usually see that they are occupied with furniture that's suitable for the room's designated

questions to ask yourself

- *Who in your household would benefit from a Poyo?*

- *Are there any obvious spots available? If not, can you carve out an alcove in an existing room to create one? (See "Creating an Alcove" on p. 233 for suggestions.)*

- *What functions would the Poyo accommodate?*

- *If the purpose is to engage in a passion or hobby, are there any specific spatial or storage requirements? (For example, a painter would need a place to store paints and canvases, good lighting, and a spot for an easel.)*

- *Is there a need for any remodeling to make the space work?*

  - *More windows*

  - *New or different flooring*

  - *Better visual and/or acoustical separation—screen, door, or drape*

  - *Shelving or other built-ins*

  - *Adding color*

CREATING SPACE FOR A PLACE OF YOUR OWN

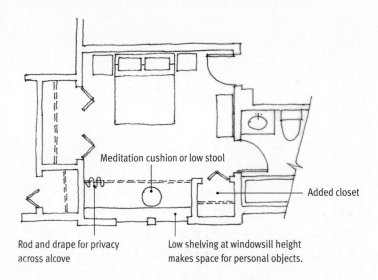

Meditation cushion or low stool

Added closet

Rod and drape for privacy across alcove

Low shelving at windowsill height makes space for personal objects.

In this bedroom with a vaulted ceiling, there's just enough space above the 8-ft.-high closet for a small Poyo.

function. Living rooms are filled with chairs, couches, and coffee tables; dining rooms are filled with a table and chairs; bedrooms are filled with beds and dressers. We are so used to looking in this way that we don't see the space *surrounding* the furniture. Sometimes there's a different way of configuring the furniture layout to open up a small area of floor space that can then be used for something else.

Let's take a look at a couple of examples. Suppose you have a good-size master bedroom that is furnished with only the bed, two side tables, and a dresser, as shown in the drawing above. Although you may not be aware of it, there's some extra square footage here that can be repurposed. By adding a closet to one side of the window, you also create a beautiful and well-lit alcove with the adjacent space. If you lower the ceiling over this area as well, you further accentuate and differentiate the space from the rest of the room. Add a drape or sliding screens and you have a small private space that can readily serve as a Poyo.

As another example, suppose you have a bedroom with a vaulted ceiling and a closet within that room that has only an 8-ft. ceiling. Though the space between the 8-ft. mark and the vaulted ceiling above is hidden behind a vertical surface, there's plenty of space up there for a little Poyo that could be accessed by a ship's ladder (see the photo above).

Or perhaps you have an attic that's filled with boxes of forgotten treasures and accessed by a pull-down ladder. That space, with a little thoughtful design work, can be converted into some additional living space. In the example shown in the bottom photo on p. 236, a ship's ladder was built into a 2-ft. swath of space taken from the guest bedroom, which added a 10-ft.-wide strip of attic space. The stairway hatch separates the attic into two sections—a Poyo at one end and a home office at the other.

a bathing sanctuary

For some, deep water and a beautiful, serene place to soak can provide the same kind of private retreat that a Poyo does. A Japanese soaking tub, or *ofuro*, such as the one shown here, is an ideal bathing sanctuary. These traditional tubs are deep but small, usually just the right size for one person. You shower and wash outside the tub, and then lower yourself into the hot water to relax and simply sit.

Making It Personal

The aspect of a Poyo that is most attractive to the people who long for one is that it can be made completely their own. We all have treasures of one type or another, but when we are married or living with other adults in close, shared proximity, there's no place to put those treasures other than in a box, hidden from view.

One of the true delights of a Poyo is that you can reintegrate those special items from your past into the room's décor if you want to, and in the process have it reflect more of your life experiences back to you. Alternatively, you can make it spare and elegant—a place that is peaceful and serene, without any reference to the past at all. There are no rules for this space other than your own preferences.

The Poyo in Sarah's old house was tucked under the eaves of a steep attic-level gable, accessed by a ship's ladder.

Sarah's own Poyo is filled with things from her past that have special meaning for her. The room is painted one of her favorite colors, two walls are lined with books, and the comfortable chair is the place she sits to do most of her writing and reading.

18. bedrooms

One of the most common motivations for a remodeling is the need for more bedrooms. While children are quite happy to share a room when they are young, as they move beyond grade-school age, the desire for a room of their own becomes increasingly pressing. Just as many adults value a "place of their own," the same holds true for children.

Another common motivator these days occurs with newly blended families, when two sets of children suddenly become siblings. This is not always an easy transition, but if the house is remodeled appropriately it can help to make it a little less traumatic. Again the solution lies in giving each child his or her own space, however small.

In this chapter, we're going to look at how to increase the number of bedrooms, as well as how to create a single room with multiple sleeping quarters, each with its own sense of privacy. We'll also look at ways to make an existing bedroom more appealing and engaging.

For this modest home, remodeling the second floor involved dividing a space to create separate rooms for two children as well as improving the character of the parents' room (seen here).

strategies for creating more bedrooms

1. Dividing One into Two

The first option to consider is that of dividing a large single bedroom into two smaller ones. By code, you are allowed to make a bedroom as small as 70 to 90 sq. ft. of open floor area, though anything smaller than 10 ft. by 10 ft. definitely feels cramped to most Americans. Since building codes vary and ceiling heights are also a factor, if you are pushing the limit, check with your local authorities before assuming you can divide a room.

2. Converting a Room

The next option is to repurpose an existing room, such as a rarely used dining room, back porch, or den. If you live in a house with a basement, you may be able to convert some space to make a bedroom or two. This option is typically more appealing for teenagers than for young children, who may be frightened at night if they feel too far away from their parents. If you're considering a basement remodeling, be aware that there are some design basics that must be applied to meet code (see "Egress Windows" at right).

3. Making Private Bunks

If the need for additional sleeping space is short term, another strategy for kids who get along well is to create separate bunks within an existing room. This takes up very little space—just the size of a regular twin or

---

egress windows

An egress window, which is required for every bedroom, must have a clear opening of at least 5.7 sq. ft. This is large enough to allow a firefighter to enter through the window. Every egress window must also be at least 20 in. wide and 24 in. high, and the bottom of the window opening must be no more than 44 in. from the floor. If you are planning a basement bedroom, there are also window well requirements that vary somewhat depending upon your location, so be sure to check carefully with your local building inspections department for specifics before proceeding with design.

All major window manufacturers list in their catalogs the net free opening for each of their windows and skylights, and indicate which ones will meet egress requirements, so although this list of dimensions sounds complicated, the hard work has already been done for you if you are buying a new window. Casement windows will typically be the smallest to meet egress requirements because almost the whole window area is openable, while less than half of a double-hung or gliding window is openable.

Note that to obtain the required 5.7 sq. ft., net opening dimensions have to exceed minimum width and height requirements.

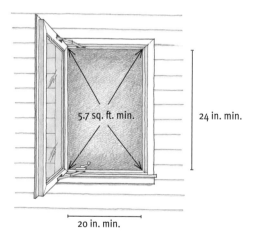

5.7 sq. ft. min.

24 in. min.

20 in. min.

questions to ask yourself

Here are some questions to consider as you plan your new or remodeled bedroom(s):

- *Who will be using each bedroom?*

- *If the room is for guests, how long do guests typically stay?*

- *What activities does the room need to accommodate in addition to sleeping?*

- *What size bed or beds are you planning?*

- *Will there be a bedside table or tables?*

- *What other objects and furnishings will occupy the room?*

- *How much closet space do you need in each bedroom?*

- *Is there a way to create an alcove or a secondary space either for sitting or playing?*

- *If the room will be used on occasion by guests, can you make a place to set a suitcase?*

- *Is there a way to add extra storage in the eaves?*

- *Is there any need for bookshelves or toy shelves?*

- *Are there any places for additional storage?*

- *Would it be valuable to redesign the existing closet layout?*

- *If the room will do double duty as a sitting room, office, or den, is there a way to build in a Murphy bed rather than a standard bed?*

BEDROOM BY ADDITION

before

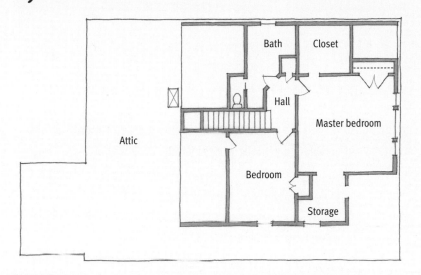

after

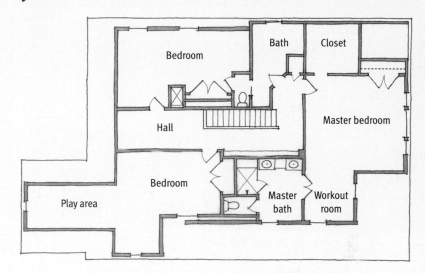

double bed—and the bunks can even be placed in an area with lower than standard head height. If you provide drapes for each bed alcove, the child has a wonderfully cozy private cave. I've used this strategy in a number of homes over the years, and I've never met a kid who didn't love the idea.

4. Adding On

If none of the above options will work, it's time to consider an addition. A common way to add on is to lengthen, widen, or add height to an existing second floor to house additional bedrooms (as shown in the plans above). In many older homes built in the era before roof trusses became the norm, the second floor is built into the roof structure, so that the upstairs rooms have sloped walls, with dormers along the front of the house to accommodate windows. The back side of the house often sports a lean-to dormer, making second-floor ceilings on this side of the house low and sloped across its width—not a particularly comfortable shape of space.

Adding bedrooms to a second floor afforded an opportunity to widen the central hall (see the floor plans above) and include built-in bookshelves.

add up or out?

If you don't already have a second floor but are considering adding up, you may be surprised at the amount of work to be done. You'll need to find a place for a stairway for example, which will mean some major remodeling to the main level as well as all the structural and finish work to add a new level to the house. So although it is conceptually simple, it's not cheap. Usually though, adding up is less expensive than adding out because there is no foundation work to be done. This is really beyond the scope of this book, but it's worth mentioning because it is such a common desire.

In the example below, the whole roof has been raised by increasing its slope, and the rear dormer lengthened. Three elegantly proportioned dormers have been added along the front of the house as well, to give it an entirely new look and feel both inside and out. Although this is not an inexpensive approach to expansion, the increased scale and much improved character of the exterior make this kind of modification a good investment if you can afford it.

working with an existing bedroom

If the bedroom you are planning to remodel already has enough square footage but is lacking in character or is simply awkward in layout, there are many things you can do to improve it. Children's bedrooms in particular offer ample opportunity for creative design. Kids almost always love nooks and crannies that are sized just right for them, so there's no need to leave the room in its conventional rectangular box form.

But if that's what you've got, how do you make it more interesting? The answer lies in built-ins and creative storage. As we saw in the last chapter, you can create the appearance of more space by actually carving out a section or two to use for storage. Or you can add play platforms, bunk-bed units, and all manner of other built-ins to enhance a child's bedroom in a less permanent way, of course.

With a room that is intended as a guest bedroom, the same kinds of strategies apply. If most of your guests tend to stay for only a day or two, the closet and storage needs will be different from those needed for a

Adding dormers to this Cape expanded the bedrooms upstairs while improving the look of the house from the front.

Staying within the existing roof instead of adding on a full story results in spaces with shelter around activity areas (in this case, a dormer play area, a sitting area, and a guest bedroom) and character as varied as the geometry of the roof.

the bump-in

A good way to create interest in a room—even at the expense of square footage—is to create what I call a "bump-in." In the photo below, two closets have been added to either side of a window to create a window seat. Without the closets, this would be a standard rectangular room with a plain window plunked in the center of the outside wall. Adding the closets makes the room much more interesting and useful, with more storage and a new place to sit as well, both assets to any bedroom.

Another way to accomplish a similar effect, even if there's no window available, is to place a closet or a section of deep shelving a few feet from an adjacent wall and to fill the remaining space with a small desk or dresser space. If the ceiling can also be lowered over this alcove, the space will become its own little room within the larger room.

full-time resident. A guest closet can be small, with just a few hangers and one or two drawers. Ideally, the room should have a good spot to place a suitcase and with a chair or dresser for placing other odds and end. If there's room to include a small sitting place for reading or watching TV, your guest will feel well cared for.

not so big principles

Innovative Everyday Closets

A major player in any bedroom is the functionality of its closet space. So many older houses have inadequate closet space, which places significant hardship on household members as they try to make do with a closet designed for an era when people clearly owned less stuff. In a room for an adult, the closet serves primarily as a place for clothing storage, but in a child's or teenager's room, the closet usually also attempts to fulfill a toy storage role as well. It's no wonder that toys tend to be spread throughout the house these days. There's simply no place else for them to go.

As you redesign the bedrooms, make certain to pay close attention to what kinds of stuff—and how much of it—there is to be stored in addition to clothes. I am a strong believer in getting a design consultant to help with closet layout. Today there are many excellent closet and storage system companies that can help you. (If you are working with an architect or interior designer, he or she can help you as well.)

Shelving as Display

Shelving, as we've discussed in several other chapters, can be an effective way to obtain a lot of extra storage with minimal impact to a room's square footage. For example, in the first house I owned, I added a single

A four-poster bed creates an implied ceiling in a bedroom with a high ceiling.

shelf above all the doorways on the second-floor landing, and I used the space to display many of my favorite fiction books. I didn't use them every day so they didn't need to be particularly accessible, yet I was certainly not ready to part with them at the time.

A similar technique is used in the child's bedroom below right, where a collection of fire trucks is exhibited and stored at the same time. If shelving is brought all the way to the floor, then the room becomes smaller by the amount of the depth of the shelf—usually around 12 in. In most rooms, the loss of this space isn't even noticed because the visual stimulation of all the objects on the shelving gives the sense of increased room size.

Shelter around Activity

Any activity area will be more effective in supporting its intended function if it offers a sense of shelter. This is true no matter the scale of the activity, from a house of worship to a house for everyday living to a playhouse. We gravitate to places where we feel both protected and inspired.

One of the simplest ways to accomplish a sense of protection is to lower the section of ceiling that's directly over the bed. If you have an 8-ft. ceiling, you can lower the height to 7 ft. And if you have a taller ceiling, you can introduce either a floating shelf, a dropped soffit, or even draped fabric to help make the space more cozy. This is especially important when the bed has its head against a very tall wall: For some people, the feeling of vulnerability can be overwhelming, making it almost impossible to sleep.

If there's not the budget to alter the ceiling shape, another option for creating the sense of shelter is to use a four-poster bed. Whether or not you drape fabric across the top of the rectangle created by the posts, the ceiling is implied, and most bodies will settle down and feel comfortable.

(far left) A lowered ceiling over the bed provides a sense of shelter and protection.

(left) Built-in display shelving slightly decreases square footage but makes up for it with the visual impact of the displayed objects.

138 square feet of serenity

Woodworker and designer Burt Miller and his wife, Misa, chose their apartment in Washington, D.C., for its proximity to the serene natural surroundings of Rock Creek Park. When it came time to remodel the small bedroom in their 800-sq.-ft. home, they wanted to capture a similar atmosphere of serenity inside. Burt and Misa, a native of Japan, also wanted to infuse the room with the qualities of traditional Japanese architecture and furnishings, with a nod to modern minimalism. What you see in the room is a showcase of Asian-influenced woodwork, all done by Burt with an equal measure of skill and restraint. What you don't see is just as important. The shoji screens hide closet space, and a trim maple soffit conceals a heating and cooling unit. But the real hidden secret is the soundproofing. Burt constructed what amounts to a room within a room by installing a secondary wall whose framing is mounted on cork and rubber pads. The ceiling and floor are also soundproofed. The room went from feeling cold and oppressive to feeling cozy and private, and it's filled with small details Burt and Misa cherish every day.

The closet space behind the 4-ft. by 8-ft. sliding shoji screens is as carefully ordered as the bedroom itself. Pull-down rods allow hanging clothes to be placed high, leaving room at the base of the closet for cedar-lined, weather-stripped drawers for storing kimonos.

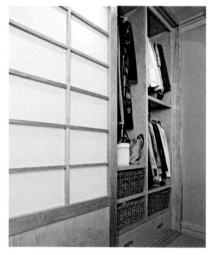

To create a feeling of buoyant calm and to increase both the actual and perceived floor space in the little bedroom, built-in fixtures are suspended from the wall or ceiling.

The serene atmosphere of the bedroom results, in part, from a lack of clutter; everything is hidden behind the shoji screens. But it also results from color and material choices: light maple wood, soothing sage green paint, and a paper-based floor covering. Simple details also contribute: The small nightstands float off the floor; the speakers hang from a slot in the crown molding; and the sconces glow softly.

❶ The nightstands float above the floor to either side of the bed, hung from the wall just like the maple sconces and the elegant three-panel chip carving above the bed.

❷ In keeping with the floating theme, stereo equipment is suspended from a corner shelf. While much is hidden behind the shoji screens, the media equipment is integrated into the look of the room.

❸ The original heating and cooling unit rested on the floor beneath the window. The new unit hangs from the ceiling, concealed behind a maple soffit.

"Although the soundproofing reduced the bedroom from 156 sq. ft. to 138 sq. ft., the trade-off was well worth it."
— Burt Miller, designer

a bedroom to share

Susan and Dan have worked with several architects over the years as they've remodeled their 1950s ranch outside Minneapolis, Minnesota. For the latest phase, they turned to architect Tom Vermeland. At issue was a common problem: more kids than bedrooms. Tom's solution was less common: There are still just two bedrooms for Susan and Dan's son and two daughters, but now the girls share a larger room. The shared bedroom is part of a larger remodeling that includes the master suite (which you can see in the next chapter on p. 257). In fact, the 8-ft. depth of the master bath addition sets the depth of the added space in the girls' room. The addition has space for one alcove containing a bed, nightstand, desk, and built-in shelving. A second alcove fits within the original bedroom. The alcoves have standard 8-ft.-high ceilings, but above the shared play area, the ceiling slopes up to clerestory windows, a fine example of *ceiling height variety*. Tom also makes marvelous use of fat walls.

"We considered giving each of the three children his or her own bedroom, but the house wasn't set up for it. Better to have the two girls share."

— Tom Vermeland, architect

bed alcoves

In a game of give-and-take, the addition provides space for a new master bath and closet; the space occupied by the old master bath and closet is now occupied by the children's bath. In turn, the space that had been the children's bath has become part of the expanded girls' bedroom, which has also expanded into the addition.

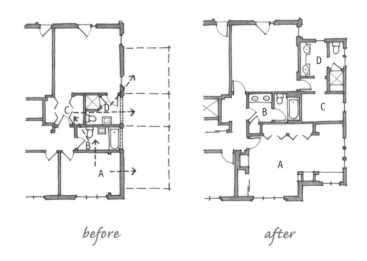

before   *after*

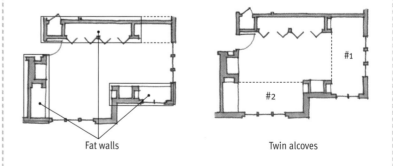

Fat walls   Twin alcoves

Standard 8-ft.-high flat ceilings define the alcoves and lend them a feeling of intimacy. The shared play space feels more open under a high, sloped ceiling. The fat walls provide thickness for built-in storage and desk nooks while helping to define the alcoves.

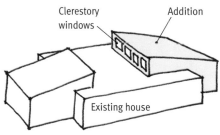

The addition extends over the existing flat-roofed section of the house, allowing the clerestory windows to be placed above the shared bedroom and adjacent bath. The form of the addition is sympathetic to that of the house.

light from above

Clerestory windows throw light deep into the bedroom and the adjacent bath. In addition, interior windows (seen in the far left photo) allow light from the clerestories to penetrate the inner area of the bath.

tots in the attic

As architect Mindy Sloo and her husband, Mark, took over the second-floor bedrooms in their Minneapolis, Minnesota, foursquare as home offices, they looked to the attic as bedroom space for their two growing daughters. The attic was unfinished but blessed with easy access via a wide staircase. Like the house, the attic was a near-perfect square in plan. Above it, a hipped roof sloped down on all four sides like a pyramid; there were no gable ends or vertical exterior walls. Mindy designed a wide dormer for the center of each side: two as bed alcoves, one for a full bath, and one for light and space above the stairs. The four dormers pinch off the four corners of the attic; these spaces were perfect for built-in desks and full-height closets with knee-high storage cubbies behind them. At the high center of the largely open attic is a ventilation fan, which gets covered with a panel of rigid insulation during the winter. Mindy and Mark did much of the work themselves, but for the girls, the remodeled attic is child's play.

(top left and right) Built-in desks, one for each child, utilize the space behind the kneewalls in two corners of the attic. The desk units roll out to allow access to storage cubbies.

(bottom) The dormer above the stairs adds light, increases headroom, and captures a little space to one side of the stair railing for toy storage. The door opens to a closet, one of two, that takes advantage of the space under the sloped ceiling at a corner of the attic.

"The attic floorboards turned out to be fir, not pine. There are bad surprises in remodeling and good surprises. This was a good one."

— *Mindy Sloo, architect*

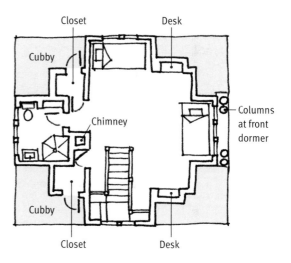

Closet

Desk

Cubby

Chimney

Columns at front dormer

Cubby

Closet

Desk

The girls may be carefree in their charmed bed alcove, but setting up bedrooms in an attic isn't without its challenges. The double-hung windows in the dormer are too small to pass fire-code requirements for egress; to create a large enough opening, the entire window unit in the middle of the three swings open on hinges like a door.

19. master suites

In my own experience, master bedroom suites are the third most common remodeling projects undertaken, after a redo of the kitchen or bathroom. There are a number of ways to improve a master suite, from reworking the existing space to borrowing some square footage from adjacent rooms to adding on. Although throughout this book we've avoided spending much time on major additions, in this chapter we are going to look at a couple of examples in which a master bedroom has been added above a new family room addition. Building this kind of addition onto the back or side of a house that is simply too small for its inhabitants is common, and there are a few guidelines that will help you to make the new master suite both comfortable and functional.

In this master suite, a closet has been transformed into a delightful bed alcove; the closet was replaced with a walk-in closet (behind the curved wall at left) that improves the proportions of what had been an overly long room.

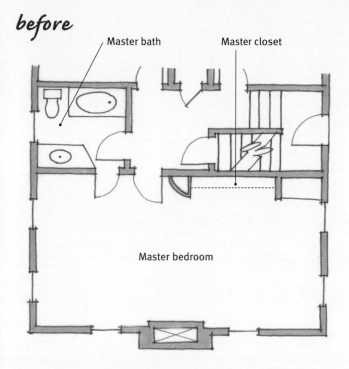

Master bath   Master closet

Master bedroom

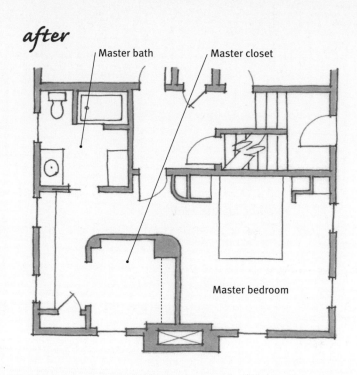

Master bath   Master closet

Master bedroom

reworking the existing space

Many older homes have tiny master bathrooms and closets, which make the bedroom suite feel cramped and awkward. If you are lucky enough to own a house that has a spacious master bedroom despite its inadequate closet and bathroom, your biggest hurdle is coming to terms with losing some of the open floor space in the bedroom. Despite the fact that the area is there and not used very much, for most people the idea of making a room smaller is hard to accept.

In fact, it is sometimes possible to make the room seem larger than it was before, even though the actual floor area is smaller, simply by making intelligent use of some Not So Big principles. If it is possible to configure the space so that both bathroom and closet are accessed from a short hallway, the bedroom will seem less cluttered with doors, and the hallway will give the bedroom a larger feeling, especially if there is a window or lighted painting at the far end (see the examples on the facing page and in the floor plans above).

borrowing space from adjacent rooms

If the existing room is already small though, or if the existing master bedroom has no bathroom of its own so that significantly more space is needed, then another strategy must be implemented. Before you decide to add on, a decision that many homeowners jump to at this point, take a look at the adjacent bedrooms to see if there is another way to configure them so that you can obtain the extra square footage you need for the master suite.

If you are doing more remodeling within the house at the same time, you may realize, for example, that by moving one of the kids' bedrooms to the lower level, you can then make the vacated bedroom into a part of an expanded master suite. Alternatively, if you have more bedrooms than you need, you could remove one and use it to enhance the master suite. Although a four-bedroom house may be slightly more valuable in

questions to ask yourself

- Which of these four strategies best fits your needs?

  - Reworking the existing space

  - Borrowing space from adjacent rooms

  - Adding on just a little

  - Adding on above a new family room

- Ideally, do you want one closet or two?

- Would you prefer a walk-in closet or a wall closet?

- What features would you like to have in each closet?

- How many linear feet of full-length hanging space do you need?

- How many linear feet of half-length hanging space do you need?

- How much drawer space and other shelf storage space do you need?

- How many pairs of shoes will you need space for?

- Do you have other items that require specialized hanging space, such as ties, necklaces, belts, or scarves? If so, how many are to be accommodated?

- What special features and fixtures would you like to have in the bathroom?

- Are you planning to have a jetted or soaking tub in the master bathroom? (If so, be sure to look at the dimensions early on in the design process so that you can appropriately integrate it into the design.)

- Do you want the toilet in a separate room or compartment?

- Do you need two sinks or is one sufficient? (Two has become the standard, so if there's room it's best to provide a second one.)

- Do you have any preferences related to the design of the shower, such as size, type or number of shower-heads, or door style or configuration?

- How much linen storage do you need in or close to the bathroom?

- What size of bed or beds do you need to accommodate?

- What size side tables will you be using?

- Do you have any freestanding dressers, chairs, or other pieces of furniture that need to be designed for? If so, what are the dimensions of each—length, width, and height?

- Do you like to have daylight entering your bedroom in the morning?

- Do you prefer a dark room until it is time to get up?

- If the room is being used by a couple, do you both agree on this; if not, who has the last word?

the resale market than a three bedroom, a three-bedroom house with a beautiful master suite will trump a four-bedroom house with an average master suite every time.

adding on just a little

Just as you can add a small bump-out to a kitchen to accommodate a better layout or an informal eating area (see chapter 8), you can use the same strategy in the design of a master suite. Typically, you don't need a lot of extra space—adding just a few feet can make a big difference. If the eaves on the house are wide enough, you may be able to tuck

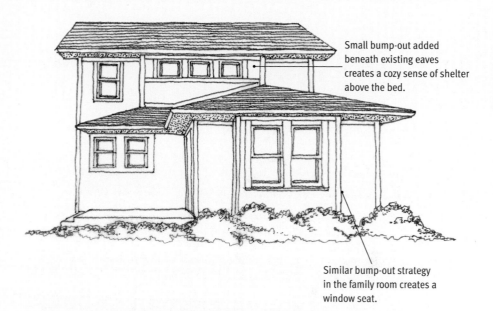

Small bump-out added beneath existing eaves creates a cozy sense of shelter above the bed.

Similar bump-out strategy in the family room creates a window seat.

In this master suite, one of two existing windows became a door to a bath and closet addition, but the other window was left in place, unobstructed by the addition—hiding, in effect, behind the bed's headboard.

the new bump-out under the existing roof, which will help to keep costs down and project scope contained. A more elaborate roof solution will automatically cost more.

In the example on p. 257, which was also featured in case study 35 on p. 250, an 8-ft.-wide extension to the bedroom wing of the house provides space for both an expanded children's bedroom and for the remodeled master suite. In this instance, the master suite has been upgraded from "not bad" to "terrific," not by making it much larger, but by paying close attention to detail. In fact, the square footage of the whole suite, including closet and bathroom, has increased by only 120 sq. ft., but the quality and character of the space is dramatically improved, a perfect example of what the Not So Big sensibility is all about.

adding on above a new family room

When a family room is being added on to the main level of a house, the temptation to add a new master suite to the second floor at the same time can be almost insurmountable. After all, the foundation work is being done anyway, and there's still a roof required whether the addition is one story high or two. So if the second-floor square footage is added along with the family room, it's not as expensive as it would be if it were a separate project.

But additions come with their own challenges. For an addition to be desirable, it needs to fit in with the existing character of the house, and it needs to maintain or even improve the functionality of the existing upper level as well, which is not always easy to accomplish. As I described in chapter 10, whenever you are thinking about adding on, it is critical to begin with the roof. The addition shown below not only fits with the house's character but actually enhances it. To do this successfully, you need to work with an experienced architect. If you are

This master suite was added above an existing family room, but it occupies a smaller footprint than the room below, more in tune with its function as a bedroom and better proportioned to the overall mass of the house.

trying to design the addition yourself (which I don't recommend), keep your roof solution simple.

The interior flow of the upstairs—what architects call the "circulation"—can also be a major challenge. The second floor was designed to work for the number of existing bedrooms and bathrooms only. Designing in a hallway to access the new addition can often require some major reworking of one or two of the existing rooms. If the new hallway forces you to slice through a bedroom, it may override any additional value you might get from a new master suite. Since it is so easy to damage the functionality of the rest of the upstairs when adding on, approach this kind of project with care and ideally with a professional at your side to help you.

not so big principles

Ceiling Shape

One common characteristic of bedrooms is their unrelievedly rectangular shape. You can make a dull room quite beautiful and a lot more comfortable just by giving the ceiling a new shape.

In the master bedroom remodeling shown on p. 257, a soffit runs around the perimeter of the room and the ceiling is left full height in the center, directly above the bed. By continuing the soffit behind the headboard to give the head of the bed some sense of shelter, and by adding two recessed lights to highlight a painting above the bed, the whole room gains a focal point in a graceful way.

designing a not so big closet

The real art of the small closet is to tailor it to fit your particular needs. In my own "not quite big enough" walk-in closet, I had a classic problem—a space that was just under 6 ft. wide, which is simply not enough to comfortably accommodate hanging space on both sides of the room without feeling squeezed as you enter. So I came up with a design that stayed within the existing footprint and that gave me more hanging space than I'd had previously. The full-length hanging space is turned sideways so that the center walkway can be a little wider than it was prior to the remodeling, and the dressers to either side of the door make the entry process less compressed.

Having a beautiful space to step into has made a significant difference to my demeanor first thing in the morning. Instead of feeling frustrated, now I enjoy the process because I can see everything easily, there's a place for all my stuff, including shoes, necklaces, and scarves, and I can move around inside it with ease. Sometimes it's the little things that make the biggest difference!

pod of space

When you have a large open space, such as an attic, that you want to convert into a master bedroom suite or guest suite, it's a natural temptation to use walls to separate the various functions. Instead, consider using a *pod of space*—a room that's not attached to any of the side walls but that floats unattached within the larger space. In the remodeling shown here, a pod of space partially encloses the bathroom, giving the bed a wall to rest on and partitioning the rest of the room into closet and sitting area. The beauty of this solution is that it maintains the sense of openness—and avoids all the tricky carpentry work entailed in meeting the complex ceiling shapes that are present in an attic.

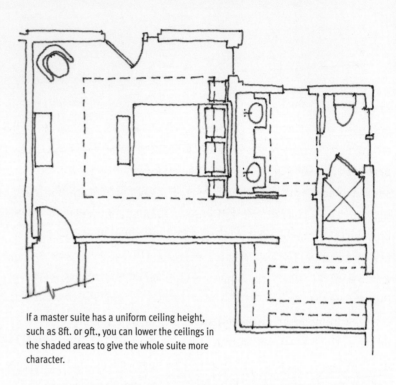

If a master suite has a uniform ceiling height, such as 8ft. or 9ft., you can lower the ceilings in the shaded areas to give the whole suite more character.

I often continue the use of this detail elsewhere in the master suite as well, by extending the lowered ceiling along the hallway, if there is one, to the bathroom and closets. The net effect is one first of compression, within the narrower space of the hallway, and then release as you enter the larger room. This almost always has the effect of making a smaller space seem larger than it really is. It's not so much the size of the room at the end of the hallway that counts as it is the contrast between the heights of the passageway and the room it adjoins. This was one of the spatial devices that Frank Lloyd Wright frequently used to evoke a sense of expansiveness.

Another alternative for adding some shape to the ceiling is to build a barrel vault below the existing ceiling surface. This can be done even when the ceiling height you have to work with is only 8 ft. tall.

Bed Alcove

Another way to alleviate the rectangularity of a master bedroom is to create an alcove for the bed to sit in. This gives the room two parts: the bed place and the walking and sitting place. Although this might seem like a small and not particularly significant alteration, the effect for the users of the bed can be quite dramatic. If you don't want to use walls or a framed opening to create the alcove, you can also use a four-poster bed or a fabric enclosure. The objective in each case is to give a sense of a room within a room, a place that is more private, more protected, and cozier than the rest of the room.

In the remodeling we saw on page 254 and below right, an existing closet was turned into an alcove for the bed. The unique shape of the closet was retained, but the doors were removed and bedside-tables and recessed lights added. The result is a focal point for the room and a sense of protection for the head of the bed. Although in this instance the alcove is not large enough to contain the entire bed, the effect is similar. If the alcove's structure were removed, it would be a standard square room.

Signature Pattern

If you want to distinguish your home, your remodeling, or a particular room in the house such as the master bedroom suite, you can add a special feature pattern as shown above with this unique composition of trim bands. In place of the typical ranch-style casing, the owners wanted to use a wider flat casing and to make it out of wood from a hardwood stockpile that they'd collected over the years. They selected maple for the main casings, with a narrow band of walnut added both above and below to give a unique signature pattern to the whole house.

With all the old trim replaced with the new signature pattern, the house gained an entirely new look and feel. When architect Tom Vermeland worked with the owners many years later to remodel the master bedroom suite, the continuation of this signature pattern became a major player in tying together the old with the new.

A bed alcove feels like a sheltered room within a room whether it's large enough to contain all or just some of the bed.

up in
the roof

Len and Vicki's remodeled house in West Hartford, Connecticut, is a jewel box—plain on the outside, dazzling within—thanks to the inspired work of architectural designer Jamie Wolf and interior designer Peter Robin. We wrote mostly about the first floor in *Inside the Not So Big House;* now we have an opportunity to look upstairs, where Jamie and Peter have turned the whole floor into a master suite. When guests stay the night, the three rooms and bath upstairs revert to private bedrooms and a shared bath, but empty-nesters Len and Vicki generally have the rooms to themselves. The second floor functions as a suite because double doors open the master bedroom to the bath just across the hall and to a study a few steps away. It feels like a suite because the hall and each room are unified with a consistent palette of colors, textures, materials, and details. Not that each space in the suite is equal; the master bedroom, with its ceiling soaring high into the former attic to a three-sided skylight, is clearly the sanctum sanctorum.

"As I ascended into the pyramidal attic space, I immediately saw the attraction of using this fascinating form to give character to the bedroom below."

—Jamie Wolf, designer

(above) The bedroom is a quiet sanctuary, with no furnishings other than the bed, backed by a linen drape that softens the space and hides one of the two lower, street-facing windows. The original flat ceiling has been cut away to reveal a dramatic peaked space within the steep front gable, capturing the former attic window in the gable for the space below.

(right) His-and-hers dressing rooms to either side of the bed can be closed off by translucent shoji screens. The screens slide behind backlit fabric panels; the lighting and the layers of material adding a subtle drama at night.

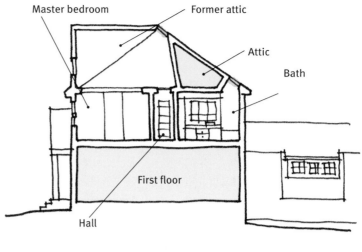

Master bedroom   Former attic

Attic

Bath

First floor

Hall

attic breakthrough

The curved and tilted walls encircling the former attic space above the bedroom were inspired by sculptor Richard Serra's torqued ellipses. Light from a three-sided skylight at the peak of the roof washes sublimely over the planes and surfaces across the day.

The rooms on the second floor function independently when guests stay over; otherwise, the entire floor is a master suite, held together by details that are variations on a theme. Translucent panels appear on the double doors to the bedroom, above the stairs at the end of the hall, on the door to the bath, and in the soffit above the vanity.

occupying the attic

Built in the 1920s as a mill house, Nancy and Susan's home in Carborro, North Carolina, is typical of many single-story houses of its era. Although it had ample square footage on the first floor, its unfinished attic was compromised by a low-sloped roof, stairs that arrived in the dark middle of the attic, and two chimneys that interrupted the most promising areas for remodeling. On the other hand, the attic had windows in its gable ends and good-sized dormers with windows at the front and the back. Nancy and Susan didn't want to expand the footprint of the house, so the attic, in spite of its challenges, was the obvious place for accommodating a much-needed master suite.

Nancy and Susan called on architect Sophie Piesse to figure out how to fit a bedroom, bath, home office, and storage into the attic without changing the shallow roofline. They wanted the new rooms upstairs to feel private yet not closed off from the main floor. And it was on the main floor that Sophie made a move to improve the central hall—in many ways the dominant space of the house—while also solving the puzzle of the attic. Sophie took down the old staircase and turned the stairs around. Instead of beginning at the front door, the stairs now start at the back of the house and climb to the dormer windows above the front porch.

working within the roof

There's ample floor area in this attic but not a lot of headroom. Still, there's enough ceiling height in the dormers and at the ridge of the roof for a crucifix of small but useful spaces: a window seat in one dormer, an office in the other (with a new screened porch extending from it), a bedroom and closets at one gable end, a bath at the other—all connected by a wide central hall. The corners of the attic floor, under the low eaves, are used for utilities and storage.

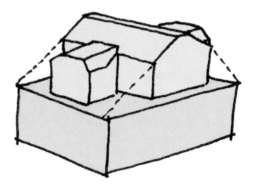

It might be counterintuitive to bring the stairs up from the private back of the house instead of from the public front entry, but as Sophie says, "There's no rule about where a stair has to come out." The new staircase connects the private master suite more directly to the kitchen; at the same time, it prevents arriving guests from looking straight up into the master suite.

No windows were added in the attic, but the most has been made of light from the existing windows. A vintage stained-glass window that had been stored in the attic now warms the bedroom and lets in a little light from the center hall. Lining up the bedroom door roughly with the bathroom door allows a long view toward light at the far gable end.

staircase switcheroo

Switching the direction of the stairs was the key not only to the new master suite in the attic but also to the remodeled rooms on the main floor . . . and to the integration of upstairs and downstairs. The stairs had climbed from the front entry to the middle of the unfinished attic; now they connect the family spaces at the back of the house to a delightful landing with a window seat. The oak for the handrail and newel post comes from old joists removed from the remodeled kitchen.

"You know, there's no rule about where a stair has to come out."
—Sophie Piesse, architect

one chimney less, one room more

In addition to switching the direction of the stairs, architect Sophie Piesse took a bold approach to the chimney that punched through the middle of the attic. She took the chimney out, making room for the master bedroom (giving up a little-used guest bedroom fireplace downstairs). The bricks were used to pave a garden path.

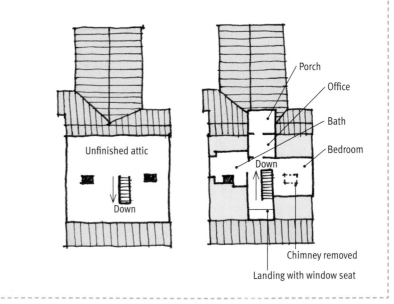

❶ ❸ The charm and coziness of the bedroom and bath are rewards for working within the shelter of the existing roof, which all but guarantees *ceiling height variety*. Adding a full second story would have resulted in more full-height space but much less character.

❷ Even in a Not So Big remodeling, you can find a little room for flair. Nancy's 8-ft. by 8-ft. office doesn't feel cramped because it opens onto a screened porch of the same dimensions, created simply by extending the existing dormer.

a modest addition

In chapter 4, we looked at a mudroom on a 1920s Bungalow in Newton, Massachusetts, owned by architect Todd Sloane and his wife, Elizabeth (see pp. 68–69). The tiny mudroom, created by enclosing an existing porch, exemplifies Todd's dictum to keep it simple, stay on budget, and respect what's there. The same spirit, writ a little larger, informs the addition of a family room with a master bedroom above it to the north side of the house. As noted earlier in this chapter, a two-story addition of this sort is one of the most common. But Todd and Elizabeth's take on it is uncommonly modest. Setbacks dictated the footprint of the family room, which in turn set the size of the bedroom above. The two spaces together total just 350 sq. ft. Keeping the addition this small kept costs in line and—more important—prevented the addition from competing with the original house. It's not a big master suite—suite is almost a misnomer for it—but it makes a big difference.

Placing the addition toward the rear of the house and setting its roofline lower than that of the existing house ensure that the original Bungalow roof remains the dominant form. On the other hand, proportions and details borrowed from the old house help the new addition blend in.

"I learned a lot from the original house; it was my map to solving issues raised by the addition in terms of proportions, window casings, rafter tails, and other details."

— Todd Sloane, architect

The bedroom is just large enough for a bed alcove with drawers built within the knee-walls of the dormer at the back. A short hall connects the bedroom to the bath and the upstairs hall, adding some privacy.

Family room   Kitchen

Master bedroom

first floor

second floor

family room below, master suite above: a common addition, done not so big

Many additions of this type include a large family room on the first floor with a complete master suite—bedroom, walk-in-closets, and his-and-her baths—above it. Here, just a small bedroom has been added over a family room no larger than a typical media room. To complete the suite, a former child's bedroom has been converted to a master bath (the bedroom closet remains in place), while the former master bedroom has become a child's bedroom.

PART IV

Pulling It All Together

20. too bigness

The idea of remodeling a house to make it feel *smaller* may seem pretty outlandish, but the truth is that many houses built today are just too big to feel comfortable in. All over the country, there are houses with floor plans that are just about perfect but that are nearly uninhabitable because of a third dimension on steroids—that is, with ceiling heights that overwhelm the spaces they shelter. A room that's taller than it is wide is a terrific spot for practicing hoops but not the place to have a quiet conversation after dinner or to watch TV while paying the bills. Not only will the acoustics make you run for a pair of earplugs, but also the lack of overhead containment can make you feel quite unsettled, as though you are on show—an exhibit in your own house.

There are also a growing number of houses in which the dimensions are too big in every direction—length, width, *and* height. For these buildings, there's a bit more surgery required to remedy the situation. I'll give you some tips to evaluate whether it makes sense to try to fix the house, or if you'd be better off selling it to someone who really wants that much space in the first place.

So this chapter is for anyone living in a house that suffers from too bigness in any one or all dimensions. With the application of some fairly simple techniques, you'll be able to find that comfortable spot to feel at home. And as you'll see, with sufficient care, attention to detail, and influx of dollars, it's even possible to transform an uninspiring sack of a house into a well-tailored and elegantly proportioned suit.

proportion

The concept of proportion—the harmonious relation of parts to each other or to the whole—is one that we've all but forgotten in much of what we build, eat, and otherwise consume these days. When it comes to houses, the remedy is to start with the proportions of your own body. If you are 6 ft. or more, you'll likely want different dimensions for the spaces you inhabit than will someone who is 5 ft. That is as it should be. The spaces that will feel comfortable to the shorter person may feel cramped to the taller individual, while a space that feels just right to the taller person will most likely feel too big if you are short. The point is that your house should first and foremost fit you and the other members of your household.

You can assess the appropriateness of your home's proportions by asking yourself the questions in the sidebar on the next page. If you answer "yes" to any question, parts of your house are most likely proportioned for a larger creature than the normal human; if you answer "yes" to five or more questions, your house is definitely suffering from a case of too bigness. To bring it down to human scale here are some strategies that may help.

1. create a hierarchy of ceiling heights

On the interior of a too big house, the first step should be to identify areas of the floor plan that would benefit from a lower ceiling height than at present. Although it is often difficult for homeowners to believe that

An entry that's too tall can feel intimidating. Lowering the ceiling just inside the door and adding human-scaled detail, as North Carolina architect Tina Govan did with this large, amorphous interior, makes for a more welcoming entry sequence and helps differentiate the entry area from the larger, taller main living spaces.

questions to ask yourself

- *Are there any living areas in the house that are taller than they are wide?*

- *Are there any spaces that feel comfortable to be in only when the house is full of people?*

- *Are there any spaces that are particularly echoey?*

- *Are there any spaces that rarely if ever get used and that you don't really need to find another function for because there's already plenty of room in the house?*

- *Does the house look huge from any exterior angle?*

- *Do you sometimes feel as though you are rattling around in the house—that there's too much space and not enough of a sense of place in any of it?*

- *Do you sometimes wander around the house looking for a comfortable place to sit and read or have a cup of coffee?*

- *Is your house so large that you can coexist with other household members without running into them except when there's a prearranged time and place to do so?*

- *Is the first reflex of a guest stepping into your foyer or living room for the first time to look upward and say, "Wow"? (This is not always an indication of approval, just awe.)*

- *When you are in the kitchen and another member of the household is in the adjacent family room, do you have to shout to be heard?*

- *Do you have any rooms that are more than 16 ft. tall?*

More than enough space, but perhaps too little of the quality we call home.

less volume will mean more comfort, if a ceiling height hierarchy is done well it can completely transform the home's interior. The only time when this is a bad idea is when your ceiling height is already *less than* 8 ft. high, which is usually not the case in a too big house.

Here's a list of the things I'll typically do to improve the ceiling height hierarchy:

- Create a distinction in ceiling height between the main gathering places and hallways and alcoves; the larger spaces should have the taller ceilings, and the subordinate spaces should have lower ceilings.

- Consider establishing a third in-between ceiling height for subordinate spaces, such as kitchens, informal eating areas, and small alcoves. Alternatively, you can drop the ceiling height in these subordinate spaces to the height of the hallways.

- Consider running a dropped soffit around the perimeter of the main gathering places. I will often make this continuous soffit at the same height as either the subordinate spaces described above or at the height of the hallways.

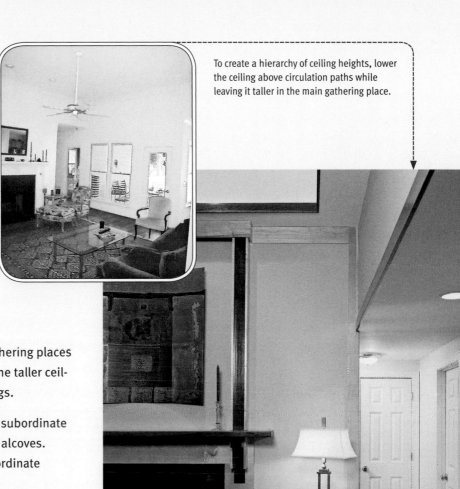

To create a hierarchy of ceiling heights, lower the ceiling above circulation paths while leaving it taller in the main gathering place.

A dropped soffit around the perimeter of a room adds intimacy while preserving the openness of the space.

2. include some more intimate places

If your house is too big in its horizontal dimensions as well as the vertical, look for places in the house that would benefit from some downsizing. For example, maybe you have a main family room or living room that is really big enough for several seating arrangements though you'd prefer only one. Or perhaps the kitchen eating area is at sea in an ocean of space that's too far from the kitchen to feel connected. In situations like these, you have some opportunities for big improvements, but the way to accomplish them may never have occurred to you. With extra space to spare, you can actually increase the thickness of some of your existing walls in order to sculpt new rooms and alcoves within the existing space.

We usually build our interior walls out of 2x4s, so the finished wall is around 4 in. deep. We do this because it is economical and because we usually want to make the space we have as accessible for everyday use as possible. But if space is not an issue—if you have more than you need—your walls can in fact be any thickness you want and they can define an entirely different shape of space on one side than they do on the other.

You can see a good example of this in the plan of the White House, where the "Blue Room" in the residential part of the house is shaped in an oval form, though it could have been a rectangle with a rounded front face just as easily. Of course, at the time this house was designed, back in the 1790s, walls weren't typically built out of wood, so the thicknesses were related to the building materials of the day. But you can see throughout the plan that walls were more malleable than they are today, with all manner of indents, niches, and curvatures.

So if you have more than enough space in your house but not many well-defined smaller places, take a lesson from this past era of home design and add some thickness to your walls to sculpt some new places and to give new shape to the existing ones. You can give each new place its own unique form and character, making some of them cozy and intimate in contrast to the vast acreage of space that currently confronts you. (For an example of this kind of spatial sculpting, see p. 155–157.)

WHITE HOUSE FIRST FLOOR PLAN

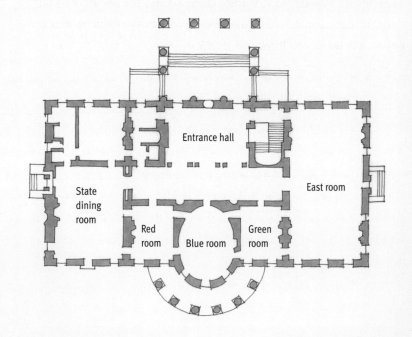

A key ingredient of exterior proportioning is to make sure that every dormer, every shutter, and every round-top window is of the appropriate scale for its situation. When any of these elements is the wrong size (as with the round top shown here), it shrieks its awkwardness to the neighborhood.

3. make the exterior less monumental

Many large houses have little or no grace to their exterior composition. Their various surfaces are a random assemblage of windows, doorways, vinyl, and brick or stone veneer, sometimes with a couple of Palladian windows and some extra-tall columns thrown in on the front facade for good measure—or rather, to impress the neighbors.

If this is your challenge, you'd be well advised to hire an architect or designer to help you. The remedy will take someone with a practiced eye for composition to help you bring the home's true potential to the surface. The art of it usually requires some paring away of the unnecessary, some reorganization of the surface components, and some newly introduced design elements to help break up the massive surfaces into more bite-sized pieces. You'll see one excellent example of this strategy in the case study that follows on p. 280.

not so big principles

Implied Ceilings

When it's not possible to add a soffit or floating shelf to a space, there are other ways of creating the appearance of a ceiling without it being something structural. At the simplest level, a hanging light above a dining room table will accomplish this. But there are other ways of implying a ceiling that in many cases can be more attractive than a solid surface overhead, while still giving a sense of shelter to the area beneath. For example, you can add a lattice of wood or metal around the periphery of a room or a floating shelf or soffit (see the drawing below). This still allows light to penetrate but brings the apparent height of the room down significantly.

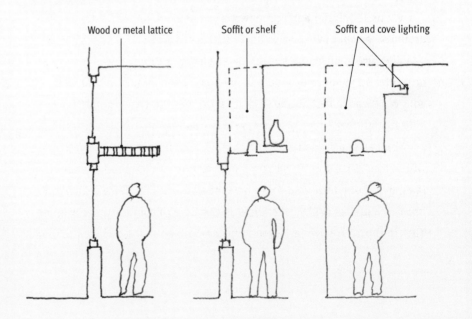

Wood or metal lattice   Soffit or shelf   Soffit and cove lighting

Hanging a light fixture above a dining table is a simple way to imply the presence of a low ceiling.

fabric implied ceiling

A less expensive version of an implied ceiling is to drape fabric over a series of rods extending from the wall. (You'll sometimes see a version of this detail in restaurants.) All you need is a few metal angles or kitchen towel rods, a narrow band of fabric, and a couple of hours of time and you'll have yourself an effective implied ceiling that can be removed with ease when it's time to move. This is an excellent idea for renters, incidentally.

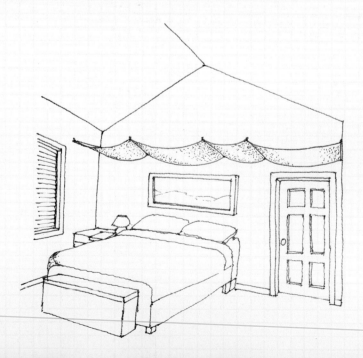

Interior Lighting

Lighting is important no matter what the remodeling challenge, but when it comes to too bigness, lighting can play a major role in improving the appearance of the space and in making it better scaled to our human forms. As shown in the remodeling featured here, the main living space, although still tall, benefits from a prominent trim band with bright cove lighting above. The ceiling height is now overshadowed by its sky-like quality, the ceiling appearing to be delineated by the trim band. The added feature lighting above the mantel also plays an important role, directing attention to the focal piece of artwork above the fireplace.

In a big space, the eye needs several places to land, and a directed light source helps accentuate those places. Although this may be counterintuitive, you don't want to have the whole space equally well lit. Doing so will have a homogenizing effect that can further exacerbate the already overwhelming character that comes with bigness. So although you may want some recessed down lights to give an ambient light level for the room, don't rely on this kind of lighting to do the whole job. Provide some indirect lighting that uses the ceiling and wall surfaces to bounce light around in the space. Then supplement with some pools of light for tasks like reading and eating. Finally, add some feature lighting to highlight the focal points of the room's décor.

The human scale of this tall living room benefits from the addition of a prominent trim band with bright cove lighting above it.

breaking up a box

Sue and David settled on a builder Colonial they didn't love because they liked its location in Granby, Connecticut, and its large backyard abutting a farm and woodlands. They soon became frustrated by the entry sequence from the garage through a cramped mudroom. It was an aggravating way to come home and an ungracious way to welcome guests (no one ever entered through the front door into the two-story atrium entry). The kitchen was little more than a passage to the dining room; the living room was too large, with few walls for furniture; and the back of the house was a two-story blank wall onto which was appended a utilitarian deck with a long staircase down to the yard.

From the back, the house looked too tall by a half. Here was a house just waiting for designer Jamie Wolf's favorite remodeling move, *The Jamie*, in which a narrow band of space added to the back of the house transforms nearly everything, inside and out. Jamie added 60 sq. ft. in the form of two bump-outs and turned an odd garage corner into a powder room. He unclogged the back entry area, opened the kitchen to the eating area and living room, and closed off the living room to the study, making both rooms easier to use.

Outside, Jamie ran a covered porch the length of the house, culminating at a screened porch with the pavilion-like quality of a gazebo. The porches and a stone patio just a step below establish an intimate connection between the house and the backyard. In the best spirit of *doing double duty,* the porches, bump-outs, and attendant details turned the house from a vinyl-sided box into a home that is also *at home* with its surroundings.

The original rear facade looked blank and way too tall, its verticality exaggerated by the thin chimney and a lack of a strong horizontal element, its blankness resulting from a lack of detail. The hovering quality of the raised deck and the long staircase only compounded the vertical feel. The new covered porch adds the missing horizontal touch, breaking up the facade and hiding much of the chimney and the curious notch in the existing second-floor bay. The screened porch elongates the footprint of the house and anchors it to the ground.

a house transformed, inside and out

The terraced garden and stone patio eliminate the need for a porch railing, improving the view from inside and the connection of the house to the backyard. While the vinyl siding and minimally trimmed windows were left above the porch, the walls under the porch are shingled and the windows have wide trim and upper sashes divided by mullions. The artfully curved columns and stained fir porch floor add still more human-scaled detail, further softening the facade under the porch roof where you experience it close at hand. The porch roof also shades the first-floor rooms from the harsh summer sun.

"When we first approached designers about making changes to the back of the house, we were met with incredulity. They couldn't believe we'd spend good money to make our home more livable, without adding to its curb appeal. But I just had to do it. You need your home to welcome you in its embrace, and my house wasn't doing that for me."

—Sue, homeowner

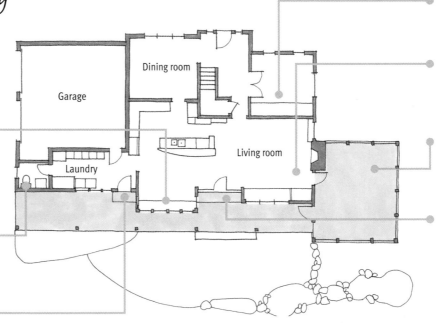

The kitchen was cramped and difficult to access.

Reaching the kitchen from the driveway required walking through three cramped spaces: an odd corner of the garage, the laundry room, and the mudroom.

Connected to the living room by French doors, the study was actually too open.

The living room lacked wall space, making furniture placement difficult.

The only door to the backyard cut right through the small eating area.

Garage

Dining room

Living room

Laundry

Powder room

Deck

before

"Our plan was to introduce a whole new relationship between the house and the yard with a long, covered porch breaking up the rear facade and culminating in a screened porch."
—*Jamie Wolf, designer*

With its French doors turned to face the entry hall, the study is now a quiet retreat.

Removing the French doors from the study gave the living room an uninterrupted wall for additional sitting area.

The screened porch adds relatively inexpensive, fair-weather living space and blurs the distinction between indoors and out.

Sheltered under the porch roof, a French door opens to a spot between the eating area and living room with a clear path to the front of the house.

A 3-ft. bump-out bench allows the table to be tight to the exterior wall, opening up circulation between the mudroom and the kitchen.

The odd, seemingly leftover corner of the garage is the perfect spot for the relocated powder room.

The new entry door is sheltered by the porch roof and opens to a tidy mudroom just off the kitchen.

Garage

Dining room

Living room

Laundry

after

❶ The window-seat bump-out in the living room, sheltered beneath a lowered soffit, adds seating while preserving circulation space. The built-in media cabinet tucked in the corner holds a TV that swivels out for viewing.

❷ The kitchen now opens across an island to the eating area, living room, and backyard. The tidy mudroom, seen beyond the kitchen, welcomes family and guests from either the back door or the garage.

❸ Bumping out 3 ft. for a window seat allowed the table in the eating area to shift closer to the rear wall, creating a clear circulation path to the new back door and to the living room and screened porch beyond.

21. whole house transformations

We've looked at a lot of strategies for making the various parts of your home better than before, but now it's time to consider what's possible when you weave all these design ideas together to create an entirely new house that's built more or less within the existing frame. Although it obviously costs more to accomplish a whole house transformation than it does to remodel only a room or two, it can still be done in a way that keeps costs to a reasonable minimum and dramatically increases the value of the house at the same time. In fact, if you've really learned the lessons of the preceding chapters, you will almost certainly be able to make your investments of time and money pay for themselves very quickly, both in terms of increased value and improved quality of life.

TRANSFORMATION WITHIN THE FOOTPRINT

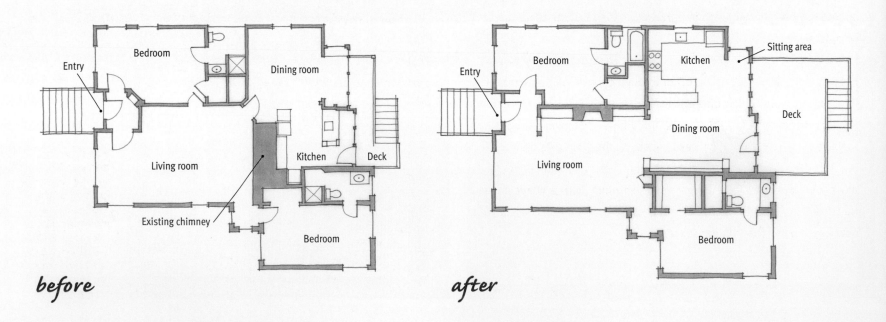

before

after

rethinking the circulation

One of the biggest problems with many existing homes is that the layout doesn't work for the efficient movement of people through the house— what architects refer to as "circulation." To a non-architect, it may not seem that anything is wrong, but if parts of the house are rarely used because they're not visible, or if you have to go out of your way to get to a room that you use all the time, chances are there's room for improvement.

We looked at this issue when we were discussing the kitchen as catalyst for bigger changes back in chapter 11, but when you begin the design process knowing that you are planning to redo the whole house, your first step should be to look for any obstacles that block smooth movement and visual connection between places. The two houses illustrated in this chapter both began with this clearing of obstacles as their primary objective. As you'll see, although there has been no new square footage added in either case, the circulation and interconnectivity of spaces has been dramatically improved, and the resulting houses seem completely new.

In the case studies that follow, you'll see that some transformations happen within the existing footprint, through opening up and connecting; others employ bump-outs and small additions to expand the existing square footage just a little; while still others add upward or outward to find the new rooms and spaces needed. All the strategies and Not So Big Principles described throughout this book are fair game as you rethink your house. And don't forget that even when doing a whole house transformation, it's not necessarily new space that you need but rather a new way of using the existing space.

Framed openings, built-ins, ceiling height variety, lighting, and a unifying color scheme have transformed this entire house within the existing footprint (see the before and after plans on the facing page).

questions to ask yourself

- Are there any rooms or spaces that you'd like to have but currently don't have room for? Some commonly requested rooms are:

  - Family room

  - Away room

  - Porch

  - Sunroom

  - Place of Your Own

  - Mudroom/pet room

  - Mail-sorting place

  - Laundry room

  - Bathroom—accessible, full, or powder

  - Pantry

  - Hobby/craft room

  - Master bedroom suite

  - Extra bedroom

  - Home office

  - Storage room

- Will the inclusion of the spaces you want require an addition, or are there underutilized spaces within the existing footprint that can be repurposed?

- Using the tools for rethinking the floor plan that you learned in chapter 6, are there appropriate places within the existing footprint to accommodate the additional rooms and spaces you want?

- Which of the spaces listed are "must-haves" and which are in the "it would be nice to have but I can live without it" category?

- Are there any existing rooms or spaces that you would like to update or improve?

- If you were to tie together all the rooms and spaces in the house aesthetically, are there any particular characteristics you would like to include (such as a continuous trim band, a series of newly introduced framed openings, or a hierarchy of ceiling heights)?

- Are there pictures from magazines and websites of spaces you like the look of?

- Have you considered hiring an architect to help you redesign your home? When you are planning to do a whole house transformation, the value of professional help is hard to overstate. Almost all the images in this book are the result of an architect's involvement.

not so big principles

Let There Be Daylight

One of the best ways to increase the apparent size of a home without adding on is to bring more daylight into the interior. You can do this by increasing the size and placement of existing windows and by opening up some of the more internal spaces so that they receive more of the already available daylight. The farther a space is from a window, the harder it is to make it feel comfortable and enjoyable to sit in for any length of time. This is one of the unintended consequences of a home with a larger footprint: There's more central space that's far away from a source of natural light, which makes it dark and uninviting.

There are a number of ways to broadcast daylight farther into the house. In chapter 9, we saw how a window can be located adjacent to a perpendicular wall so that it serves as a big daylight reflector, which can make a home appreciably lighter. Especially when considering an addition, make sure that you are not inadvertently eliminating the utility and charm of some previously light-filled room by cutting it off from its source of daylight.

Light shelves If your ceiling is high enough, there's another way to bounce light farther back into a space. Just as you can use a perpendicular wall surface to reflect light, you can also use a light shelf and the ceiling surface above as reflectors. This requires the introduction of transom windows above the main windows and a shelf with a light-colored top surface to bounce the light from these upper windows onto the ceiling surface above.

Not only is the use of light shelves a great technique for brightening the home, but it is also an excellent way to weave disparate spaces together. Here the connecting medium is daylight itself, and though we tend not to think of light as a surface treatment, it is in fact a powerful integrator because it enlivens every surface it strikes.

A simple Dutch door and an open seating alcove around a large window brighten the entry area and allow light into the main living space.

LIGHT SHELVES

You can use this technique for windows facing any direction. Although there will be more daylight bounced into the house from windows receiving direct sunlight, a softer and often more manageable light will come from windows receiving more diffuse daylight.

Connection to the Outdoors

When undertaking a whole house transformation, you have a terrific opportunity to expand the perceived boundaries of your home to the edge of your property line, or beyond if you have access to a longer view. No matter what climate zone you live in, you'll find that your house will feel several times larger if you locate doors and windows to draw in surrounding views and to allow easy movement outside when weather permits.

Wherever there's a view to the outdoors, always look for opportunities to make a stronger visual or circulation connection between the two. For example, ask yourself if there's a way to better locate a window or doorway to take advantage of the surrounding landscape when you're sitting at the kitchen table. Is there something that can be done with the landscaping itself to shape the view you look at from here?

If you provide an exterior sitting space that is sheltered from the elements by the roof above, you will have created another room from which to enjoy the outdoors even when it is raining. In many climates, the addition of a screened porch off the kitchen or main living space can serve as an excellent connector between inside and out, and during the summer months can turn into the most heavily used living space of all.

Doing Double Duty

Even when you are planning a major overhaul of your home's interior, it's important to keep in mind that many spaces can play two or more roles. Doing double duty is not only a concept to be used when space is tight. It can simply be a strategy for rooms that don't get used all the time or for complementary functions that occur at different times during the day.

A whole house transformation affords an opportunity to improve the connection between the inside of your house and the outdoors. Here, the remodeled kitchen opens to a translucent-roofed deck.

No matter how well organized you are, and no matter how good your contractor is, living through a major remodeling can be one of life's most challenging experiences. There is no way to prepare yourself for the changes to your life that occur during this period. It's not just the construction dust and general disorganization of living space that is at issue. Remodelers typically start each day early and often end late. There's constant noise, and if there are any difficulties that arise between the contractors and home-owners during the process, there's no place to escape to.

Here are some words of advice:

1. *If you are doing a significant amount of remodeling to your home in addition to the kitchen, you'll enjoy the process much more if you move out during construction.*

2. *If you decide to stay put, make sure you have a temporary kitchen located somewhere away from the worst of the noise and mess of construction.*

3. *Find remodelers who are sensitive to the needs of the homeowners during construction and who clean up well at the end of each day.*

And, most important of all:

4. *Never begin a substantial remodeling project to accommodate any of the following:*

   a. *a new baby when you find out you are newly pregnant (wait until the baby is born)*

   b. *a wedding reception for your son or daughter within the coming year*

   c. *a family reunion or large-scale party within the coming year*

   d. *any major event within the coming year where the completion of the remodeling project is required for the event's success*

Large-scale remodelings often take longer than planned and can be fraught with unforeseen problems and emotional challenges that can derail the planning of the major event in question. If your heart is set on hosting a major event or accommodating a new addition to the family, give yourself at least 18 months to complete the project, even if this seems way more time than necessary. You never know what will happen.

Taking this approach will make your home feel both more intimate and better tailored.

Sometimes double-duty functioning can even happen by accident, as occurred in the master bedroom for the same house. In sprucing up the closet, expanding the opening to the closet's full width, the architect used sliding shoji screens instead of closet doors and added an interior closet light for convenience. When the light is on and the doors are closed, the homeowners discovered that the backlit shoji panels provide a wonderfully soft ambient lighting for the bedroom.

Always look for opportunities to do double duty. The shoji screens (top photo) hide a closet and also cast soft, ambient light into the bedroom when the closet light is on. The sliding solid doors cleverly conceal the TV or focus attention on the TV rather than on the side display shelves.

three small additions, one much better house

When Amy and John contacted their neighbor, architect Bruce Anderson, they were the third set of owners of the same house in Indianapolis, Indiana, who had talked about doing something to improve it. As Amy and John explained it to Bruce, the entire first floor was one big hallway; a leaky front door opened into the center of the living room; and the first floor lacked a powder room—all of which impinged not only on Amy and John but also on Amy's home-based business, which she was running out of the dining room. Happily, Amy and John had 7½ ft. of driveway on the south side of the house onto which they could build. Within this narrow but sufficient confine, Bruce placed two small additions: a breakfast nook extending off the kitchen, and an entry vestibule and powder room extending from the living room. At the back of the house, Bruce added a dedicated home office adjacent to the dining room, which could still serve as a conference room.

The additions gave the house a measure of clarity and utility it had lacked, as well as a more pleasing exterior look. But even three additions would not have solved the circulation problems in the original rooms if Amy and John had not been willing to give up half their coat closet in favor of a direct passageway between the front of the house and the kitchen. That half a closet sacrificed made all the difference.

additive forms

This two-story house has a large, dominant form onto which two smaller, subordinate forms had been added: a front porch and a shed-roofed pantry at the back. So when the remodeling called for more space, it was in keeping with the original house to expand the two existing additive forms, wrapping the front porch around one side to create an entry area and powder room; turning the corner with the pantry to create a breakfast nook; and extending the pantry across the back and outward to create a home office.

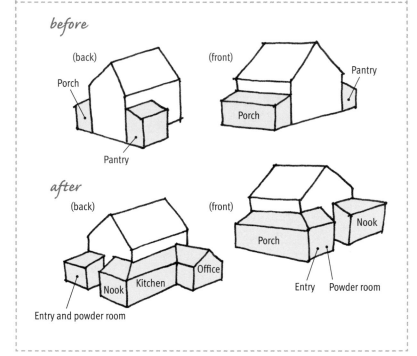

before
(back) Porch Pantry
(front) Pantry Porch

after
(back) Nook Kitchen Office
Entry and powder room
(front) Nook Porch Entry Powder room

"It was going to be a larger project, with a master suite above the office addition, but Amy and John decided they really didn't need all that space."

— Bruce Anderson, architect

The original house was modest from the front but well proportioned. The remodeled porch gives the house a much more substantial feel, and the enclosed entry in the corner is the key to improving the circulation within.

The back of the house had a utilitarian quality about it that called out for a more generous composition of forms. The expanded addition and the new home-office addition break down the mass of the main house and ease its connection to the backyard. Remodeling was also an opportunity to bury the many utility wires that clung to the house.

whole house transformations   293

before

Each of the three spaces on the first floor had a circulation path running right through it. The kitchen was effectively cut in two by circulation from the front of the house and from a side entry. Worse, the front door opened directly into the center of the living room. Compounding the situation, the dining room served as the office of a home-based business, so clients trekked through the middle of the living room.

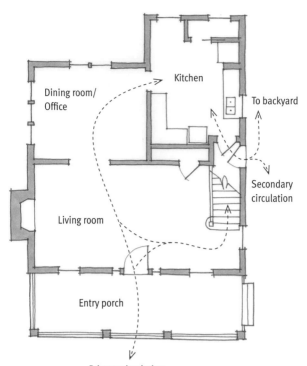

Dining room/ Office

Kitchen

To backyard

Secondary circulation

Living room

Entry porch

Primary circulation

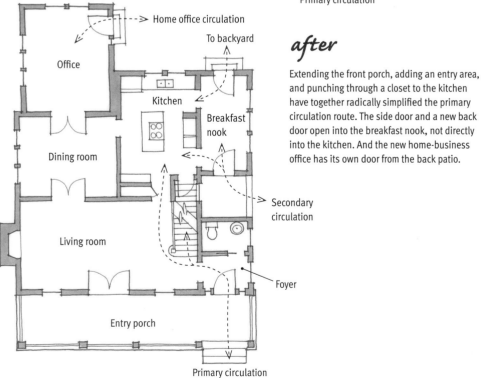

Home office circulation

To backyard

Office

Kitchen

Breakfast nook

Dining room

Secondary circulation

Living room

Foyer

Entry porch

Primary circulation

after

Extending the front porch, adding an entry area, and punching through a closet to the kitchen have together radically simplified the primary circulation route. The side door and a new back door open into the breakfast nook, not directly into the kitchen. And the new home-business office has its own door from the back patio.

❶ Opening the back of an existing coat closet created a wide passageway to the kitchen, improving circulation while maintaining a little distance between the living room and kitchen.

❷ The breakfast nook is just wide enough to serve as both a side entry and a place for a quick bite to eat.

❸ Light and views flow easily from the home office (in the foreground) through the dining room, into the living room, and across the front porch. French doors allow each space to be closed off as necessary.

❹ Carpeting the living room saved money, which was spent instead on a signature door and hard-

wood flooring at the entry and along the base of the stairs.

❺ The old kitchen was cut off from the backyard. The new kitchen features two rear-facing windows above the sink and easy access to the backyard via the adjacent breakfast nook.

making a little house a little more commodious

One way to turn a house of just 874 sq. ft. into a house that lives larger would be to add a second story or perhaps several full-size rooms on the ground floor. But suppose the house was on a narrow lot with tight restrictions on how much could be added to it. How to get the feeling and functionality of more space while only adding a little? This, in effect, was the question single homeowner Meryl put to architect Carol Cozen, her neighbor around the corner in Hermosa Beach, California. Carol's answer was to open the kitchen, living room, and dining room to each other and to extend the living room, bath, and master bedroom roughly 5 ft. out to one side and to the backyard. In the end, the house is just 284 sq. ft. larger, but the feel of each existing space has been amplified. Meryl can cook in the kitchen while engaging guests in the living room; she has a more generous bedroom and bath; and she feels more connected to the side yard and backyard.

The original hearth wasn't bad, but the new one looks better and works harder, with deep shelves, an intimate nook, and an opaque window that lets in light but maintains privacy by the front door.

"The challenge was to work within the confines of the setbacks and still maximize the size and feel of the house."
—Carol Cozen, architect

The kitchen incorporates the side door to what had been the laundry room, while using the old laundry-room space for a wall of cabinets.

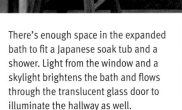

There's enough space in the expanded bath to fit a Japanese soak tub and a shower. Light from the window and a skylight brightens the bath and flows through the translucent glass door to illuminate the hallway as well.

squeezing a little addition within the setbacks

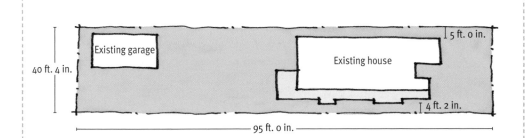

Existing garage

Existing house

5 ft. 0 in.

40 ft. 4 in.

4 ft. 2 in.

95 ft. 0 in.

❶ Sliding glass doors connect the master bedroom to a backyard garden and the detached garage, which now houses the laundry area.

❷ Removing the wall between the kitchen and living room creates a more generous entry area and lets the cook interact with guests.

❸ The eucalyptus trees felt cozy even before the remodeling. The added window seat draws the trees even closer into the sphere of the living room.

a lot of little moves add up

It isn't the amount of added square feet but the number of design issues addressed that makes this remodeled house so much more livable than it used to be.

before

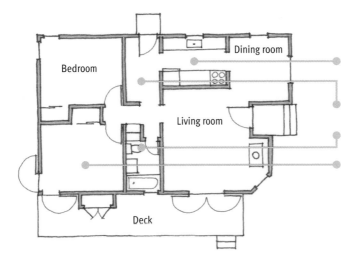

The kitchen was tight and closed off to the dining room and living room.

The washer and dryer were crammed into a small side-entry area.

The bath was cramped and dark.

The master bedroom was too small, lacking closet space.

after

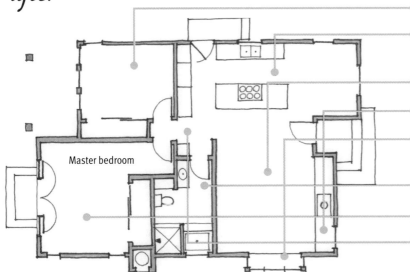

More windows add light and connect the bedroom to the backyard.

The kitchen opens to the living room and dining room and connects directly outside.

The living room gains volume by opening up into the roof.

A new hearth with built-in shelving adds storage and display space.

A window seat extends the living room outward toward the eucalyptus trees.

The bath is now wide enough for both a shower and a soak tub.

The larger master bedroom opens to the backyard garden.

The hall opens into the kitchen, borrowing natural light from skylights in the adjacent bedroom and bath.

a bungalow reimagined

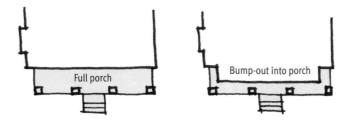

Full porch

Bump-out into porch

Architect Tom Bosworth and his wife, Ellen, had the luxury of staying in their longtime home in Seattle, Washington, while they spent a year remodeling a nearby Bungalow. Listening to Tom explain the remodeling, you'd think there was nothing to it. Every move appears to have suggested itself. The truth is that Tom, a patriarch of Northwest architecture, applied six decades of design experience onto every inch of this modest house. The big moves, if you can call them that, are five bump-outs that don't appreciably add square footage yet completely transform the usefulness and character of each of the house's small rooms.

The most prominent bump-out is a 3-ft. extension of the front facade onto the front porch. This bump-out steals space from the porch but ingeniously improves the entry sequence, a sore point in the original design. Tom also converted the one-car garage into his studio. Otherwise, the remodeling comprises little moves, scores of them, from a graceful skylight down to the smallest trim detail. It's still a simple Bungalow—in many ways the same as it was when first built—but in its quiet way, it's a masterpiece.

A long bump-out extends onto the original porch, adding much needed pockets of space. The use of the porch was sacrificed (it was too narrow to serve as a porch anyway) but not its character or scale. Indeed, the new housefront, with its tapered columns and wooden railing, actually looks more porchlike.

enlightened garage

Tom turned the existing one-car garage into a light-filled studio with a few deft moves: He raised the roof 3 ft., increasing headroom and creating enough height for a bank of tall, 8-ft. 6-in. French doors; he installed skylights on the north-facing roof to balance the light inside; and he lengthened the garage by a few feet to sneak in a closet and half bath. The French doors open to a courtyard surrounded by dense plantings. "The size of the studio," Tom says, "is really the size of the whole courtyard." The studio doesn't feel like a converted garage because the French doors on the long side of the structure shift the orientation to the courtyard, whereas new doors fitted to the old garage-door opening would have favored the driveway and given away the structure's original purpose.

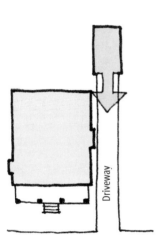

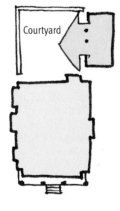

The dining room has been turned into a library by virtue of built-in bookshelves and a writing table placed off to one corner rather than in the center. The reading chair sits within a deep alcove that combines the depth of a bump-out bay and a bump-in bookcase.

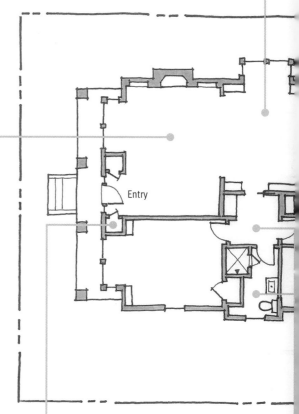

Entry

The living room benefits from a dedicated entry area and a generous bay for additional seating. The hearth and built-in bookcases were left just the way they were, a testament to the craftsmanship that went into the original house.

"Except for the lack of a front vestibule, it was a good plan. The question became how to make it nice and not just utilitarian."
— *Thomas L. Bosworth, architect*

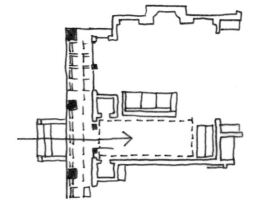

Narrow coat closets to either side of the front door create a vestibule that extends into an arrival space defined within the larger living room by the back of a sofa and a prominent furniture piece at the far end of the room, on axis with the front door.

In a kitchen not much larger than a ship's galley, open shelves span a bump-out window bay. The marble countertop is new, but the stainless-steel sink was left in place for its rich patina. The art-glass door was made for Tom and Ellen's former house by an artist friend and brought with them to this one.

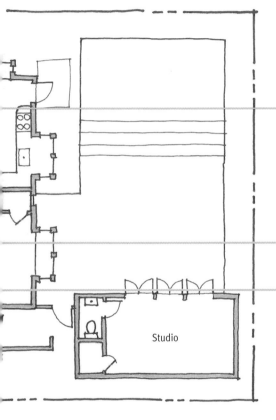

Studio

In the master bedroom, the deep bay is a window seat with ample storage below. The entire wall behind the headboard (not visible in the photo) is a mirror, so in a way, you experience the window seat twice.

A skylight atop a high, tapered ceiling introduces light from above not in the largest, most important spot in the house, but where it's needed most, in what had been a dark, windowless hall between bedrooms.

The bath (the one bump-out original to the house) was enlarged for a shower by stealing closet space from the front bedroom. Tom kept the old sink and commode and enhanced the vintage feel of the room with a narrow marble shelf above wainscoting.

whole house transformations   303

22. green remodeling

When you do a remodeling of any size, you have the opportunity to make your house a little greener. Even if you believe your house is a lost cause—it leaks like a sieve and was built in an era long before the terms *energy efficient* and *green* were in vogue—there are many things you can do to make the structure a better custodian of our planet's resources, to say nothing of reducing your energy bills.

With today's gas, oil, and electricity prices fluctuating so widely, the financial pinch is fueling the desire to make significant shifts to the way our homes consume energy. No matter where you live, fuel costs have an immediate impact on quality of life and are no longer something we can easily overlook. And in terms of planetary sustainability, the entire population is becoming more aware by the day of the role we each play. Our homes are an integral part of the solution. It is a little known fact that more than 20 percent of greenhouse gas emissions comes from our dwellings.

This remodeling of a very leaky and drab North Carolina ranch house (featured on pp. 304-308) gave architect Sophie Piesse the opportunity to do some significant "greening" of the home inside and out. The first step, making a home more beautiful, is an eminently sustainable strategy because people tend to look after places they love.

So taking the opportunity to replace the components that are not up to present-day standards will not only enhance the livability and reduce utility costs today but will also rehabilitate the house and extend its life span considerably. While you are doing a significant amount of remodeling, it's an excellent time to do some "greening" where it counts the most—the roof, walls, windows, and doors that make up the building envelope.

upgrading the energy efficiency of your home

My goal here is to give you some simple strategies for improving the energy efficiency of what is already there and to help you make better choices when it comes to selecting materials for any remodeling you do. You can implement as many items on the list below as budget allows. If at any point you feel overwhelmed, just pick one and do that well. This is how we can collectively upgrade our existing housing stock: one small step at a time.

1. Obtain an energy audit

Begin by obtaining an energy audit for your home. You can do some basic energy auditing yourself using this list as a guide, but for a complete audit, you'll want an energy expert to help you. Go to www.energystar.gov and search "Energy Audit" to find some excellent resources to help you. These experts will assess the relative benefits associated with each of the strategies that follows and can help streamline the process of improving your home's energy efficiency to get you the best results for the dollars you have available.

not so big and beautifully green

I define the term *green* slightly differently than many other people. To me, it refers not only to the sustainability of the materials of construction and the energy efficiency, indoor air quality, and durability of the structure, but also to the appropriateness of its size and its innate beauty. I often say that Not So Big should be the first step in sustainability because when a house is right-sized for its inhabitants and beautifully designed and crafted for everyday inspiration, not only is it performing its current function efficiently, but it is also likely to be looked after by its future residents for many decades to come—and perhaps even centuries.

Something that is beautiful tends to be well cared for by all its owners over time. But somehow this simple and rather obvious truth has been overlooked in much of what gets built today. So in my estimation, if a house is not beautiful, it is not truly sustainable, no matter how many green features it sports. By implementing some of the strategies presented in this book, you are automatically increasing the durability of the house, and thus its sustainability, simply because it will be more appealing to all future residents.

2. Assess the state of your heating and cooling system

In most homes, a large part of the inefficiencies lies in the heating and cooling system. You'd have to replace an awful lot of standard light bulbs with more efficient ones to get the kind of energy savings that can be obtained by simply doing a better job of sealing the ductwork, for example.

- Have your existing heating and cooling system checked out by a good (HVAC) heating, ventilation, and air-conditioning contractor.

- Seal major air leaks in the system identified by the energy audit, replace any defective, substandard, or inappropriately sized ductwork, and insulate all ductwork in unconditioned spaces. The right sizing of ducts can substantially lower utility bills.

- Install a programmable thermostat, or if you are technologically challenged and prefer a standard model, make sure you set the temperature to conserve energy at night when you do not need as much heating or cooling.

3. Simple strategies for reducing utility bills

- Replace furnace filters regularly. Once a month is ideal for most furnaces.

- Weather-strip doors and windows.

- Replace light bulbs with more energy-efficient ones, such as compact fluorescent or LED. (Do a test first to make sure you like the color and quality of light provided by the bulbs being considered.)

- Insulate the hot-water heater.

- Seal air leaks in and around the building envelope to reduce the loss of already conditioned air. Be sure to provide controlled ventilation to maintain indoor air quality.

All the original single-pane windows were replaced with double-paned low-e argon-filled units, and all the new doors were properly weatherstripped. The amount of glass on the north side, the front of the house, was reduced to minimize heat loss, and the new light-colored exterior reflects heat in the summer, making it easier and less expensive to cool.

- Have your HVAC system maintained by a professional on a regular basis, ideally once or twice a year.

4. Improve indoor air quality

- Test for back drafting—a condition in which flue gases are drawn back through the flue and into living spaces.

- Install a low-level carbon monoxide monitor.

The original floors were stripped and refinished with nontoxic materials, and the walls and ceiling were painted a light color using low-VOC paints to reflect more of the natural light entering the home.

The new cabinetry is made with FSC-certified wood and veneers; countertops are Alkemi, a product made from aluminum milling scrap; appliances and lighting are all Energy Star rated; and all the new plumbing is low flow to reduce water consumption.

- If your house is relatively tight, make sure that you have adequate air exchange. Check with your energy auditor or HVAC contractor for recommendations. In more extreme climates, install an air-to-air heat exchanger, and in more temperate zones add some mechanical ventilation.

- Add a better filtration system or air-purification system to further improve indoor air quality.

- Have your basement or crawl space evaluated for the presence of moisture and mold and upgrade as necessary to create a healthy environment.

- Paint with low- or no-volatile organic compounds (VOC) finishes.

- If you plan to use carpet, use natural fibers such as wool or sisal.

Other things to do when you remodel

- Use Forestry Stewardship Council (FSC) certified woods and engineered wood products.

- When replacing appliances, look for products that are Energy Star rated.

- Avoid recessed lights in insulated ceiling areas; if they're already there, add insulated boxes around them to avoid attic bypasses.

- Consider installing an instant hot-water system.

- If you have largely unobstructed south-facing roof surface, consider installing a solar hot-water system.

- Consider increasing the level of insulation in the house if it's below standard. Attics and crawl spaces are common culprits.

More expensive strategies worth considering

- Replace single-pane windows with double or triple pane, ideally with a low-emissivity coating, known as "low e."

- Consider replacing your heating and cooling system if it's older and less efficient. Air conditioners, for example, have a seasonal energy efficiency rating (SEER); the higher the number the better the efficiency.

- Consider adding a solar domestic hot water heater and/or a photovoltaic array if you have an area of roof with largely unobstructed south-facing access to sunlight.

what I did to green my own house

When I moved from Minnesota to North Carolina, I didn't have the time or resources to build a new home for myself, so I bought an existing house—the one I described back in chapter 1. Along with its various design shortcomings, it was also much leakier than the house I had built for myself in Minnesota. In fact, it came as quite a shock that houses in the South are typically built with much less attention to energy efficiency.

I began the process of tightening and greening my new home with some obvious steps. I did some simple things, like adding weather stripping and replacing some old appliances with new Energy Star ones. I also replaced some single-pane windows in the sunroom with new double-pane ones, and I insulated the existing attic with Icynene, an excellent sprayed-in foam insulation that also serves as an air barrier and expands to seal all wall and ceiling cavities against air movement.

But it wasn't until recently, with our utility bills climbing every month because of increasing fuel costs, that I decided it was time to take the next steps. I hired a local expert in energy efficiency to conduct a complete energy audit. They recommended a number of strategies, and at the top of their list, not surprisingly, was a whole house sealing to reduce the air leakage. Equally important, they told me, was to have the ductwork sealed or replaced. And at the same time, if it were in my budget, they suggested replacing the HVAC system with a more efficient system. Although our heating and cooling system still worked well, it was inefficient and excessively noisy. So that was an item that was high on my list of priorities as well.

By switching to a high-efficiency 19 SEER heat pump system with an excellent air-filtration system and by replacing all the old ductwork, our utility bills have decreased substantially and the air quality has improved noticeably as well. And though the cost of the new system and upgraded ductwork was fairly expensive, the system will likely pay for itself within five to ten years—a return on investment that is not only of value to us personally but will also reduce the home's carbon footprint for the long haul, thus contributing to the planet's well-being as well.

The biggest benefit of all is one that I hadn't fully anticipated. The house is dramatically more comfortable now, and we no longer have to make do with less-than-ideal temperatures at the far ends of duct runs or with the stratification between main and upper level temperatures. And I no longer have to try to tune out the sound of the compressor every time the unit kicks on. Our new system is so quiet I barely hear it. So replacing the heating system may have been a good move for the environment and for our utility bills, but it has proven to be an excellent strategy for our personal sense of well-being as well.

To determine how much air is leaking out through walls and windows, an energy auditor conducts a blower door test, which is designed to pull air out of the house with a powerful fan. This allows the auditor to measure the air infiltration rate as outside air flows in through otherwise invisible cracks and openings.

green rambler

I n 2006, Peter Lytle and his wife, Vivian, founded Live Green, Live Smart®, an educational organization dedicated to creating and promoting sustainable shelter. The following year, Live Green, Live Smart® teamed up with architect Steve Kleineman to transform a postwar rambler in suburban Minneapolis into the first remodeled home to achieve a LEED Platinum certification, the highest rating awarded by the U.S. Green Building Council.

It's now a demonstration house called, aptly enough, The Sustainable House™, and it's also home to Peter, Vivian, and their daughter. Built in 1948, the house had leaky windows and doors, substandard wiring, peeling stucco, marginal insulation, and an old furnace. Needing improvements in both livability and sustainability, it was the perfect test case.

As architect, Steve's goal was to update the visual appearance without changing the scale of the house. The key was to move the stairs that access the basement rooms from the middle of the interior, where they cut up the main living space, to a new front entry. Steve converted the existing garage into a bed and bath suite and added a small laundry room and mudroom, connecting to a new garage. Beyond that, the changes were small ones, many of them strictly green, some of them primarily aesthetic, and several of them, like the extended roof overhangs, an inspired blend of both.

extending the roof overhang

Extending the roof overhang to nearly 4 ft. from the exterior wall of the house accomplished several things at once. The shallow roof now has a dual pitch, giving it an Asian-influenced and suitably Prairie Style feel. The deep overhang also protects the exterior from weather and shades the house from the high summer sun. The overhang is a perfect example of the place where Not So Big and green meet.

The shallow, 4-in. soffit along the perimeter of the interior is there to allow for additional insulation above the exterior walls, though it also adds visual interest. The deeper soffits that help define functional areas within the larger space were created by raising the ceiling to 9 ft., stealing a little attic space but leaving more than enough for a thick layer of insulation. Note how much brighter the living area is now that it extends visually to the light-filled front entry.

Placing the stairs in the new front entry space took the sting out of the trip down to the basement rooms. But more than that, removing the old stairway unclogged the main living space, making possible the multifunctional living/dining/kitchen area.

"Our goal was to find an ordinary home people can relate to and turn it into a demonstration of sustainability that fits the neighborhood."
— Steve Kleineman, architect

before

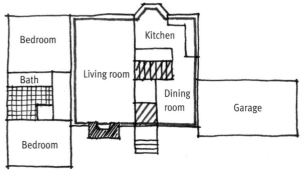

Bedroom

Bath

Bedroom

Living room

Kitchen

Dining room

Garage

after

Because it is so open, the main living space feels larger than it is. Within it, areas for cooking, eating, and sitting are defined by dropped soffits (the dotted lines on the plan).

Garage

Mudroom

Laundry

Bedroom

The only addition other than the front entry and stairway is a laundry room and a mudroom that connects to a new garage.

A bump-out extended over the existing foundation gives the master bedroom a little elbow room.

Widening the bath within the existing footprint by a few feet and converting the front bedroom to a walk-in closet turned the former bedroom wing into a master suite.

Moving the stairway and entry area to a modest (roughly 11-ft. by 16-ft.) addition opens up the whole interior and improves the entry sequence.

The garage was converted to a second bedroom with a full bath that also serves as a powder room.

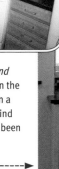

The kitchen remodel is a classic *U-to-Island* move. As in the living area, a deep soffit in the kitchen defines it as a discrete area within a larger space. The countertop extends behind the kitchen sink to fill in the bay that had been a cramped breakfast nook.

not so big and green

Some of the changes employed in The Sustainable House™, like switching to a geothermal heating and cooling system, recycling gray water, and installing photovoltaic panels to generate solar electricity, represent a significant effort. They're smart moves and should be considered. But the smaller changes are ones that all Not So Big remodels can embrace. Here's a quick look at a few of these:

- Every lightbulb in the house is an energy-efficient compact fluorescent or LED.

- Paints and varnishes are free of harmful VOCs and formaldehyde.

- Appliances are Energy Star rated.

- Low-flow, dual-flush toilets flush once for liquids and twice for solid waste.

- Most of the new wood is FSC certified, guaranteed by the Forest Stewardship Council to have come from sustainable forests.

- As many of the original components as possible were reused. 2x6 wall studs were reused to extend the eaves out from the house. Old stucco was ground up and used for a driveway base. Anything that could not be reused was responsibly recycled.

- Rigid foam insulation was added to the exterior of the walls, and a closed-cell, no-VOC foam insulation was sprayed between the studs, creating walls with an insulation value of R-29. Closed-cell spray foam and blown-in fiberglass insulation created ceilings with an insulation value of R-50.

- New windows are triple-glazed and argon-filled to reduce heat transfer.

- Foundation concrete for the additions was made with 40 percent fly ash, which recycles waste from coal plants and actually creates a stronger mixture than the standard.

For more information about The Sustainable House™ and remodeling green, visit http://livegreenlivesmart.org.

February 2007: The rambler before remodeling.

March 2007: Extended roof overhangs and a new front entry.

May 2007: Rigid foam insulation board covers the exterior.

August 2007: Triple-glazed windows replace the leaky old single panes.

23. my not so big addition

Back in chapter 1, I described the changes I made to my house in Raleigh so that my husband and I could move in and feel at home. You may recall that these modifications fell into two broad categories: what needed to be changed right away to make the house more livable; and what we decided to do to improve the character of what was already there. In this concluding chapter, I'll focus on two other categories: what we changed a couple of years after we moved in to accommodate some new developments in our lives; and what would be nice to do someday but which we haven't done yet either to avoid life disruption or because it seems to cost too much for the added benefit.

All the concepts and strategies you've learned about throughout this book can be applied to any type of change to an existing home, whether remodeling or addition. By regularly revisiting the strategies I've described, you can continue to tailor your home to fit your needs as they change, instead of having to move every few years. That's what I did with our house.

The two workspaces in the office addition are mirror images of each other, with a lowered section of ceiling creating an alcove at either end of the main office to shelter the side desk space. Corner windows offer a contained but panoramic view to the surrounding garden below.

adding on just a little

After we'd been living in our remodeled house for a few years, I finally accepted the fact that my office space was simply too small and lacked the qualities of beauty and harmony that lie at the core of the Not So Big sensibility. It seemed ironic that I was writing about all these wonderful houses and design ideas while working with my friend and assistant, Marie, in a *not big enough* converted bedroom and a *not so commodious* bonus room.

Every square foot of available space was already in full use every day, the guest bedroom doing double duty as my office's conference room and the original living room and dining room serving as my husband's home office. So I either needed to rent some office space elsewhere, move to a new house with more square footage to spare, or add on. I chose the latter, adding just 200 sq. ft. of space to my existing office

By raising the ridge over the roof of the family room a little (photo above), the whole roof solution for the back of the house could be resolved. The new skylight centered on the family room window became a defining feature of the remodeled office. (The photo at left shows the house before remodeling.)

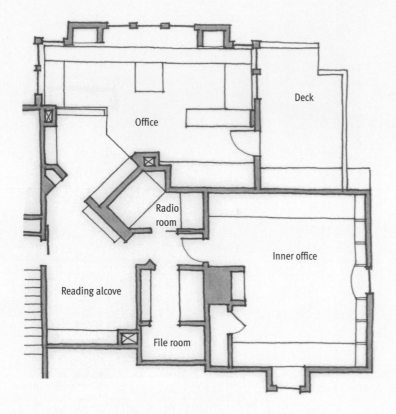

Deck

Office

Radio room

Inner office

Reading alcove

File room

area. What it has allowed in terms of business expansion and creative expression is beyond measure.

For a long time, however, I couldn't figure out how to integrate the addition of new space into the existing form of the house. I'd been pretty sure that the addition should go above the existing garden room because that would require no new foundation work, but the combination of roof forms on the back of the house was pretty complicated, and I couldn't easily see how to resolve them. And then one day, while I was standing in front of the house, it came to me.

If you look at the roof configuration from the front (see the photos on p. 315), you'll see that there's a lower middle section over the family room. This is where our office sat—in the sloped roof directly above. What had stumped me until that moment was that I had assumed that by increasing the height of this segment of roof, it would seem out of proportion with the rest of the house. Now I realized that I would only need to increase the ridge height slightly. It didn't need to extend above the ridge of the larger mass of the house to its left. But with this small amount of

The raised ridge allowed the addition to attach gracefully to the existing roof forms to either side, and to dramatically improve the look of the whole composition at the same time.

The "radio" room, an acoustically private nook to one side of the upstairs hallway, is just about the right size for a sauna or closet, should some future owner want to convert it.

increase I could resolve the much more complicated combination of roof forms on the back (see the photos on the facing page).

This example reinforces the point I made in chapter 8 that to add on successfully you *must* begin with what the roof allows you to do. If I hadn't waited for inspiration to strike, I could really have messed up the look of the house, both front and back. A good architectural solution, just like a good recipe, often takes time, especially when the existing conditions are complicated.

designing the interior

So with the vision for a solution in mind, I began to design the interior of the space. We needed a way to create a gracious entry into the office, a way to bring more daylight into this area. We needed space for both Marie and me to work. We needed a storage room and plenty of bookshelf and layout space. And I needed a soundproof room in which to conduct radio interviews. I also wanted to improve my inner office, where I do most of my writing, adding some bookshelves and some more daylight.

The key to the interior solution was one very simple design move on the front of the house. I knew we needed to introduce some daylight into the sloped section of roof where Marie's desk had been—a space that would now be in the office entry area—and the only way to do this without it looking like a mistake on the front facade was to center a skylight directly above the family room window (see the top photo on p. 315). With this one act, the rest of the design fell into place.

Entering: The beauty of the door itself and the detailing of the surrounding trimwork help to define the sense of a gateway between home and office.

from siding to trim

To make a house look more carefully detailed than it actually is, paint the bottom board of a wall of siding and it will appear to be trim rather than siding. Only on close inspection can you tell that it is no different than the other siding boards above it—just a different color. This simple application of paint can make the house look much more finished and a lot more handsome to the eye.

Entering the Office

One of the biggest challenges in successfully integrating a work-place into a home is to give it its own identity, to make it feel like a different place, even though it is under the same roof as the rest of the house. In my own case, I also wanted the office to illustrate many of the design principles I've described in my books, so the whole area involved in this phase of the remodeling needed to do double duty in more than a purely functional sense.

As you enter the office, you come through a new sliding door that, when open, appears to be no more than a framed opening but when closed separates the worlds on either side from one another. The entry space itself provides a quiet sitting place to read and have a cup of tea, and it also doubles as a place for magazine storage.

Another function of the entry area is to orient guests. There are two zones of the office—the more public open office area, where the everyday business of Susanka Studios is conducted, and the more private writing and designing realm of my inner office. I decided to introduce a diagonal wall across from the sliding door, with an opening to the public realm at the left end and an opening to the private realm at the right end. By adding a dropped soffit above this diagonal wall, the whole composition acts as another suggestion of a gateway and a strong orientation device for the whole design.

❶ Reflecting Surfaces: Locating a perpendicular wall adjacent to the new skylight bounces daylight throughout the new office entry area.

❷ Visual Weight: The wall directly across from the entry door is painted an intense color to ground the space and give it a point of focus. As you step through the opening into the main office, you pass a tiny, lighted niche, which is painted the same color and contains a fountain. The sound of the water sets the mood for the whole office.

❸ Long View Through: The view through the entry area into my inner office is in fact visible all the way from the master bedroom when the door to the office is open, giving an intriguing glimpse into the very different character of the newly remodeled space.

❹ A Place for Everything: From counterspace for a cutting board and postage machine, to a small shelf for all the odds and ends needed in an office, to a built-in CD rack, everything was designed in from scratch.

Point of Focus: In this space the windows steal the show. The three stained-glass art pieces hanging in the main windows look as though they were made to fit the windows, but in fact it's the other way around: I designed the windows to fit the art pieces.

The Public Realm

The main office is clearly the architectural highlight of the addition, with its sloped barrel-vaulted ceiling and ample woodwork. In *The Not So Big House,* I wrote about the potential of our homes to emulate boat design and to be just as beautifully designed for the functions they serve. In a way this new office space is like the interior of a yacht, a place where everything is designed and everything has a specific place (see the photo on the facing page). This is truly a boat for living.

The Private Realm

My "Poyo," accessed by the hallway on the other side of the diagonal wall, has been through the biggest transformation of any room in the house. Before we bought the house it was barely habitable, but today it is easily my favorite space. . .both because of its sheltering form and because it is filled with the things I love. I don't have a phone here, so it's a perfect retreat place and private work space. When I have the door closed, it sends a clear signal that I need to concentrate—a necessity for me when I'm writing, designing, or meditating.

a few additional refinements

Since we added on, we've also made a few other alterations that have significantly improved the look, feel, and livability of the house, even though each change is itself quite small. One such recent remodel was to reconfigure the family room fireplace design. Although I liked the arched form of the fireplace itself, the height and design of the existing mantel had always bothered me. I contacted the craftsman who had made the mantel for my previous house in St. Paul, and he made me another, just like it, for this house.

I placed the new mantel about a foot lower than the existing mantel to correct the awkward proportioning of the original composition. Rather

Three phases of the inner-office metamorphosis, from ugly duckling bonus room (replete with dark wood paneling and shag carpet) to comfortable retreat and writing garret lined with a wall of bookshelves and counterspace along both low walls. A new dormer was also added with the final remodeling.

The fireplace in the family room had an interesting shape, but the mantel was less than charming and at an odd height that made the whole composition look awkward. The new mantel gives the whole family room a sense of balance.

Something Places: Small places for both utility and artwork are strategically placed throughout the office, both to inspire and to catch the attention.

than remove the brickwork above, I simply covered it over with wallboard that was then painted a deep maroon color like the diagonal wall in my office. The results were instant and dramatic.

More recent changes include the remodeling of the master bedroom closets and the reconfiguration of the laundry. I wasn't anticipating how big a difference these seemingly incidental remodelings would make on my attitude toward the house. The spaces are still tiny, but now they are a pleasure to be in, the lighting is good, and their design is much more satisfying.

all in good time

Of course, there are other changes still to be made that fall into that last category of "things that would be nice to do one day." I'd love, for example, to replace all the doors and trim work in the house with a super-green alternative to solid wood—a high-density fiberboard wrapped in a natural cherry veneer. This would significantly improve the character of the house, but it would affect every wall surface, requiring paint touch up at the very least, and more likely significant patching as well.

I'd love to add windows behind the bed in the master bedroom bed alcove, so that there would be light at the end of the long view from my inner office back to the other end of the house. And I'd really like to modify the master bedroom ceiling, adding some ceiling height variety by lowering the dormer ceilings and the ceiling of the hallway to the bathroom.

But every time I think about these potential changes, I also realize that there is really nothing wrong with the existing trim and doors or with the bedroom ceiling height, other than their ordinariness. Maybe we will make these changes, maybe we won't.

Looking at each of the remodelings we've done so far, this house has evolved from standard to well above average without our having to break the bank to make it so. It is still only 2,400 sq. ft. and serves as workplace for two separate businesses and everyday living place for my husband and myself. It's perfectly tailored for the way we live, and it has become so not by figuring it all out ahead of time, before we moved in, but by making changes incrementally as our needs have shifted.

the not so big way to a sustainable future

The reason I've told the story of this house in such detail, and taken you through the thought processes at each step along the way, is to illustrate that remodeling is really a lifelong process. It's not something you can do once, complete, and forget about forever more. Our houses change as we change, and if you can allow your remodeling projects to evolve with you, your dwelling will continue to feed your spirit in ways you'd never believed possible.

It's my fervent belief that when you've made your home fit you to a tee, after you've moved on there will be others who'll recognize the love and attention that has gone into its making and who in turn will want to take care of it with the same diligence you have. "Well building," to use Vitruvius's term, is contagious. Each new owner will make a few changes of their own, and the home will continue to live on, gaining in character and patina with each set of new inhabitants. This is how it has happened over the centuries in Europe and other parts of the world where they know how to build for centuries rather than decades, and this is how it can happen here. We don't have to keep tearing down and starting over. By learning the lessons of this book, you will be taking a giant step toward realizing a vastly more sustainable future in which we too can start to look after what we've already made.

That's the potential of *all* our homes. There's so much that's possible in home design, so much that can make every dwelling place a better fit and a more expressive reflector of its owners' lifestyles and passions, but to realize the potential, we have to start thinking more creatively, more durably, and more three-dimensionally. No matter what your house challenges are, and no matter your budget, there *are* things you can do to make it a better place to live, both for today and for centuries to come. The only limit is your imagination. Good remodeling to you.

There's a story just like mine behind every one of the homes shown in this book. Marc and I have described the architectural decision-making process and have shown the results that can be obtained when you learn to think in a Not So Big way, but the personal back story for each home is at least as important in shaping the end product.

credits

Note: All "before" photos are courtesy of the architect listed, except where noted. For contact information on each of the architects and designers included in the book, please visit www.notsobighouse.com/ nsb_remodelingcredits.asp

p. vi: **Photo © Ken Gutmaker, Architect:** Bruce Anderson

p. 3: **Photo © Greg Premru, Architect: Amory Architects**

Chapter 1
pp. 4–21: **Photos © Randy O'Rourke, except inset Photos courtesy Sarah Susanka, FAIA, Architect: Sarah Susanka, FAIA**

Chapter 2
p. 22: **Photo © Anice Hoachlander, Hoachlander Davis Photography, Architect: Moore Architects**

p 24: **Photos courtesy Michele and Eric Van Hyfte, Architect: Michele Van Hyfte, AIA**

p. 26: **Photos © Anice Hoachlander, Hoachlander Davis Photography, Architect: Moore Architects**

p. 27: **Photos courtesy Peter Tart, Architect: Peter Tart Architect**

p. 28: **Photos © Stanley Livingston, Architect: Michael Klement, AIA, Architectural Resource**

p. 29: **Photos courtesy Marcus DiPietro, Architect: Marcus DiPietro, Architect**

p. 30: **Photo courtesy Michele and Eric Van Hyfte, Architect: Michele Van Hyfte, AIA**

p. 31: **Photo © Ken Gutmaker, Architect: Rehkamp Larson Architects**

p. 32: **Photo © Koz Digital Photography, Architect: Steve Jaskowiak, West Studio Architects**

p. 33: **(top) Photo © Stanley Livingston, Architect: Michael Klement, AIA, Architectural Resource; (bottom) Photo © Michael Jensen, Architect: Bosworth Hoedemaker**

pp. 34–37: **Photos © Randy O'Rourke, Architects: Eric Odor, AIA, with Chris Babser, SALA Architects**

pp. 38–39: **Photos © Anice Hoachlander, Hoachlander Davis Photography, Architect: Moore Architects**

pp. 40–41: **Photos © Steve Oleson, Architect: Nick Deaver Architect**

p. 43: **Photos © Randy O'Rourke, Architect: Lloyd Architects**

p. 45: **Photos © Anice Hoachlander, Hoachlander Davis Photography, Architect: Moore Architects**

Chapter 3
p. 46: **Photo © Dave Adams, Architect: Sage Architecture**

p. 49: **Photo © Steve Oleson, Architect: Nick Deaver Architects**

p. 50: **(top) Photo © Steve Oleson, Architect: Nick Deaver Architects; (bottom) Photo courtesy William Wadell, Distinctive Architecture, Architect: William Wadell, Distinctive Architecture**

p. 51: **(top) Photo © Dave Adams, Architects: Sage Architecture; (bottom) Photo courtesy David Peabody, Architect: Peabody Architects**

p. 52: **Photo © Steve Oleson, Architect: Nick Deaver Architects**

p. 53: **(top and bottom left) Photos © Randy O'Rourke, Architects: SmithLewis Architecture; (bottom right) Photo © Eric Camden, Architect: Sarah Susanka, FAIA**

pp. 54–55: **Photos courtesy TEA₂ Architects, Architect: Dan Nepp, AIA, TEA₂ Architects**

pp. 56–59: **Photos © Randy O'Rourke, Architect: Stephen Robinson, AIA, Axios Architecture**

Chapter 4
p. 60: **Photos © Robert Benson, Designer: Jamie Wolf, Wolfworks**

p. 61: **(top) Photo © Robert Benson, Designer: Jamie Wolf, Wolfworks; (bottom) Photo © Ken Gutmaker, Architect: Rehkamp Larson Architects**

p. 62: **Photo © Ken Gutmaker, Designer: Sonya Carel, Assoc. AIA**

p. 64: **(left) Photo courtesy Sarah Susanka; (right) Photo © Randy O'Rourke, Architect: Sarah Susanka, FAIA**

p. 65: **(left) Photo courtesy Ned Engs, Architect: Ned Engs, AIA, E4 Architects; (top and bottom right) Photos © Ross Chapin, Architect: Ross Chapin Architects**

p. 66: **Photo © Greg Hadley, Architect: Peabody Architects**

p. 67: **Photo © Anne Gummerson, Architect: Laura Thomas, Melville Thomas Architects**

pp. 68–69: **Photos © Randy O'Rourke, Architect: Todd Sloane, AIA**

p. 70: **Photo © Michael Kaskel, Architect: Harold Forrest Dietrich Architects**

p. 71: **Photo © Bud Dietrich, Architect: Harold Forrest Dietrich Architects**

Chapter 5
p. 72: **Photo courtesy Ned Engs, Architect: Ned Engs, AIA, E4 Architects**

p. 74: **Photo © Greg Premru, Architect: Amory Architects**

p. 77: **Photo courtesy Gregory Thomas, Architect, Architect: Gregory Thomas, Architect**

p. 78: **Photo © Chad Brown, Architect; Gail L. Wong Architects**

p. 79: **Photo © Randy O'Rourke, Architect: Todd Sloane**

p. 80: **Photo courtesy Amy Hetletvedt, Architect: Van Dyke Lawrence Architects**

p. 81: **Photos © Greg Premru, Architects: Amory Architects**

pp. 82–83: **Photos courtesy Harriet Christina Chu, AIA, Architect: Harriet Christina Chu, AIA**

Chapter 6
p. 84: **Photos © Anice Hoachlander, Hoachlander Davis Photography, Architect: Moore Architects**

p. 86: **Photo courtesy Sarah Susanka, FAIA; Architect; Sarah Susanka, FAIA**

p. 88: **(top left) Photo © Ken Gutmaker, Architect: Gail L. Wong Architects; (bottom left) Photo © Anice Hoachlander, Hoachlander Davis Photography, Architect: Moore Architects; (bottom right) Photo © Karen Melvin, Architect: McMonigal Architects**

p. 89: **Photos © Greg Premru, Architect: Amory Architects**

pp. 90–93: **Photos © Ken Gutmaker, Architect: Gail L. Wong Architects**

pp. 94–97: **Photos © Seth Tice-Lewis, Architect: Sophie Piesse Architect**

Chapter 7
p. 99: **Photos © Ken Gutmaker, Architect: Mark Parry, AIA, Idea Studios**

p. 101: **Photo © Greg Premru, Architect: Amory Architects**

p. 102: **Photo courtesy Robert Harrison, AIA; Architect: Harrison Architects**

p. 103: **(left) Photo courtesy Robert Harrison, AIA, Architect: Harrison Architects; (right) Photo courtesy William Wadell, Distinctive Architecture, Architect: William Wadell, Distinctive Architecture**

p. 104: **Photo courtesy Harriet Christina Chu, AIA, Architect: Harriet Christina Chu, AIA**

p. 105: **(top) Photo courtesy Dawn Blobaum, Architects: Dawn Blobaum, AIA, and James Bartl; (bottom) Photo © Greg Premru, Architect: Amory Architects**

p. 106: **(top) Photo © Randy O'Rourke, Architect: Steve Robinson, AIA, Axios Architecture; (bottom) Photo Eric Camden, Architect: Sarah Susanka, FAIA**

p. 211: **Photo © Greg Hadley, Architect: Peabody Architects**

pp. 212–213: **Photos © Randy O'Rourke, Architect: Elizabeth Craver, Craver Architects**

p. 215: **Photo © Art Grice, Architect: Russell Hamlet, Studio Hamlet**

pp. 216–217: **Photos © Ken Gutmaker, Architect: Kelly Davis, SALA Architects**

Chapter 16
p. 218: **Photo courtesy Mira Jean Steinbrecher, AIA, Architect: Jean Steinbrecher Architects**

p. 221: **(top) Photo by Rob Yagid, courtesy** *Fine Homebuilding,* **© The Taunton Press, Inc., Architect: Tina Govan Architect; (bottom) Photos © Ken Gutmaker, Architect: Kelly Davis, SALA Architects**

p. 222: **Photos © Randy O'Rourke, Architect: Lloyd Architects**

p. 223: **Photo © Randy O'Rourke, Architect: Sarah Susanka, FAIA**

p. 224: **(left) Photo courtesy Richard Wagner and Robyn Chrabascz, Architect: David H. Gleason Associates; (right) Photo courtesy Mira Jean Steinbrecher, AIA, Architect: Jean Steinbrecher Architects**

pp. 225–227: **Photos © Shawn Glen Pierson and Architétc, Architects: Richard Wieboldt & Associates Architects, with Shawn Glen Pierson**

pp. 228–229: **Photos © Randy O'Rourke, Architect: Jim Thornhill, AIA, Luna Design Group**

pp. 230–231: **(left and middle) Photos © Randy O'Rourke; (right) Photos courtesy Jo Machinist Architect, Architect: Jo Machinist Architect**

Chapter 17
pp. 233–234: **Photos © Ross Chapin, Architect: Ross Chapin Architects**

p. 235: **Photo courtesy of Richard Klecka, Architect: Bryna Rapp**

p. 236: **(top left) Photo © William Enos, Emerald Light Photography, Designer: Lisa Sten, Harrell Remodeling; (top right) Photo © Elisabeth Groh, Architect: Sarah Susanka, FAIA; (bottom right) Photo © Elisabeth Groh, Architect: Sarah Susanka, FAIA**

p. 237: **Photo © Elisabeth Groh, Architect: Sarah Susanka, FAIA**

pp. 238–239: **Photos courtesy Jo Moniz, Architect: Jo Moniz, AIA**

Chapter 18
p. 240: **Photo © Randy O'Rourke, Architect: Elaine Gallagher Adams, AIA**

p. 242: **Photo © Randy O'Rourke, Architect: Elaine Gallagher Adams, AIA**

p. 243: **Photo © Scott Wang Photography, Designer: Sawhorse**

p. 244: **Photos courtesy Sharyl Stropkay, Lifestyle Interiors & Organization, Designer: Sharyl Stropkay, Lifestyle Interiors & Organization**

p. 245: **Photos © Randy O'Rourke, Designer: Allison Jones, Insight Design**

p. 246: **Photo © John Fabel, Architect: Kraus-Fitch Architects**

p. 247: **(bottom left) Photo © Randy O'Rourke, Architect: Mary Staikos, AIA, Staikos Associates Architects; (top and bottom right) Photos courtesy Sharyl Stropkay, Lifestyle Interiors & Organization, Architect: Sharyl Stropkay, Lifestyle Interiors & Organization**

pp. 248–249: **Photos © Randy O'Rourke, Designer: Burt Miller, Nami Designs**

p. 251: **Photos © Randy O'Rourke, Architect: Tom Vermeland, Vermeland Architects**

pp. 252–253: **Photos © Randy O'Rourke, Designer: Mindy Sloo, M&M Restoration**

Chapter 19
p. 254: **Photo © John Banks, Architect: Chris Hawley, Stahl Architects**

p. 257: **Photo © Randy O'Rourke, Architect: Tom Vermeland, Vermeland Architects**

p. 258: **Photos © Shawn Glen Pierson and Architétc, Architect: Richard Wieboldt & Assoc. Architects, with Shawn Glen Pierson**

p. 259: **Photos © Randy O'Rourke, Architect: Sarah Susanka, FAIA**

p. 260: **Photos courtesy Robert T. Coolidge, AIA, Architect: Robert T. Coolidge, AIA**

p. 261: **(bottom left) Photo © Ross Chapin, Architect: Ross Chapin Architects; (top right) Photo © Randy O'Rourke, Architect: Tom Vermeland, Vermeland Architects; (bottom right) Photo © John Banks, Architect: Chris Hawley, Stahl Architects**

p. 262: **Photo © Robert Benson; Designer: Jamie Wolf, Wolfworks**

p. 263: **(top left) Photo © Robert Benson; (right) Photos © Ken Gutmaker, Designer: Jamie Wolf, Wolfworks**

pp. 265–267: **Photos © Seth Tice-Lewis, Architect: Sophie Piesse**

pp. 268–269: **Photos © Randy O'Rourke, Architect: Todd Sloane, AIA**

Chapter 20
p. 270: **Photo © Robert Benson, Designer: Jamie Wolf, Wolfworks**

p. 273: **Photo © Randy O'Rourke, Architect: Tina Govan Architect**

p. 274: **Photo © Bill O'Luanaigh**

p. 275: **Photos © Randy O'Rourke, Architect: Tina Govan Architect**

p. 277: **Photo courtesy Sarah Susanka, FAIA**

p. 278: **Photo courtesy Dan Nepp, TEA₂ Architects, Architects: Stephen Nordgaard and Dan Nepp, TEA₂ Architects**

p. 279: **Photo © Randy O'Rourke, Architect: Tina Govan Architect**

pp. 280–283: **Photos © Robert Benson, Designer: Jamie Wolf, Wolfworks**

Chapter 21
p. 285: **Photos © Dave Adams, Architect: Sage Architecture**

pp. 287–289: **Photos © Ken Gutmaker, Designer: Robin Barker, M. Arch.**

p. 291: **Photos © Ken Gutmaker, Designer: Robin Barker, M. Arch.**

pp. 292–295: **Photos © Ken Gutmaker, Architect: Bruce Anderson**

pp. 296–298: **Photos © Ken Gutmaker, Architect: Carol Cozen, AIA, Cozen Architecture**

pp. 300–303: **Photos © Michael Jensen, Architect: Bowsworth Hoedemaker**

Chapter 22
p. 304: **Photo © Michael Sanford, Architect: Sophie Piesse Architect**

p. 305: **Photo © Dave Adams, Architect: Sage Architecture**

pp. 306-308: **Photos © Michael Sanford, Architect: Sophie Piesse Architect**

p. 309: **Photo courtesy Sarah Susanka, FAIA**

pp. 310–313: **Photos courtesy Peter Lytle, Live Green, Live Smart Institute, Architect: Steve Kleinman/Live Green, Live Smart™**

Chapter 23
pp. 314–324: **Photos © Randy O'Rourke, Architect: Sarah Susanka, FAIA**

All illustrations are by Martha Garstang Hill, except:

©Sarah Susanka: pp. 6, 27, 28, 30, 47, 64, 75, 77, 78, 81, 87, 106, 116, 126, 142, 144, 177, 182, 187, 219, 223, 235, 257, 260, 277, 278, 288

Marc Vassallo: pp. 34, 36, 39, 42, 44, 57, 69, 70, 83, 90, 93, 96, 111, 121, 122, 137, 149, 175, 185, 188, 214, 226, 239, 251, 253, 263, 264, 266, 280, 292, 297, 300, 301, 312

index